A WOMAN OF UNCERTAIN
CHARACTER

Also by Clancy Sigal

Weekend in Dinlock

Going Away

Zone of the Interior

The Secret Defector

A WOMAN OF UNCERTAIN CHARACTER

The Amorous and Radical Adventures
of My Mother Jennie
(Who Always Wanted to Be a Respectable Jewish Mom)

by Her Bastard Son

CLANCY SIGAL

CARROLL & GRAF PUBLISHERS
NEW YORK

A WOMAN OF UNCERTAIN CHARACTER
The Amorous and Radical Adventures of My Mother Jennie (Who Always Wanted to Be a Respectable Jewish Mom)

Carroll & Craf Publishers
An Imprint of Avalon Publishing Group, Inc.
245 West 17th Street
11th Floor
New York, NY 10011

AVALON
publishing group incorporated

Library of Congress Cataloging-in-Publication Data is available.

ISBN-13: 978-0-78671-748-4
ISBN-10: 0-78671-748-3

9 8 7 6 5 4 3 2 1

Designed by Maria E. Torres

Printed in the United States of America
Distributed by Publishers Group West

For my son, Joe Sigal,
and
His mother, Janice Tidwell

Contents

Prologue

Chicago, 1935

The state's attorney's office in the Loop, at night. The building is empty of daytime workers except for the detectives and uniformed cops on the eleventh floor gathered to grill a suspect, my mother, Jennie Persily. They picked her up at work, but she resisted until they agreed to drive her home to dress for the occasion and to drag me along. In all her dealings with the police she refuses to look anything less than her best. Makeup just right, cloche hat tipped over one eye concealed by half veil, navy-striped linen jacket, white rayon blouse cut low, long coral-red rayon skirt with large black buttons, gauntlet-style black kidskin gloves, and vamp silk pumps with three-inch heels. She gazes directly into the desk lamp shining in her face, behind which shadows pump questions at her.

One of the shadows leans over and takes her face in his hand, a major liberty. She shakes him off contemptuously. "Tough guy, eh? Try that on your wife at home." The shadow moves in threateningly and another says, "Take it easy, Ed."

Ma calmly demands, "You promised someone to care for my boy. Either take him outside or bring a nurse."

They ignore her demand, thank God. Fascinated, I perch on a wooden bench in the semidarkness, pretending to read a Big Little comic book on my lap. They're treating my mother like John Dillinger or Ma Barker, who they'd just shot full of holes down South somewhere. *Who had she murdered and would they beat her up?* I wondered.

I can't follow the grilling. Words like "extortion," "executive board," "intimidation," local this and local that. Ma finally leans over and gently twists the lamp so the glare is on the detectives behind the desk. They look like Halloween ghosts. "Cut it out, Jennie!" barks one of the cops, putting the light back where it was. Ma recrosses her silk-stockinged legs, reaches into her purse, pulls out a Pall Mall, and takes her time lighting it. Blows a perfect smoke ring. She offers the pack to the darkness. Nobody accepts.

I have to go to the bathroom but am afraid to ask. Whatever happens, I don't want to be away from Ma. Somebody notices me fidgeting and sighs. "Okay Jennie, g'wan home with your brat. But watch your step next time."

Ma sits smoking, taking her time. "C'mon," urges another cop, "it's been a long night." Satisfied, she gets up, straightens her outfit, pulls the veil down, and says to me, "Kalman, we're through with the gentlemen." *She* was through with *them*.

We sail through the outer office toward the elevators. Nobody follows us into the hallway. At the elevator two men get on. Silence. One of them lays an envelope on her chest and says, "You don't have to do anything for this, Jennie. Just stay home for a couple of weeks until things blow over." Ma fakes accepting the envelope, but just before we get out on the ground floor she smartly slaps the envelope back on the guy who'd given it to her. When the door opens there are more plainclothes in the lobby waiting to take us by surprise. Ma hasn't taken the envelope. As she steps out she says to the cops, "What do you take me for—a greenhorn?" She pushes me through revolving doors out onto State Street.

In the taxi home I pester Ma to tell me what it's all about. Carefully removing her hat, she explains that the men were state's attorney detectives waiting to arrest her for accepting a bribe to help them break the sweater makers' strike. "Marked money. They take me for a fool just off the boat." She shakes her head, so full of rich red auburn permanent-waved hair, and stares out into the Chicago night. "There's no excuse for stupidity." She turns to me and lifts an educating finger. "Not all cops are this dumb, Kalman. Just some. They're the ones to be afraid of."

"But how do you tell the difference?" I ask.

She laughs. "Oh, they'll let you know, don't worry."

Then she reaches over to hug and draw me close to her in the backseat. "You did well tonight."

"I didn't do anything," I say.

"Exactly, my sweet child," she says.

1

A Chat with Grandma

Like Dr. Frankenstein, I, Jennie's son, bring the dead back to life. In Hollywood, where I write movies, I helped raise Frida Kahlo from her grave, gave the kiss of life to Sandra Bullock as the wartime nurse who was Hemingway's first love, and resurrected Maria Callas and Simone de Beauvoir. The only woman who has resisted my touch is my own mother. It should be a piece of cake, since no producer is leaning over my shoulder to demand a "money shot."

A story comes easier if you imagine the actress who plays the lead, so I'm casting not one, but three stars in Jennie's role: Reese Witherspoon (in a red wig) as my mother the teenage sweatshop worker and strike leader; Julia Roberts with her glorious swagger as the single mother of a mutinous son; and Susan Sarandon or Kathy Bates as the scandalous, liberated older woman putting it all out there. Jennie hated sentimental self-sacrifice, so Meg Ryan is all wrong for the part. Ma, who loved movies, might have preferred Myrna Loy or Ginger Rogers, but that's not possible.

The story that follows tracks my obsession with—and journey toward—a woman it has taken all my life to find through her miasma of lies and half-truths and evasions. What a genius she was at covering her trail. Why do our parents do it? What's in it for them?

I'd make a good cold-case detective, slow but tenacious.

❋ ❋ ❋

Author's note: Writing Jennie's story is to violate the most fundamental compact between my mother and me—to keep it strictly between ourselves. Squealing—informing—was lower than murder, worse than the ultimate crime of scabbing on a picket line. Our conspiracy of silence became second nature, as it is in Mafia families. Style was ultra-important to my mother, and her mode was extreme poise under stress, iron calmness at all costs. She did not warn, prompt, or sermonize on the absolute need for secrecy, but enforced our Jewish form of *omerta* merely by a single lift of her arched eyebrow or a quick sidelong glance. For a long time I felt that talking or writing about her would be like ratting out—a violent betrayal of everything in our culture.

But now that I am a father and tempted to veil from my son certain facts of my own life, I see where family mystery gets us: Nowhere.

❋ ❋ ❋

Even before I was ten—my son Joe's age now—I was already Jennie's accomplice and partner in crime. It was like being a

Mob kid, except in reverse. We were the good guys, the union people, against whom Al Capone and Meyer Lansky supplied the paid goons who beat up my parents and their friends. But this wasn't like *The Untouchables*. In real life, the lines of morality got all twisty and tangled. Our little household, moving from city to city and state to state, had an *in* with "connected" guys, tank town gorillas who could be lured away from strikebreaking by a decent enough bribe. We lived in a twilight world between law and lawless and were comfortable in the commute.

In the 1930s there was no clear boundary between honest trade unionist and hoodlum-for-hire because, in a world of shifting alliances and desperate men and women, you couldn't afford legalistic ethical judgments. Leo Sigal, my dad, packed a Colt .45 model 1911 with a five-inch barrel; Jennie Persily, my mother, although a sworn pacifist, used her fists, as well as her strong voice, on scabs. In the furnished rooms we kept moving in and out of, Jennie and Leo entertained a cosmopolitan cocktail of small-time criminals, professional and accidental hoboes, drifters, curbstone philosophers, Prohibition-era ex-bootleggers, Wobblies (International Workers of the World) committed to industrial sabotage ("propaganda of the deed"), anarchists, and freeloaders, a swirling soup of men and a few women devoted, in one degree or another, to the union faith. Until I was an adult I thought every home was like this.

This story is for Joe.

❖ ❖ ❖

San Fernando Valley, a day before yesterday.

It's a furnace-hot day in Los Angeles. From a free kick, the

3

(Photo by Janice Tidwell)

Clancy and Joe at Jennie's grave in Los Angeles.

little green soccer ball arcs high into the eye-achingly blue cloudless sky over Kagel Canyon, which lies in the northeast corner of "the valley" not far from the Charles Manson ranch across the Santa Susannah mountains and the 118 freeway. My son, Joseph Franklin Sigal, a husky blond boy, toe-nurses the soccer ball among rusty bronze grave markers that are inscribed with names like Zaretsky, Cohen, Friedman, and Zimmerman. He's brought along a baseball and glove for insurance and our Australian shepherd Kelly, who's going crazy in the dry grass.

Joe hopscotches atop the markers to retrieve his soccer ball at the goalpost he has invented—Grave H, Plot 77—on a sunny slope in the Workmen's Circle section of the Glen Haven cemetery. The plaque here does not say, as others do, "Beloved Mother and Grandmother" or "Beloved Wife and Mother," but reads simply, "Jennie Persily Sigal—a woman of the working class." The soccer ball rests on the little mound of earth where my wife Janice—Joe's mother—and I bend to clean away the accumulated leaves and weeds from Jennie's marker. Then Joe dribbles the ball away from the grave while idly munching a peanut butter sandwich.

"Hey Joe," I call, "be more respectful. Grandma is sleeping."

"No, she isn't," he responds in that surprisingly deep voice for a ten-year-old. "She's dead." He may still believe in Santa Claus and the tooth fairy but is strict about being fibbed to.

Over the graves, we start lobbing his Eric Gagne-signed ball and I teach him my side-arm splitter "slurve" from a recently recovered baseball memory.

When Joe moves away to inspect some ants under an elm tree, Janice leaves me alone with Jennie. I kneel on the grass and, as usual, confide my troubles to Ma, like George C. Scott in *Patton* muttering holy thoughts to his wounded GIs.

Joseph Franklin is getting restless. Janice takes him by the hand and they stand over Jennie's modest marker, which is oxydized almost green by rain and sun. Joe asks, "What do you and Granma Jennie talk about?" "Oh," I say, "world politics, the Academy Awards, and does the Yankee shortstop Derek Jeter have a girlfriend?" "No, really," he demands. Like Jennie, he hates being patronized. "We talk about you," I tell him truthfully. This satisfies him, and now he wants to go home.

Clancy, Janice Tidwell (Joe's mother), and Joe, two and a half.

As we stroll down the hill to the car he turns and waves. "Bye, Jennie."

All the way home—under gathering rain clouds over the mountains, past the mysterious eucalyptus-shrouded canyons where they keep horses, Harleys, and meth labs hidden in the mustard scrub, past the post-World War II tracts with tiny, sunbaked front lawns (the kind of flat-roofed, single-storey GI loan house Jennie dreamed one day we might buy and live in surrounded by rose bushes), down to Lakeview Terrace, where the LAPD whaled on Rodney King and where I have a cousin who is a porno projectionist in a Pussycat Theater (union job, of course), onto the Foothill 210 to the Ronald Reagan 118 to the 405—the kid's got something on his mind. Finally blurts:

"Dad, who is Jennie?"

"Your grandmother on my side," I remind him.

"No," he stubbornly shakes his head, "who *is* she?"

How do you raise a child in a time so very different from your own? I'm a Flapper Age hootchy-kootchy speakeasy baby; my Joe is a child of the "war on terror." He had just been born when Tim McVeigh murdered 168 men, women, and children in the Oklahoma City bombing, and six when — arms tightly around each other — we watched on TV as nineteen men armed only with box cutters crashed their planes into the Twin Towers. Osama bin Laden, not Adolph Hitler, is his Darth Vader.

Joe age four and Clancy. We can't wait for it to rain to go splashing together.

He's into gangsta rap, Randy Johnson's late-inning relief stats, and Captain Underpants. I come from this distant other time, before SATs, playdates, Lizzie McGuire, Grand Theft Auto, and not speaking to strangers. I had half a dozen names before I was Joe's age, but he *knows* he is Joseph Franklin Sigal. The Franklin is for the president who shaped my life and Jennie's—

2

First Memories: Red Hair, Ruby Lips

1929—*Black Friday stock market crash triggers the Great Depression. Six Chicago gangsters gunned down in St. Valentine's Day Massacre. "Talkies" kill silent movies.*

The German shepherd dog, leashless in the streets of Brighton Beach, Brooklyn, leaps howling between two parked cars and bites me, age three. I flee, screaming, into the path of an ice truck that drags me half a block down Neptune Avenue. Voices ring in my knocked-out head. *"Kook! Der kleiner starbt! Es izt die blot fun im!"* ("He's dead! Look! It's blood!") My eyes fly open. I'm in Ma's lap; she's sprawled in a chair in the drugstore wiping my gashed knee with a cotton swab. Customers crowd in like medical students, each with an opinion on the cadaver — me. Everyone except Ma is convinced that I am dead. "Wake up, Kalman," she commands. "You hear me? Open your eyes! Do it now!" I know that tone. It means, *Don't you dare die on me.*

I sit up and hug her. How splendid she looks, flame-colored hair framing her strong, round, freckled face, blue eyes as steady as God's, red-ruby lips pursed in relief and reprimand. Shedding tears is unthinkable for either of us. Has she paused for a moment to put on makeup before dashing out of the house?

Tomorrow, we'll stroll down to the swarming sand of Coney Island, the salty-smelling boardwalk, and the terror-eyed plaster horses of the musical merry-go-round, and I'll play the game of hunting and picking through the cracked-leather satchel that a strange but familiar man, Jack—Uncle Tzak (I have a speech defect)—takes to the beach with Ma and me and where I find a constantly refreshed trove of Lincoln pennies. Uncle Tzak wears a tilted derby hat and a sly knowing smile. I never find out who he is.

Nor why we are in Brighton Beach.

What I Know Now about Jennie Then

Her maiden name Persily translates as "porcelain" from Russian. She was born in 1895, in the pogrom-ravaged town of Proskurov, which lies on a low marshy plain in the province of Podolia—on the railroad line between Odessa and Lemberg at the confluence of the Bug and Ploskaya rivers in the Russian Ukraine. Her father, Kalman, was a grain merchant or an itinerant peddler, depending on who is telling the story. A middleman between peasants and wholesalers, he fit the superstitious peasants' profile of bloodsucking Jew and exploiter of the masses. Czar Alexander II's assassination in the 1880s set off a vicious wave of anti-Jewish pogroms on Proskurov's 25,000 Jews, half the town's total population. The little girl Jennie Persily witnessed the random ethnic-cleansing raids by armed *kreɟtynanin* who roared "Christ has risen!" and fierce mounted Cossacks wielding sabres who responded, "Indeed he has!", and she never forgot the carnage, later transferring to me, her only child, a deep foreboding that nothing in life was secure. From then on, her natural disarming smile never quite lost the shadow of an anxious frown that somewhere, somehow, a bad thing was about to happen.

My grandfather Kalman Persily's wife, Edith Rosenzweig, was the family's beating heart and moral guardian over Jennie, her four sisters — Fannie, Pauline, Bessie, and Surkah, and her five brothers — Arkeh, Duvid, Shiya, Usher, and Joseph. When one by one, two by two the Persilys emigrated to America, Surkah stayed behind to marry a shoemaker; it is possible she was murdered by the Germans when they invaded Russia in 1941, but nobody seems to know. All the brothers came to New York except "Yussele" (Joseph), who vanished somewhere in South America. Like so many others, the Persilys came through Ellis Island and settled on New York's Lower East Side. There the kids overnight became full-time child workers after Kalman, the family patriarch, was killed by a runaway beer wagon. An American story.

❊ ❊ ❊

Jennie, the riotous one, was labelled a "crazy bohemian" because, to compensate for her almost complete lack of formal education, she devoured books and went to Cooper Union lectures by the rebel poet John Reed, the anarchist Emma Goldman, and the fiery labor lawyer Clarence Darrow — who was Ma's friend and Dad's defense attorney — after whom she named me Clarence, a

The beating heart of the immigrant Persily family: Edis or Edith Rosenzweig, Jennie's mother, who bore five daughters and five sons. Undated, probably in New York's lower east side after 1905.

cross I bore for too long. She was sixteen when, from a sweatshop down the street, she witnessed the infamous Triangle Shirtwaist Fire in New York City that claimed the lives of 146 young immigrant workers, mostly girls and women. By then, she was already an experienced needle-trades worker on several types of machines—including overlock and high-speed single needle lockstitch—and a can-do union organizer, having called her first strike at thirteen when the boss kept putting the time-clock back. Of all the Persily sisters, she was perceived as the wildest, least predictable, and laziest because, as my Aunt Fanny explained, "She was too busy learning to be a revolutionist to settle down like the rest of us. And then that animal Sigal came along. . . ."

That animal Sigal—my dad.

Jennie was single and thirty-one when she had me. As usual, my father was not around at the time.

There is some dispute where I was born. My birth certificate indicates Michael Reese Hospital in Chicago, but my cousin Esther—who married a semipro wrestler who fought the Japanese in the Aleutians (and who's the daughter of Jennie's favorite brother Arkeh)—told me, "That Chicago certificate is a phony. Your father paid somebody off, or scared somebody into faking it. He knew how to manage such things. You were born in Kings County Hospital in Brooklyn. I was there. Why else were you and your mother in Brighton Beach?" Then Esther clammed up.

At some point, I was placed in an institution for homeless boys, whose high wooden fence and regular meals calmed me down for a while. When Jennie eventually came to claim me, I screamed bloody murder and grabbed ahold of the iron bedstead of my cot and begged the other orphans to rescue me. Matron had to pry my fingers loose before turning me over to Jennie, who got down on her knees to me.

"Aren't you glad to see me?" she begged.

I stared at her coldly. Why was she taking me away from my friends?

"I want to stay here." I squirmed out of her embrace.

Ma let go, looked at me calmly, and offered a bribe: "Let's take a train."

"Is it a Pullman?" I asked.

"Of course! And we'll never get off."

"Promise?" I loved trains more than anything.

She nodded, got to her feet, took me by the hand, bade goodbye to Matron, and hustled us off to the railroad station for what turned out to be the first of mysterious stopovers in Buffalo, Detroit, Flint, Indianapolis, St. Louis, Cape Girardoux, Cairo, Winston-Salem to . . .

ABOVE (LEFT): Jennie, age nineteen or early twenties. A passionate admirer of outspoken radicals like John Reed and Emma Goldman.

ABOVE (RIGHT): Jennie, in her early twenties, during WWI. Dressed to kill even then.

BOTTOM (LEFT): Jennie (in the middle) with her sister Pauline on her left and cousin Minnie on her right. Date unknown.

3

Jennie, Dowun Sowuth

1931—Frankenstein *a box-office boffo. Scottsboro Boys framed on a rape charge in Alabama. German millionaires support the 800,000-strong Nazi party, edging Hitler to power.*

When I was a little boy Jennie and I spent a lot of time riding soot-filled railroad coaches, sleeping cradled against each other on wicker-lattice reversible seats in our home on wheels. Lackawanna, Pennsylvania Central, Virginia & Blue Mountain, Central Pacific, Georgia Southern. The names on the passing freight cars rolling by helped teach me to read as I picked out the letters—B&O, MOP, OK, SAP. Best of all, when we had the money, I loved "going Pullman," scampering up the hooked ladder to an upper berth in a thrilling ascent second only to looping the loop in a wartime Spad like my cartoon-strip hero, Smilin' Jack. Warm and cozy, a cocoon of crisp clean white sheets and pillow slips (smelling faintly of Clorox) and tightly tucked hospital-corner brown blanket with the "property of the

Pullman Company" logo on it, no bedbugs, ticks, or cock-roaches, the noise of the wheels as soothing as a South Sea breeze to Tahitians. Back then, all "colored" porters—members of A. Philip Randolph's Brotherhood of Railway Porters—were called "George," businessmen smelling of Barbasol and wearing black-white-and-brown wingtip shoes lounged over manhattans in the rear observation car, and the Baldwin steam locomotives up front actually did go clickety-clack on iron tracks in the fastness of the American night.

There is hardly a third-rate hotel we didn't stay at in that broad lonely landscape trisecting the Great Plains, Memphis, and New York. The concept of child care was unknown. When Jennie arrived in a new town on one of her mystic missions—now I know it was clandestine organizing for the United Textile Workers or a sister union—she'd often deposit me with a passing stranger in the squalid (but to me glamorous) potted-palm lob-bies of flophouses that flaunted names like Excelsior or Grand or Regal. I'd happily loll about all day on my own—sly, obser-vant, lonely, chattering a mile a minute to the bell captain and the Prince Albert cigar stand girl, or gaping at the "prossies" who sometimes adopted me as a mascot, or annoying the "drum-mers" (traveling salesmen), and scooting out from under the flat feet of the omnipresent house dick—an off duty or discharged-for-cause local cop. My red and black $2 tin toy roulette wheel—a sort of 1931 Nintendo—and I were inseparable.

Blue curling smoke from Five Cent Mild & Mellow cigars and the prossies' Woolworth's perfume was a heady mixture to a chubby, chattery five-year-old who had already seen his mama hit upside the head by a police billy club and knew what an "agotiation" was and would soon spend time in jail along-side his mother.

Being a labor organizer's son was a kick. I was part of something bigger than myself even if I didn't understand what it was. And there were those secrets, the elixir of childhood. My main responsibility was to keep my mouth shut, because one "misspoke" from me, my mother advised, and our house of cards could come crashing down. There were strict rules: my little overnight satchel was never to be completely unpacked; lies told to strangers were relative; you told the truth to landlords, policemen, and bill collectors at your peril; you didn't arrive in a new town without a "local contact," usually an undercover union sympathizer—someone to guide you through the human geography and point out company stooges. Stool pigeons—squealers—were to be identified and stepped around like sidewalk snot.

Strategies for coping with the vertigo of terror you had to figure out for yourself. You showed no fear, ever, under any circumstance.

Confusion was my element, chaos almost comforting. If Dad suddenly showed up, he and Ma would toss me back and forth between them depending on who won the argument. Before we reached Chattanooga and grumbling a bit, Dad took me along in a borrowed LaSalle roadster to Flint, Detroit, and Cleveland when he made a circuit of the barbers, bakers, and Hebrew Trades hat blockers, candy-makers, and laundry workers he had earlier set up in union locals and from whom he collected dues (twenty cents a week). In a new town, he liked to use me as part of his sales pitch, nobody—including off duty cops—objecting when I accompanied Dad inside a smoky tavern. When the guys at the bar chuckled over his cute kid, Dad used the opening to talk up the union. ("This child is no dummy. He can tell the difference between a living wage and

17

what you're getting. . . .") I loved these times with him, including when he got into a fight with a man twice his size in a saloon and knocked him down with his first punch. I blinked the way Brandon de Wilde does in *Shane* when Alan Ladd shows him how to fire a six-gun—holy cow, that's my dad!

But then he had to hit the road again without me and I went back to being Ma's boy.

＊ ＊ ＊

Chattanooga, in the far southeast corner of Tennessee, was Bessie Smith's hometown. Despite the bad times, it was a thriving industrial city, built on and around hills, with a tense labor and race history. Everyone was armed, even the streetcar conductors, who wore pistols in braided holsters to enforce the rigid color line. Bayonet-slashing National Guardsmen and imported scabs were routinely called out to strikes that erupted all over the nearby textile towns—Erwin, Harriman, Kingsport—whose workers, down from the hollows, were just as likely to shoot back. This was Bible Belt country where a back-to-the-past evangelist like Billy Sunday was a bigger draw than Clark Gable, "blue laws" were strictly upheld, and African-Americans careful to be off the streets after sundown. The first trial ever broadcast nationwide, the sensational Scopes "monkey trial" with Clarence Darrow arguing for science against creationist and three-time presidential candidate William Jennings Bryan, had been held a few miles away in a sweltering Dayton, Tennessee, courtroom.

About the time Ma and I came to Chattanooga the local newspapers were full of the Scottsboro case in which nine young blacks just across the Alabama state line were falsely accused of raping two white hookers. Sam Liebowitz, the defense attorney, would be chased out of town by the prosecutor screaming "Jew lawyer!" at him.

Unpacking our bags in Chattanooga Jennie suggested it might not be a propitious time to reveal that we were Jewish and that I had been named for Clarence Darrow.

It didn't matter. I was five, and in love with Chattanooga.

I, Clarence Demarest.

We took fake names whatever new town we moved to. Depending on circumstance, I was Carl, Caspar, Caleb, Calvin, Charles, or Christopher—anything with a "C," I guess, to hold onto a faint shred of my own identity and, through mine, to honor Jennie's father Kalman, who had been killed in a beer wagon accident. (Several of my maternal cousins—Coleman, Clem, Carl—have "C" first names.) Surnames for us Ma chose playfully at random from a roster of Hollywood B-list actors; at the moment, she was fond of the Paramount comic William Demarest.

Was all this name changing really necessary? In the abstract, probably not. Somewhere in the South there must have been Jewish organizers who kept their real names. But over time and road trips, it had become second nature for Ma and me, a dodge to maximize safety, a travel accessory, almost. I thought, *very cool*.

It was a game of shadows, fictitious trails, bogus resumés improvised on the spot or well rehearsed depending on the location. Jennie was a lollapalooza liar; labor organizers, especially below the Mason-Dixon Line, lived that way then. If either of us made a slip, Ma repeatedly warned, there would be "consequences." That house of cards again. On this particular stop, in Chattanooga, I'd be attending a mainly Baptist public school at the top of Pine Street where we rented a room. The school, like most local businesses, closed on General Robert E. Lee's birthday. The Civil War was the War between the States. Ma's instructions were clear and precise. "Practice your new name. Don't argue. Don't talk religion. Stay out of fights. And smile, always smile."

"Couldn't I be called Tom for once?" I wheedled—for cowboy star Tom Mix. Jennie replied that Tom wasn't a Jewish name. "But we're gentiles now," I reminded her. "Forget it, Mr. Demarest, Esquire," she said giving me her famous "no more arguments" look. "Go out, make friends—and *keep smiling*," she snapped.

The conspiracy of the necessary lie between us endured beyond the era of the small towns we lived in or passed through. Later, as we settled in Chicago—repeating in various neighborhoods the restless pattern we had established in the industrial South and elsewhere, moving always moving, from street to street, room to room—the secret complicity between us grew into a habit. What once had been explicit and unambiguous—taking new names, disguises, surviving by denial—became implied, ingrained, as we both operated on the same silent assumption: *Wherever we went, we would always be waiting for Dad to show up. This was unquestioned. He was The Man.*

So that was The Deal. If Jennie did not insanely scream or break down—not her style—I was to follow her example by showing zero fear or anxiety no matter what fix we found ourselves in. If I saw her being whupped by a cop (Flint), I was to look the other way and pretend she was a stranger; if we had to make a midnight flit down a hotel fire escape (Wilkes-Barre), I was not to pester her later with "why?". Today, I'm amazed when my son Joe confesses, "Poppy, I'm scared" of this or that.

Unthinkable for Jennie and me, preposterous if Dad was around. In our improvised home movie I played the Tough Guy, with style; she played the Gun Moll, with class; Dad, in those rare times with us, prowled like a caged animal, growling, biting his tongue so hard I feared he'd get lockjaw, a werewolf without a moon to howl to.

> *Nigger nigger*
> *Pull a trigger*
> *Up and down the Trissy river*
> *Snotty nose*
> *Raggy clothes*
> *That's the way the nigger goes*

is the first poem I ever learned. At five, my best friends Billy Wilson, J.C., and Cecil taught me that poem and how to whistle "Dixie" between the spaces in my front teeth and how to bait a rusty safety pin with earthworms and tongue-wet lumps of moldy bread to catch minnows when we went pole fishing. All that Chattanooga year, Ma let me run loose and wild and barefoot, chewing three-leaf clover for its salty taste on the banks of the "Trissy" river below Lookout Mountain, or schmucking downtown alone to goggle at the passersby who took no notice of a raggedy-ass child with no shoes but lots of freckles (like Ma). Almost every summer day, I took the two-cents-a-ride cable car up the incline to the mountaintop, where old Confederate veterans sat on benches gazing out across the mist-shrouded mountains, past Missionary Ridge and Pulpit Rock; you could see all the way into Georgia and Alabama out toward Sand Mountain. A kid could hunt the battlefield for minié balls that were sunk (behind wire mesh) in the oaks still

standing from the time when Hooker's Army of the Cumber-
land, with their Parrotts cannons and bayonets, had charged
uphill and carried the day against Bragg's dug-in rifle pits
during Grant's Great Siege of Chattanooga.

When Jennie enrolled me in a Baptist Sunday school I ran
home thrilled because teacher picked me to play Joseph with
his Coat of Many Colors in the Easter play. "Do we believe in
Jesus Christ? Do we, do we?" I begged. Ma took out a Pall
Mall and slowly lit it, blowing a smoke ring that hung in the air
for what seemed hours.

"Yes," she decided for safety's sake.

I demanded, "Did Jews kill Jesus like they say?"

She turned away. "Not all the precincts are in," she replied.

❊ ❊ ❊

Chattanooga was a boys' paradise and the days were never full
enough. Jennie's "cover" as a clandestine union organizer was
clerking at the grocery store kitty-corner from our Pine Street
room, both store and house owned by our landlord, another
uncle, this time "Uncle Schwartz." He was Jennie's "local contact," a thickset, hairy, taciturn man with a permanently stub-
bled chin. For the first and only time, I had my own room. In
the middle of the night Ma would go somewhere else to sleep
but she would always be there in the morning, in bed with me
or on a cot alongside. Every day, before school, I waited for the
mailman to bring a letter from Dad, who wrote now and then,
and I'd tear off the corner of the envelope embossed by a two-
cent Minuteman stamp so I could start a collection. I'd stopped
asking Ma when he'd come for us.

Our next-door neighbor was the Hamilton County sheriff,

a kindly old soul with a white handlebar mustache who seemed to spend the whole day on his front porch rocking in his chair and bidding hello to passing townspeople. He always had a friendly word for Clarence Demarest.

The game of shadows bothered me not in the slightest. I wanted it to go on forever, except that the shadows kept changing shape and sometimes it was hard to know what was real and what was not.

One day on my way home from school, Uncle Schwartz was waiting for me outside his store and invited me in and lifted me atop an ice cream freezer, refrigerating my butt, and for the first time kissed me. Until now, we'd kept miles between us. He said he'd keep on kissing me until I stopped wiping his slobber away with the back of my hand. "I'll give you a Fudgsicle," he promised, if only I would speak on his behalf to my mother, to whom he wanted to propose marriage. "I'll be good to her," Schwartz vowed. "You be sure to tell her that. I'll give you as many Fudgsicles you want. What kind of husband leaves his wife and child? Go tell her." Slobber smooch smooch. I kicked and squirmed out of his grasp and, grabbing the Fudgsicle, ran home across the street and said no such thing to my mother. Dad would come today, tomorrow, soon.

But she found out about the other thing soon enough.

Billy Wilson, my best friend, Huck to my Tom, lived up the street in a nice house behind a picket fence. He was the boss bully of my pack of wild Chattanooga five-to-six-year-olds that included my other best friends, toothpick-thin Cecil and J. C., so-called maybe because he was the hawk-spitting image of the adorable movie juvenile, Jackie Cooper. We four played truant all the time, rambling around downtown in our bare feet and hooking rides on the tramcars, where the motormen wore live-round pistols, or lying in open spaces staring into the smoky sun to blind ourselves. Longing for acceptance, I learned to talk "suthin" by copying their thick border accents; "spoke race" like them; and fearlessly baited my safety pin hook with worms we found on creek banks. Following their lead, I handled spiders, bugs, and lizards like a Conjure Man; today, they repel me.

Then it happened. Maybe there was next-door gossip about the black working women who came to our back porch in the middle of the night for long talks with Ma. The custom was that African-Americans always used rear entrances of white folks and never stayed after supper or sundown, whichever came first. Ma's black friends, probably hosiery mill workers, came *after* supper. She'd let them in, then step outside as if breathing in fresh air but really to see which neighbors were spying. She would go back inside and they'd sit around the kitchen table, the black women not washing or cooking but speaking in low, urgent tones. A strict rule was that I wasn't to come into the kitchen at such times, but of course I peeked. I paid it all little mind, but I reckon now that Ma had just about the most dangerous job there was in the South at the time—a white woman helping organize black women into a union. The timing was right, I've looked it up, Congress had just passed the Norris-LaGuardia Act outlawing the infamous "yellow dog contract" that required workers to agree as a condition of employment never to join a union. So the working-class South was rising again.

It so happened that one day Billy Wilson challenged me to a wrestle in the school yard. You were in only if you fought to stay in, but because Jennie had ordered me never to get into fights I fled home chased by Billy leading a posse of J. C. and Cecil yelling, "Sis-see! Yellabelly!" And of course the dreaded epithet Ma had done so much to avoid, "Nigger lover!"

From then on for days afterwards, Billy, as if licensed by God himself, bashed, battered, hammered, thumped, slapped, pinched, and tripped me whenever he had a mind to. In class he shook his fist at me, making my stomach flop. His betrayal upset me more than his threats. At home I vomited, got constipated, ran a fever, and, finally, chose death before dishonor. Tom Mix—my cowboy hero and gosh I wished I could ride away on his Wonder Horse Tony—could not do otherwise. One afternoon after school I hid in a passageway between two houses, a half-brick in my hand, and smashed it down on Billy's head as he passed, chasing him like a devil-hound and cracking his skull again and again with the brick and making the blood gush until he stumbled sobbing through his front gate. When I ambled home to Uncle Schwartz's house, Jennie was pale as death, she'd got the news faster than semaphore. She said, "We're finished here," and grabbed my hand to drag me, kicking and screaming in pained outrage, down to Mrs. Wilson's house, where on their doorstep Ma made me apologize to Billy, who was still whimpering but brightening because I was in for it. His mother just stared at my mother while wiping Billy's head with a blood-smudged towel. I refused to say I was sorry, but Jennie squeezed my hand so hard an inaudible repentance somehow tumbled out. Mrs. Wilson slammed the door in our faces.

So we began packing, again.

My apology to Billy Wilson—a shame and resentment that still burns—set in motion an unstoppable chain of events. All my fault.

Soon after I walloped Billy Wilson, two of the next-door sheriff's deputies, in Sam Browne belts over their crisp khaki uniforms, came to our door. They wore big revolvers in braided holsters like the streetcar motormen. My insides froze, I feared that it must be Billy Wilson croaked. The deputies took us across the street to Uncle Schwartz's general store where the sawdust on the floor was blood-dappled. Must be Billy had made it to the store and collapsed? My head exploded with relief when the sheriff himself showed up and said it was only that Schwartz had been stabbed in the neck with an ice pick by the coal-and-ice man. Jennie wanted to go to the hospital to see Schwartz, but they wouldn't let her.

I figured and figured how two such violent incidents so close together had to be connected and I was the cause, but it happened too fast to think. I wondered if the coal-and-ice man who attacked Uncle Schwartz had been Billy's father out to take revenge.

The deputies took us home and waited while we packed. Jennie stood by the window staring down the hill and chain smoking while I squashed and squirmed the suitcases to cram everything in; I was an expert fast packer. I badly wanted Ma to say something and blame me and have it over with, but she just put this mask on her face she always wore when there was trouble, and she expected me to do the same. Schwartz was no longer the issue; he'd get better or die, but what would happen to us?

Then we were taken in the police car to the courthouse, where Ma was booked into the city jail as a material witness or something like that, or just because we were strangers in town; and because they didn't have a matron, I was put in the holding tank with her.

In the jail cage with us and our suitcases was a black woman in a flowered housedress with a bruised and bloodied face. Up to now, Jennie had been extra careful about socializing openly with "nigras" except to let them in the back door at night for their long serious talks. She'd kept her peace at my clever "Nigger nigger pull a trigger . . ." and all the other casually racist remarks I'd dropped around her, I suppose not wanting to blow her cover. But now there was nothing to lose. She went over and sat with the woman. "Ma!" I stage-whispered, "why you talkin' to th' nigger?" Jennie hunched in closer to the black woman, who looked over at me and nodded like she was agreeing with something Ma said. I was really confused. What had I done wrong? Again.

In a way, jail was like the Pullman train. The cots hung from chains hammered into the cement wall and you had to do a little climbing to get into one, but no one named George came by to announce first serving in the dining car. That night, Jennie snuggled me into her own lower cot and covered us with her coat. I was hungry.

Next morning a deputy, big and fair-haired and right chivalrous, unlocked us and drove us to the train station. He put two tickets in Jennie's hand—she always wore gloves in public situations—and said, "Now you get on that train, Mrs. Demarest, and don't you never come back to Tennessee, hear?" He bent down to me. "And you mind your mother. If she forgets, and wants to come back here, you say no never she's not welcome, okay, little friend?" Yessir. Ma was very strict about me being nice to policemen.

❖ ❖ ❖

We got off the train at Chicago's Dearborn Street station, in a raging subzero blizzard, where my father in a Homburg hat and English-style drape topcoat was waiting for us. Dad lifted me up, rubbed his unshaven cheek against mine, appraised me, and set me down, while tensely waiting for my mother's signal yes or no to them staying together. My mind was elsewhere because my Buster Brown shoes, which I hardly ever wore in Chattanooga, pinched like Hell gone mad. I had only summer clothes on and immediately began coughing, the start of a long bronchial career. My mother, surrendering, finally said, "Get us out of the cold, Leo."

In the rooming house on Wells Street that Dad rented for us, the first thing Jennie did, even before unpacking, was march me straight down the hall into the common bathroom, grab my neck—yow!—and force it down to the sink where, like a crazy woman, she scrubbed out my mouth with a bar of Lifebuoy soap. Jesus, it stung. "What's that for?" I struggled in her grasp.

She cooled down. Composed, unflappable.

She shook the wet Lifebuoy at me like the red finger of God. "Don't I *ever* hear you using that *word* again!"

I knew what word she meant.

I never did.

And I was Clarence Sigal again.

For a while, at least.

My son Joe tells me I "talk funny" on first meeting people. *"Hi y'all,"* he'll imitate me and laugh. The South left its imprint on me. I came away thinking somehow we'd always live in Chattanooga, Billy Wilson would always lend me his bent-branch fishing pole, the sheriff of Hamilton County would sit rocking while twirling his wonderful mustache, and the three-leaf clovers along the Trissy river would never lose their salt. For me they never did.

P.S. Ma left her seed behind in Tennessee. After we were

kicked out, Southern textile workers right across the Bible Belt exploded in the three-week General Strike that mill owners dealt with savagely. In Honea Path, South Carolina, seven textile hands were murdered; others elsewhere were shot, beaten, fired. The strike was lost.

The Underground Stream

Both Jennie Persily and Leo Sigal were part of an underground stream in American life that for long periods seems to vanish without trace before suddenly resurfacing, then submerges and rises in no particular cyclical pattern but rolls on, sometimes merging with the mainstream, at other times diverging, even reversing direction, and apparently getting smaller and smaller, until it dries up altogether only to burst back onto the landscape strong and certain. Underground streamers are indispensable to the health of the nation because without them very little good would be accomplished: they have whatever it takes to go against the currents of ignorance, superstition, ugliness, and injustice.

Jennie and Leo never really accommodated to the way things are. In the race to social respectability something held them back, something other than bad luck. They were un-American because they never took advantage of their advantages of personal magnetism, nimble tongues, an ability to think fast on their feet, and a gift for close-in combat and (in Ma's case) timely compromise. My parents stayed poor out of a deep faith that a working person's destiny was to "Rise with your class, not from it," a phrase that was as close to a rosary as Jennie ever made.

I was privileged as a kid to sit in on some of Ma's negotiating sessions, where I closely watched her turn her emotions on and off as a strictly tactical move, like an infinitely patient chess champion. Like my father, she could thunder, pound the table, weep, and threaten, but at the core she was dead calm, tenacious, goal-oriented, lacing her conversational gambits with ironic humor that sometimes had company executives throwing up their hands in exasperation. "Oh, I give up Jennie, have it your way, you're giving me a bad case of indigestion." At such moments, clinching a contract, she was poetry in motion. It was like watching Sandy Koufax work on his 382nd strikeout or Navratilova playing on her best day.

Jennie's world, and thus mine, was inherently violent, pitting the union's raw muscle against an employer's reflex to disorganize, disenfranchise, and demonize his worker. But machine minders like her had nothing to bargain with except their bodies and she understood that, when the impassioned rhetoric floated away, it all came down to buying and selling. In the end, there has to be a *deal*; that's what unions are about. In the garment trade, where Jennie worked most of her life, there was also an ethic, to which bosses and unions once subscribed, that the workplace was family, dysfunctional and cruel but a family, nevertheless, who needed each other. It made a kind of Talmudic sense. "He'll settle," Ma always said, "because he has to. And we'll settle because a long strike is a lost strike no matter how you slice it." Jennie Persily would have made a great Special Forces ranger—go in fast and hard and get out before you take unacceptable casualties.

4

Windy City Blues

Chicago, Chicago, that toddlin' town
Chicago, Chicago, I'll show you around
Bet your bottom dollar you'll lose the blues
In Chicago, Chicago. . . .

Chicago for my mother was like living on a western frontier
outpost, except that the savage Indians (Chicagoans) were
inside the fort. She always felt in exile from her family and
away from the source of all the world's excitement, New York.
The "Big Stink," as Native Americans called the sprawl by
Lake Michigan for its swampy odor, was for Jennie an
unwholesome stew of grey winters and dull-witted people, a
backward pioneer settlement barely out of coonskin caps. But
for my dad, Chicago was like Paris for an artist; the happening
city, the front line, labor's Command Central, a fresh start after
he lost his prestigious job for punching out the president of the
Butchers' International over some anti-Jewish remarks.

In the labor wars that shook America from 1870 to 1940, Chicago was the place you went to make your mark as an organizer. If, like Leo Sigal, you were full of zip and salesmanship and had the fists to make your pitch credible, you made it in the Big Stink or not at all. Chicago was tough, challenging, open, meritocratic, radical, violent, and ethnic. It was also American labor's Gettysburg, where the bloodiest battles between workers and capital were fought in the streets and alleys. Sheridan Drive, from Fort Sheridan to the Loop downtown, was built specifically to speed U.S. troops to labor "trouble spots."

> *1877, Battle of the Viaduct, federal troops kill thirty workers in a railroad strike.*
> *1886, Haymarket Riot, seven policemen blasted, four anarchists hanged.*
> *1893, Columbian World Exposition torched in Pullman strike.*
> *1894, federal troops kill another thirty-four union men in strike.*

What a magnificent, crooked, opportunistic, exuberant, hellish place to grow up in. Welcome to the meeting, Brother, Sister!

Venus at The Dressing Table

1935—Detroit beats Cubs in World Series. Hitler in power passes anti-Jewish laws. First meeting of Alcoholics Anonymous. Congress for Industrial Organization (CIO) breaks away from the more traditional American Federation of Labor (AFL); CIO leader John L. Lewis punches AFL carpenters union boss Hutcheson in front of cameras to make it official.

I have few photographs of my mother. Those I do have show a woman with hooded eyes, a full figure, and an almost military bearing, her eyes sending a strong, defiant, sexual message, at least to me. It's the same look that commanded me not to die after the Brighton Beach dog-biting accident, not ever to say nigger again, and to respect my absent father wherever and whatever he was.

On the road, in hotel rooms or Pullmans, her body, plump and succulent, is always *there*, impossible to avoid in the cramped spaces we share. With her silent agreement I'll sit, from toddler age, to one side of her small makeup travel case, chin cupped in my chubby hands, watching her study herself in the mirror. Each time we step off a train or bus she is pumped up for her public performance, a traveling stage actress skilled in her lines—and at reading an audience, a flair she passed on to me—in most of the languages they speak (German, Yiddish, Russian, American English, Polish, bits of Magyar, Italian, Slovak). Her role model is not the impassioned un-chic Emma Goldman, whom she counts as a friend, but the slinky soigné movie star Carole Lombard in her shimmering silvery gowns trailing the marble dance floor of a Hollywood sound stage. In Ma's mind, dowdy is unrevolutionary.

Jennie's backstage prep fascinates me.

Her genius is to use loads of makeup—powder, rouge, lipstick, scent—without appearing "cheap" or "common," the foulest words in her vocabulary. Trade names like Max Factor, Helena Rubenstein, and Elizabeth Arden are as familiar to me as Radio Flyer and Lionel Train. Jennie would rather die than not shave her leg or confront a scab feeling underdressed. It has to do with personal pride and union solidarity, the same principles that make bushy-browed John L. Lewis, the mine workers' leader, proudly flaunt a chauffeur-driven limousine as his way of educating the membership that they *deserve* no less than the best.

To me, Ma's flesh communicates a more immediate language than words, a language I spend my childhood deciphering. Rich, abundant, cascading, engulfing flesh, product of a fast-developing puberty, its physical mass caged and trapped in the mandatory undergarments of her time. The hospital-pink, iron-buckled corset, with its thousand hooks and straps, the strangulating scar-leaving girdle, the D-cup brassiere laying siege to her nipples, the shroud-like Belgian silk slip, the thigh-length silk stockings held in place by snap-ons attached to bloomer-like panties, and a flowered dress from Lane Bryant's "styles for the stout," defined, dignified, and garroted Jennie's "form-fitting" figure. A warrior queen.

Fetching Ma her lipstick and eye shadow, I pretended to be Prince Valiant, squire to royalty, before galloping off to the great jousting tournaments known as labor meetings.

That's where the private and public Jennies come together.

There was always a hall, an auditorium, a Labor Lyceum where the great public dramas unfolded. Fireworks of speech-making, grand gestures, fierce denunciations, wily maneuvers, sometimes fist fights and riots. It was a theater of hope, striving, collective dream, and personal ambition in which I, a stage brat like young Buster Keaton or Mickey Rooney, was expected to step into a full-grown role soon. Of course I was bored witless by all the "I move the resolution back to committee, Brother Chairman" rituals so important to the members, most of whom had escaped foreign tyranny where Robert's Rules of Order came from the stinging slash of an overseer's whip or the barrel of a Cossack's rifle. But it soaked into me like blood, the debating sacraments, the haggling, factionalizing, shouted Gospel songs of redemption, call-and-response, tactical debates, strategizing, and maneuvering and name-calling. It's still in my veins. Perhaps that's why today I get along so well with Christian evangelicals and fundamentalist preachers' kids.

Since child care did not exist for the poor and we were often in strange towns far from friends or family, Ma had no choice but to haul me along to these amazing, tedious, earsplittingly loud, revival jubilation jamborees. I had a front-row seat at a show that made cowboy hero Charles Starrett's *Blazing Six Shooters* look tame.

Jennie could organize anybody and anything except my absent father.

Behind a podium, in a crowded hall, she was dynamite on a slow fuse. "Comrades—brothers and sisters!—" She could drag tears from a corpse and raise Lazarus from his grave by a mere curl of her eyebrow, an ironic twitch of her full lips. Style unhysterical, manner composed, tone subdued building to a spine-tingling climax, hers was a pitch from a credible heart. People listened to Jennie because she communicated that she was one of them—yet *not* one of them. In her theatrical body language she dramatized the sweatshop issues—lousy wages, *goneff* bosses, poorly ventilated fire traps to live and work in, a humiliating and dishonest piece-work system. But, her ringing modulated speaking style also affirmed, *I am better than the system.* And she dressed the part, her frills, veils, gloves, and cosmetics sending a message: Don't let yourself down.

On a speaker's platform, she appeared taller, more imposing, than the five feet four inches inside her tightly corseted, iron-girdled, Sunday-special frock and Hattie

Carnegie knockoff brimmed hat with veil flung back. This go-to-meeting outfit might consist of a rayon pleated dress, navy blue with polka dots, a white collar she would take off, wash, iron, and painstakingly sew back on, the ensemble held in by a shiny oilcloth belt that sometimes cracked and peeled. Lisle hose, nothing sheer, and modestly "sensible" shoes, not the "Cuban heels" she adored wearing to parties. Customarily, she wore gloves to union meetings, as she did to a social date or police bust.

Jennie's combination of crisp eloquence and strong feeling had a mesmerizing power to draw from her audience their respect, even awe. ("Your mother, a mouth on her like a river of fire," my father ruefully told me years later.) Men and women workers sat up straighter for her, cupping their ears to catch every word, their eyes occasionally glistening with tears. She was a fund-raising genius (for causes, not for us), knowing instinctively how, with imagery and cadence, to bring her audience to its feet cheering.

By contrast:

Within moments of opening a speech, my father looked as if he'd been through a laundry mangle. Shirt hanging out, dark hair unkempt, eyes blazing, a cigar stub jammed between his tobacco-stained teeth, stalking up and down the platform pounding a fist into his hand, he was a dynamo, a fierce black hole of flash-tempered energy. Ma's gift was unflustered persuasion; Dad was brutal ardent fury. She played her audiences like a harp; he harangued, and practically beat them up with his mouth. You had a feeling he might jump down from the stage and kick your brains out if you raised a point of order. This wasn't just my fantasy. One night in a crowded smoky meeting hall above Carl's Restaurant on Roosevelt Road in Chicago, as

Dad paced up and down pounding home his points, an object dropped to the platform when he pulled a handkerchief from his back pocket. A man sitting next to me in the front row quietly rose and handed it back to Dad, who replaced it in his pocket without either him or the audience skipping a beat. The object was a pistol, which until then I didn't know Dad carried. But none of the other men and women in the hall seemed surprised that their featured speaker packed. I looked around and examined the lined, worn faces of these ordinary working people, the Fishbeins and Wagners and Grossmans, and wondered for the first time what kind of people they were. A few nights later I asked Dad why he had a gun and he brushed me off. "It was my cigar case. You see too many movies."

True enough, I was movie crazy. It was also true that my father and his friends, without being professional gunmen, carried weapons as an ordinary tool of the trade, just as plumbers heft a locknut wrench and carpenters a bevel-edge chisel. Life in Chicago for activists was beset by everyday dangers that included Mob musclemen, rival union goons, freelance young toughs in hostile neighborhoods, and penny ante extortionists. "It's nothing," was one of Jennie's favorite phrases, "to write home about."

✻ ✻ ✻

My Dad was in and out of our lives when the mood was on him according to cosmic laws of motion I never understood. It was like having the Lone Ranger around, here today gone tomorrow. Who *was* that Masked Man? When, without warning, he'd drop by, Jennie was transformed into a young girl, flushed and excited, flashing legs and full of sparkle. I, too, came alive, heady with male love, eager to impress Dad, aiming to be the perfect son. One night, he and I made history together when he took me down to the Loop to see the Democratic presidential candidate, Franklin Delano Roosevelt, who was on the campaign trail and riding in an open touring car. FDR was waving, grinning, the election already in his seersucker pocket. Dad lifted me astraddle his shoulders to be his human periscope over the hats of the Chicago street crowd. "What do you see?" he kept asking. And I made up stories, fabulations based on my need to keep his interest. "Oooo, there goes Tom Mix—" "Tom Mix is a Democrat?" somebody in the crowd marveled. "Then we can't lose."

Even then, I may have been planning a movie career, because I had this habit of turning union meetings into Hollywood extravaganzas, adapting the action—the close-packed, unair-conditioned, sweaty-smelling, airless, smoke-choked hall crammed with extras, all of whom had the universal immigrant look, erupting into sustained waves of earsplitting noise—into *Robin Hood* or *The Prisoner of Zenda*. I could get seriously lost in my mind writing, directing, photographing, and editing a box-office bonanza from the dissociated figures in the hall around me. My favorite scenario starred Jennie Persily and Leo Sigal (note precedence of credits) and had plenty of car chases, shootouts, dynamitings, and gangland massacres, not a whole lot different, I see now, from Mamet's *Hoffa* and Stallone's *F.I.S.T.*, except that one snowy night the fantasy turned all too real.

As streetlamps glowed blurrily in a heavy snowfall outside the Slavic Hall on Ashland Avenue, labor's Champs-Elysées, the back and side doors burst open and squads of uniformed and plainclothes cops fanned in to block the exits. "Intimidation, intimidation!" people inside the hall booed. Uproar. Angry beefy policemen sauntered up and down the aisles itching to slug somebody, anybody. All this was happening in *my* movie, except that this time somebody else was directing it.

A rough hand grabbed me by the collar and yanked me out of my folding chair.

"You're all under arrest for contributing the delinquency of this here minor!" roared the voice belonging to the fist at my neck. I dangled in this fat cop's grip. Rising pandemonium, shouts, curses, protests. Ma stepped down from the platform and began to reason with the detectives, some of whom she knew by name from the time they planted marked money on her.

In other parts of the hall, the women tried to keep the men out of it. Push, shove, tumult.

"Detective Hogan," Ma planted herself in front of the cop, "do you have children at home?"

"And that's where I keep them! In the house with their mother! Not at communist meetings!" Hogan yelled at her.

"Provocation! Cossacks!" cursed some of the union members.

Jennie coolly congratulated Detective Hogan on his good fortune in being able to keep his family at home in these troubled times because some workers were not so lucky. That's why this meeting had been called. "Don't you call me a worker!" Hogan roared, still holding me. "Yes, don't call the bastard a worker! He don't deserve it!" yelled some of the union guys. Tempers soared. Jennie, looking to avoid confrontation, declared the meeting was over anyway (untrue) so why not let everyone go home? Cries: "Don't let them get away with it, Jennie!"

That's when she really turned it on. "Please don't hurt my boy, Officer Hogan. He's sick can't you see?" Hogan, King Kong in a cheap suit, stared at me. Ma put a pink ribbon on it. "TB. Incurable," she reported falsely. I tumbled to the wooden floor when Hogan dropped me like a poisonous snake. The policemen around King Kong backed off from him. Tuberculosis was universally feared back then.

Things slowly began to calm down—until Dad showed up from a different meeting down the street. Spoiling for a fight, he ripped off his jacket. Ma knew what was coming.

She did the only thing possible, collapsed in agony, doubled over. "Oh God, my gallstones!" Several women hurried to her side as she slumped to her knees. She moaned, "The pain." The crowd rustled: "It's her gallbladder." Dad and King Kong glared at her in equal disbelief. They'd been ready, even *eager*, to tear each other apart.

In disgust King Kong turned to his colleagues. "Lying kike bitch." He knew he was being outsmarted by a woman, but the protective female phalanx around my mother was too much. With reluctant bravado, Hogan led the detectives' retreat out of the hall.

"Jennie, *du bist nicht krank? Du bist gesunt?* Are you all right?" the women asked. Ma writhed in mute agony. They helped her to a sitting position where one of the women fanned her vigorously while Dad fumed and huddled with some of his Tough Little Jew friends. Denied a role in protecting the meeting, they muttered impotently among themselves until Dad broke from the pack and walked over to Jennie. He grimaced in frustration, and for a second I thought we were in more danger from him than from the detectives.

Then the director in my head yelled *Cut!* and we went home.

* * *

Home was a storefront at 1404 South Kedzie Avenue in a neighborhood called Lawndale on Chicago's west side, halfway between Al Capone's bullet-riddled fiefdom in Cicero and high-walled Montefiore Boys' Reformatory in midcity, which was how I mentally mapped Chicago. In good times, 1404 Kedzie was a pleasant location on a bustling streetcar line and close to customers from nearby apartment houses, except this was the Depression, when people did their own wash or sent it to the Chinese laundry that opened a few doors down from us a week after we moved in. What little business there was, "the Chink" undercut, a penny here, a penny there—he was killing us.

I didn't care. I loved the store. We were a family. It said so in pink and green cursive script on a sign out front that swung creakily from a rusty pole in the wind: FAMILY HAND LAUNDRY. Jennie insisted that the name was a good omen. Dad chewed hard on his cigar and said nothing.

As usual, he'd come back to us looking like hell. Unshaven, tired, bloodshot eyes spitting dull fire, a ten-cent stogie stuck between his teeth. In ecstasy I'd watched this stranger saunter out of the night and wrap his arms around my surprised mother and swing her off her feet. "Leo, the boy is watching," she gasped as she returned his hungry kisses. Holding Ma in his grip, he looked over at me. We hadn't seen each other since I was in first grade and now I was in third. "Come here," he demanded bending down to rub my face with his hard, bristly jaw.

I grabbed him and held on.

✳ ✳ ✳

Ma had lured him off the road with an offer she told him he couldn't refuse. Ah, serpent's gift! "The comrades"—small-time owners of independent laundries all over Chicago—would buy him the lease of the Family Hand Laundry if Dad would agree to organize them in a rival union to break the grip of the crooked Teamsters Union that, in complicity with the large industrial laundry corporations, ran and corrupted the industry. Several previous organizers had been shot or otherwise disposed of by mobsters or "Chicagorillas." The comrades implored Dad, whom they saw as fearless, aggressive, and armed, to take on the *schtarkers*, the hoodlums. Jennie must have done a risk-benefit analysis and concluded the danger was worth having Dad back with us. And, who knows, the Sigals might make a dollar with the store.

This was almost our last shot together.

❋ ❋ ❋

The Family Hand Laundry home the three of us shared had a single fifteen square-foot room at the back as living quarters, a familiar setup then. The only "fixtures" were my parents' brass-knobbed four-poster bed, alongside that a swaybacked couch for me, a salt-and-pepper O'Keefe & Merritt gas stove, a wooden icebox with drip tray underneath, a corner toilet whose only privacy was a plywood chest-high partition, and my personal "office"—a folding card table on which sat an Admiral portable radio with the winking green eye and a cigar box full of baseball cards and rubber bands cut from old inner tubes, the indispensable tools of my trade as armorer and rubber-gun maker for boys on the street. (How to make an alley weapon: split the side board of a Sunkist orange crate, stretch two rubber bands lengthwise around one broken half of a wooden clothes peg so the knobby part exactly fits the top of your aiming sight, extend another rubber band—ammo—around the snout and pull it taut into the notch between peg and board. You are now ready to sneak up on your best friend and shoot him in the head.)

As much as I loved going Pullman, it was great resting in one place for a while with Dad pinned to the store like a dead butterfly.

❁ ❁ ❁

That wintry night, after the Slavic Hall near-riot, Jennie went to bed in the four-poster that occupied much of our back-of-the-store home. Pacing up and down, Dad kept his Homburg on, chewed his dead cigar furiously, then stormed out, banging the front door behind him. If his rage had been rocket fuel, the Family Hand Laundry would have exploded clean off the launch pad.

In my pajamas I climbed onto the couch and pulled the covers up to my chin. I wasn't sure what happened back there on Ashland Avenue between my parents, and didn't want to know.

"How's your gallbladder?" I called across in the dark.

"What gallbladder?" Jennie said.

Dad came back about four in the morning by the Ingraham radium clock, banging on the front door which Jennie had firmly locked after him. The door handle jiggled furiously.

I got up to let him in, but Jennie grabbed my hand and pulled me into bed with her. We hadn't been in the same bed since Dad came back from the road.

Whomp! whomp! on the front door.

"Ma," I said, "it's snowing."

She held me to her.

Eventually Dad gave up punching his fist on the door. Because the soft snow outside muffled sounds, I didn't know if he was shivering in the doorway or had faded into the night, this time for good.

I lay rigid, unmoving, afraid to upset the delicate balance of domestic terror I was sure I had somehow inspired. So I snuggled closer to Jennie's warm body and quietly, oh so quietly, played with myself.

Forward to the Past

Chicago is blessed with world-class museums including the Rosenwald Science and Industry, Shedd Aquarium, Adler planetarium, Art Institute etc. For me the best was the Field Museum of Natural History by Soldiers Field on Lake Michigan which became my sanctuary when things got too nerve-wracking at home, school or on the street.

I'd take a streetcar downtown and hide myself among the Field's exhibits, spending hours of truancy under the magnificent tusks of a North American bull mastadon while staring into a glass-encased replica of a Neanderthal family— bear-skin-covered Dad, prognathous-jawed Mom and Neanderthal Boy in waxy poses of domestic activity around a primitive fire with a stuffed sabre tooth tiger yowling just outside their cave. I came to visit so often that I felt on friendly, intimate terms with these prehistoric and pre-TV Flintstones, endowing each of them with names and moral characteristics. Dad was loving and protective; Mom nurturing and optimistic; and Neanderthal Boy a cutup. They spoke to me in Neanderthalese, and making sure no guard or witness was around I replied in the Native American speech I'd picked up from the radio serial of Tom Mix's Straight Shooters. ("Oowa oowa sa-wacka.")

Jennie appeared one day at the Museum looking for me. She might have been standing there some time, watching closely, before I noticed her, but I instantly knew she knew what I was worrying about: would Neanderthal Dad leave Mom and Neanderthal Boy. No real need to say anything.

"You're missing school again," she approached.

"Okay," I said, "let's go."

Ma said, "Say goodbye to your friends."

"Quit your kidding," I told her. "They're just dummies."

But we knew they weren't.

Mr. Gee Cuts Our Throat

The Chinese laundry next to the alley a few doors down on Kedzie Avenue was a bleak bare place with a dull red store front and simple black lettering—SAM GEE. How did "the Chink" delude himself that he could ever survive against our impressive pink and green sign outside and gold and black cash register inside? Curious, I took to pausing on my way home from school to stare balefully into Mr. Gee's coolie operation. The clammy darkness and steam mist made it hard to see inside, but I imagined they smoked opium and had tong wars. I knew all about the Chinese from *Mask of Fu Manchu*, with droopy-mustached Boris Karloff as the evil doctor and Myrna Loy as the lust-crazed "Chinee" girl.

I pushed my nose right up against his sweaty window and got a look at his bare-bones setup; two wooden planks as a counter, a *suan-pan*, or abacus wood frame with rods and beads as a cash register, a mangle made of iron with wood rollers like we had at the Family Hand Laundry to damp dry customers' wash, and an ironing board. A woman who was hand sewing at the front window glanced up at me in alarm and signaled to her husband, a youngish guy with jet-black hair who went to his wife as if protecting her from some kind of wild beast. His two kids, a little girl and a boy about my age, came to stand beside them, nervously staring at me staring at them.

I'd seen enough. Before they'd become aware of me they had been smoothly meshing as a team in the hot damp store, each silently bent to a task, with both kids involved, the little girl tying handkerchiefs together on a string and the boy ironing a shirt all by himself. Until that moment it never occurred to me to help out in our store except to mind it alone when my parents were out and I had an empire to protect, like Flash Gordon versus Ming the Terrible.

Suddenly the Chinese proprietor, Sam Gee, came out still wielding his steam iron. He knew who I was. "Go 'way. You spy." He pointed to the hand-scrawled cardboard signs at the bottom of his front window giving his prices:

One shirt one dime
Two shirts 20 ¢
Three shirts 25 ¢

"Legal!" he shouted. "All legal! Shoo!" He whirled his steam iron around his head to warn me off. At least it wasn't a dagger and he wasn't wearing a pigtail, so I backed off, giving him the customary up-you with my crooked arm.

The bastard was cut-rating us to death. We advertised "fine finish" at fifteen cents a shirt, a nickel over him, and we promised customers some items specially hand-washed, which Ma did in an old wooden tub next to our tin bathtub out back. On his desperately low prices how could Sam Gee pay off *schmeer* to the health inspector as we had to?

But he'd given me an idea. I marched into our Family Hand Laundry to announce that I wanted to learn how to iron a shirt. My father looked up astonished, Ma raised *both* eyebrows; my volunteering to help at anything was unprecedented. Ma said, "Are you feeling well, Kalman?" adding, "It took your father two years' apprentice at the Ritz-Carlton before they let him touch a shirt." My father simply gaped. At last I'd impressed him.

In the end, they gave in and under Dad's tutelage I learned how to press shirt cuffs, not the whole shirt or collars or fancy monogrammed or specially starched, just cuffs, the steam iron not too hot to burn the fabric and not so cold it was wrinkled. Thanks to Sam Gee, I was ironing my way into Dad's love, I hoped.

P.S. Since then, I have exchanged experiences with a Chinese laundryman's son, Pak Lew, and examined a PhD thesis on the subject by Dr. Paul C.P. Siu. In all likelihood, Sam Gee or his parents came from the Taishan district by the South China Sea whose peasant economy had been ruined by Western manufactured goods—and had emigrated to the "Old Gold Mountain" (America) by way of California and relocated East after the race riots of the 1870s. Isolated except for clan relationships, they were outside Chicago's complicated police-and-Mob culture in which our laundry operated. To the best of my knowledge, they were the only Chinese family in Lawndale.

I never progressed much beyond cuffs, but I'm super at that.

1936—President Franklin D. Roosevelt elected in a landslide. Bruno Richard Hauptman convicted of kidnapping and murdering the Lindbergh baby. Mussolini and Hitler proclaim an "axis." King Edward VIII, a Hitler sympathizer, abdicates British throne for "the woman I love," a randy American divorcée.

5

The Heart Is a Gregarious Hunter

We are the men of the coming generation
We are the lads who will build a mighty nation
Hopeful are we in the planting of the seeds
We are the men our country needs—
                              —school song

Huckleberry came and went of his own free will.
                              —Mark Twain, *Huckleberry Finn*

Much of this story occurs in a square mile on Chicago's west side known as Lawndale, although at the time almost nobody except precinct captains and sociologists called it by that Arcadian name; everyone else knew it as GVS—Greater Vest Side —a reference to its predominantly (95 percent plus) Jewish population.

Technically, the west side stretches from *schmatte*-haggling now-demolished Maxwell Street on the edge of the Loop way out to the western suburbs of Oak Park and Austin. But my own west side was "inner city"; ten close-packed city blocks that featured a long main drag — Roosevelt Road, or Twelfth Street — a park, sixty-five synagogues, countless storefront *schuls*, St. Agatha's church, Sears, Roebuck's world headquarters with its own railway sidings, the Labor Lyceum — an agora for displaced Old Country radicals — the Marks Nathan Jewish Orphan Home, and the Moorish-turreted "western edition" office of the nation's most widely read Yiddish newspaper, the *Forward*. Racial boundaries, the essence of neighborhood Chicago, were strictly observed then as now, though today the ethnicities have changed. The frontiers of each ethnic neighborhood were visibly marked by a streetcar track, viaduct, or tunnel or a street name that defined the exclusive territory of the Irish, Italians, and Poles who lived east, south, and west of us. You knew exactly who you were in Chicago because if you stepped across a certain curb or transgressed the wrong end of a railway bridge some stranger was sure to knock your teeth out.

* * *

My personal GVS, a feudal city-within-a-city with imaginary walls to keep us in and hostile strangers out, was perceived by more prosperous or ethnically unfriendly Chicagoans as a filthy, cockroach-infested, crime-ridden slum full of "kikes," the lowest form of Jew, crawling up from where they belonged, which was in the slime of Maxwell Street. The upwardly mobile north-side mother of the first girl I ever dated, a Senn High beauty, offered Jennie big money, $100, if she would use her influence to forbid my

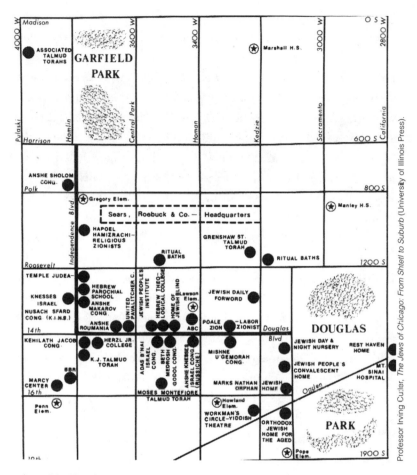

Lawndale. My "city within a city." More synagogues and schuls than Dublin has pubs.

Professor Irving Cutler, *The Jews of Chicago: From Shtetl to Suburb* (University of Illinois Press).

seeing her daughter. Such was Lawndale's disrepute. "You shoulda taken the money, Ma," I brayed. Jennie coldly looked me up and down. "Mrs. Kaiserman probably is right about you. The company you keep, the way you dress. But sell you out to a common snob, never!" The key insult here is common, not snob.

51

Real Chicago life begins west of Michigan Avenue and the Loop business district, where the vast city is a particular, parochial, and provincial patchwork of watchful neighborhoods. Only in today's distant suburbs like Highland Park and Winnetka can you get away with saying "I'm from Chicago" without an exact reference to a specific school, parish, tavern, alley. A wealthy real estate developer, who had financed the Sears Tower and was himself a west sider, once refused me an interview until I identified exactly which neighborhood I was from. "Kedzie and sixteenth," I said. "No," he demanded, "which *corner*?"

Fight the Power

On the GVS I never met an accountant, doctor or lawyer, not even an insurance salesman. If such species existed they lived beyond the known limits of my universe. "Middle class" was anyone who had a job no matter how lowly. Studs Terkel once told me he was amazed that so few—almost none—of the Rockets became white-collar professionals. "Neighborhood bums—don't get me wrong," he laughed. "But you guys are a statistical improbability."

One exception. Mr Freyer, a "people's lawyer," lived down the street from us with his wife and a pretty daughter my age named Annette. Jennie moved heaven and earth to make a *shi-dach*, a romantic match, between Annette and me because in her mind this would boost me up a social notch. "Such a clean, *nice* girl," Ma breathed. Didn't she know this was the kiss of death? Indeed, the Freyers invited me to dinner, once, and never repeated the experience. When I asked Ma why she just leaned on the Family Hand Laundry counter and looked me up and down appraisingly. "They concede you were polite and well mannered and ate everything they put before you. You didn't make dirty jokes or raise your voice."

"So?" I badgered her.

She shrugged. "So . . . they know."

"Know what?"

Ma sighed. "It's written all over you. Kedzie Avenue."

I protested that Mr. Freyer lived on the same street as us.

She shook her head. "You'll never be one of them. What's to become of you?"

"One thing for sure," I crowed. "Annette Freyer is the big loser on this deal."

Of course, Annette became one of the few Lawndale girls to go to college, even more rarely became a lawyer like her dad and married a judge. The judge, like so many in Chicago, later went to jail on a graft charge so I came out winners after all, is how I see it.

* * *

I was a perfectly ordinary Kedzie Avenue kid with an IQ tested—twice—as "low normal," an embarrassment to Jennie but a matter of stubborn pride to me. My main ambition was to remain *in situ* in GVS for the rest of my life and never leave it or my rabble—the Rockets Athletic Club of Greater West Side Chicago, fake red satin jackets and all. The cement sidewalk under my feet was reassuringly solid; the low skyline and long straight streets and prairie perspectives stretching to infinity on the flat Illinois urban plain never changed because in economically sick Chicago time itself stood still, and it was great.

Clancy, age nine, in Chicago. A Teamster thug in embryo.

The Great Depression, which for the poor lasted twelve years, from Black Monday 1929 until after Pearl Harbor, was for us boys a sort of stop-time paradise, an anarchic kingdom of our very own.

Life was full of danger but remarkably stable. Divorce was nonexistent because nobody could afford a lawyer. The neighborhood was physically intact as there was no cash incentive for developers to tear down and rebuild. The synagogue, church, school, boys' club, and street corner that were here in 1933 still stood ten years later. Permanence, of a sort, ruled.

For us preteenage Rockets, the "slum" neighborhood, perceived from the outside as a fetid swamp of crime, vice, and violence, was a vastly amusing playground served by six majestic Greek-columned elementary schools, two high schools and — glory be to the Balaban & Katz theater chain — seven movie houses within easy walking distance. I am a born spy, and just to park my backside on a busy curb and scan the rumbling traffic—pushcart peddlers, street singers, horse-drawn ice wagons, itinerant scissors grinders, roaring streetcars with swaying sparking electric poles, and kids galore running shouting pushing—was better than the best movie ever made.

Without irony, the Rocket-boys I grew up with call Depression-time Lawndale an "endless summer" of time-wasting, with nothing to do but mooch about and dream, bull-shit, and fight. Of course, it's partly nostalgia but also a still-strong sense of what the army calls "unit cohesion." Most west siders felt so attached to Lawndale that, when they socially scrambled up a notch after World War II, many moved as a group to Rogers Park or Morton Grove and took the old street signs with them; even today, sixty years later, when they are in tonier suburbs like Lincolnwood and Buffalo Grove, west siders continue to see each other, sometimes daily. I know of one poker game consisting of neighborhood guys that has gone on for more than half a century. And three of my best Rocket friends—Ike, Julie, and Hy—have dinner with one another and their families most Monday nights.

Although the crime rackets (whorehouses, bookie joints, fences for stolen merchandise) were Mob-controlled, "civilian" murder was rare in GVS, possibly because the weapons were unobtainable or too expensive. But suicide was a ready option for parents driven to the edge by hard times. Barely anyone we knew shot themselves; gas or rat poison, usually administered by women to themselves, was the preferred method. Even Jennie—for whom self-control under pressure was a kind of religion—when she was off-balance or screaming inside, would suddenly drop to her knees like a penitent in front of the gas stove and flick on the jets without striking a match. Watching in terror, I'd pretend to be bored and yawn, "Ma, be yourself." Her distraught eyes would slowly refocus. Still kneeling, she'd calmly fix her hair, rise, and walk away in serene composure, and I'd turn off the gas, listening to my beating heart slow down.

Almost all GVS apartments had their "small dark back room" holding a reclusive old country *bubbeh* or a mother half dead with mental or physical exhaustion, a crazed spinster sister or a depressed father, victims of culture shock compounded by poverty. While we sons enjoyed an astonishing freedom and autonomy, the grown-ups killed themselves, either with one sharp twist of an O'Keefe & Merritt spigot or by degrees with stress and anxiety. The despairing rage that simmered just under the neighborhood skin, sometimes erupting in family brawls, wife beatings, or ax attacks, must have—I'm told—affected us boys for the rest of our lives. But our west side culture survived on denial and iron will. Or, as my best friend and fellow Rocket, Ike Lerman (103d Infantry Division, 112 straight days in the line), says, "The reason we won the war was because our generation went into combat already experienced in doing what we were told to do in dangerous situations. That's what the Depression was all about. You ate shit and didn't complain."

But for Ike, Deaf Augie, Julie, Oscar, Marvin, Mendy, Albie, Hy, Legs, and Barney, the troubled 1930s was a time of unparalleled freedom.

My ten-year-old son Joe protests, "Movies cost only a dime? And your mother let you go alone? No way!"

Rules Is Rules

Today's gang warfare is random, impulsive, drive-by, Uzis and Glocks spraying innocent bystanders; our GVS violence was contained within a neighborhood crime structure that had natural laws and limits. The organized syndicate out of Capone's Cicero ran all the "legit" crime, like bookies and whores, and in that world only guys who skimmed or didn't pay up on time had their legs broken, or, if the infraction was serious enough, targeted for a hit. Betting on a fixed race was okay, but collecting twice through a dummy bettor was a cause for capital punishment. Everyone, including children, knew the code, the hierarchy, and where the operations were located. Every block had its fixer. "Zimmy," precinct captain under Arthur Elrod (who served God himself, Jake Arvey, alderman and kingmaker of the twenty-fourth ward) was our fixer. In return for my mother's vote and some cash, Zimmy got my name erased from the Pulaski Street police station blotter, and in return for Ma's promise to pet out the people on our side of the street for Democrats we received a Thanksgiving basket and a vague promise of a city job when the Irish quota was full. Cops routinely protected the rackets according to a fixed fee schedule. (In the 1960s, after a series of unusually flagrant scandals, a new police superintendent, Orlando Wilson, cracked down on institutionalized bribery, a reform that shook the moral foundations of Chicago citizenry long acclimatized to cop graft. One police lieutenant complained to me that, as a result of the anticorruption rules, his income was halved overnight. "This new system," he sighed, "nobody knows where they stand anymore. Yesterday I stop this car for speeding on Outer Drive. Driver holds out the usual twenty with his driver's license. I step back and say, "No thank you." I thought the guy would faint.")

There were hardly any gang murders on the west side because there were no competing mobs. The chance that Jesus could set up a table at Temple Anshe Sholem was as good as rival gangsters surviving Capone retribution. The poolroom/bookie joints where I hung out—Davey Miller's, Putty Anixter's, Zucky's—suffered no competition. Occasionally some half-brained entrepeneur would try to open a lunchroom or horse parlor across from an already established crook joint, but it was always followed by a mysterious explosion and fire.

The only exception to this tightly structured system of controlled crime was Davey Miller's poolroom near our store where super-tough but un-Mob-organized Jewish guys hung out. They were the muscle armed with baseball bats and tire chains who went after the Italians ganging up on Jews or fought down at the beach when *goyim* tried to keep Jews off of it. For Davey Miller's boys, the Jewish role models were not Albert Einstein or Justice Felix Frankfurter but two neighborhood pugs: Barney Ross (Barnet Rosofsky), a Capone apprentice (and son of an Orthodox rabbi murdered in a dairy store robbery) whose three hundreth bout was an epic fifteen-rounder against the three-time titleholder Henry Louis Armstrong; and "Kingfish" Levinsky, who fought all comers even after Joe Louis knocked him out in the first round. (Later, Barney Ross became a Marine hero on Guadalcanal, and the Kingfish ended his own career by hawking men's ties all over GVS.)

In our child's kingdom, a high level of physical aggression was accepted as a normal expression of friendship, and we'd flail away at each other on no pretext other than the sheer joy of hitting and getting hit. Some nights I'd return home with a smashed eye or blood-snotted nose and Jennie would cry, "Did a car hit you?" "No, just playing with the guys," I'd say truthfully.

We Rockets had a strict sense of honor with clear rules: (a)

Nobody was to earn a higher classroom grade than anybody else; (b) Status was conferred ambiguously; I became a Rocket hero when left behind in a "subnormal" (retarded, or special-ed) class along with the deafies, pink-eyed albinos, and other local dummies; (c) You never left the group for any reason other than death.

One incident: On the first day of school after summer break there was a Howland Elementary assembly to distribute prizes to deserving pupils. No Rocket had ever won a school prize, and on pain of torture none ever would. We lounged arrogantly in the back row, kicking the seats in front of us, when out of the blue, to my horror, the principal called my name. "To Clarence Sigal—for reading the most library books over the summer vacation." The branch librarian, whom I'd sworn to secrecy, had ratted me out! Half a dozen pairs of Rocket eyes launched themselves like missiles at me. I was caught. Reading was my secret pleasure, like jacking off in Mrs. Zaretzky's bathtub.

"Get up, pansy," Albie Lesher hissed, the guys staring at me as if I was a total stranger. The principal called out cheerily, "Don't be bashful, Clarence. Please come up and accept your award." In agonizingly slow motion I squirmed out of my seat and edged toward the aisle, my face burning with shame, as each of the Rockets savagely kicked, punched, and tore at me. By the time I fell headlong into the aisle I had a cut lip and my clean white shirt was out of my knickers and ripped down my back.

Clambering onstage, I numbly accepted the school prize, a rosette of Howland school colors, blue and white with a ribbon hanging down. The assembly politely applauded, and I tried skulking away, but the principal pulled me back and made me face the audience. Way in back I saw Albie, Nate, Ike, Deaf Augie, and the others rollicking with sneering laughter. How to preserve my honor? On brilliant impulse I stuffed the blue ribbon into my mouth and in slow, grinding, clownish movements began chewing it to pieces. The principal and the teachers in the front row simply stared, but my boys burst into thunderous, approving hand claps that continued until the ribbon disappeared into my balloon cheeks and halfway down my gullet, leaving the rosette to scrape my bruised lips and almost choking me with the little pin stuck in the ribbon. Thus, honor restored, I held up my arms like Max Baer after winning a fight and made a little war dance, proving once and for all that I was no snitch, no brain. Rockets now and forever!

Who They Were

One boy equals one brain
Two boys equal two brains
Three or more boys equal no brain.
                    —old saying

The Rockets, all nine or ten of us, moved and thought collectively as a slug-like amoeba, expanding and contracting on whim, sometimes more cellular than distinctly human. There was no leader, no charismatic crack-the-whip boss, no agenda, no purpose or point. *That* was the point. The club—gang, posse, whatever—existed within its own contradictions; you asserted your individual autonomy through its mass-think. I felt most comfortable and *independent* inside a conformist mob of undisciplined, mouthy, and impulsive Rockets. They gave me the strength to ultimately leave them.

There was nothing smudgy or indeterminate about each

Rocket's personality. Character was bound up in the all-important look that you were either born with or had improved with hair oil, Mennen's aftershave lotion, or a particular article of clothing regarded as ultimate cool. Albie (Albert) Lesher, the only one of us reputed to have actually "done it" with a girl, was almost bald at thirteen, with a sexual smirk permanently planted on his Arthur Millerish face. Even in his adolescence, Heshie (Hillel) Wolinsky looked middle-aged and sober. He, too, was losing his hair; thoughtful where we were careless, his surface calm was subverted only by startling outbursts of obscenity directed at girls, remarks nauseating even by our abysmal standards. My best friend, Ike (Isaac) Lerman, was an open-faced, gentle (at most times), hard-punching (at other times) slugger who policed our conduct for club rule infractions; lonely and troubled, he hated to go home at night to his dark apartment (electricity cut off), which was virtually barren of food. (Jennie fed him Jello and Pepsi-Cola, which he'd never tasted before.) Legs (Ben) Glasser was a bookie runner earning a significant income and the only one of us in organized sports—a second-string varsity basketball center for the all-city Marshall High team. Built like a young Mr. Universe, he already knew he was going to marry Marion Lebedeff. He was a scrappy young Maccabee with a grown man's outlook. Deaf Augie (August Bauer), plumply passive, smiled at everyone all the time and would do anything you hand-signaled him to do; later, in his early twenties, it was discovered he had been mis-diagnosed and he regained his hearing after surgery to remove the wax in his ears. The freckled redhead Julie (Julius) Wax had the meanest punch and played the nastiest pranks—you'd turn a corner and he'd smash a lemon crème pie in your face. He was a math whiz though none of us knew it at the time because we would have whipped his ass for being superior. Oscar Guttierez's father was serving time in Joliet prison for burglary; Jennie washed my mouth out with Lifebuoy soap for the last time when I called his dad a "jailbird" and made Oscar, ordinarily tough as nails, cry; he was a sweet quiet boy, a go-along get-along kid and dynamite in street fights. Mendy (Mordecai) Rapp was pure corner bum, foulmouthed and affable, a permanent school truant who spent most of his time roaming the streets and looking for trouble. He later teamed with a couple of neighborhood toughs, "Indian" and "Charley," to work as a strong-arm artist and, maybe because he'd seen too many crime movies, crashed out of a second-story apartment window during a police barricade. High-wired Hy (Hyman) Zimmerman, the most jittery Rocket, had a crush on his own sister, over whose sexual life he appointed himself supervisor with our lynch-mob assistance. And Nate (Nathan) Manoff, the smallest and most cunning Rocket, provoked street-corner brawls from which he somehow always seemed to escape while others took their lumps; Nate tootled clarinet in the school orchestra and ambled along Roosevelt Road humming Mozart and had a habit of jumping on my back and hammering me for no particular reason.

Roughhousing, wrestling, and punching one another to leave purple bruises functioned to restore something in the common order, a sense of assertion and self to right a balance thrown askew by the life around us.

But each of us had a secret vice, an intellectual perversion, unknown to and hidden from the others because it might betray our group-think. Ike snuck off to Grant Park symphonic concerts; Oscar solved chemistry problems in his basement; Legs built frontier-style Conestaga covered wagons out of old cigar boxes; Julie Wax tinkered with math problems from his older brother's textbook; and so on. Yet no Rocket dared import his secret pleasure into the club: better to be known as an ignoramus than a snob. The one time I dared enter the Chicago Art Institute, instead of merely riding on one of the bronze lions outside, I was thrown out by a guard for climbing up on the naked and armless Venus to touch her white marble breasts. By pure coincidence, a couple of the Rockets were passing by on Michigan Avenue and they chased and jeered at me all the way to the State Street L station.

Low culture was our high culture. Despite the mild scorn of Jennie, who loved Russian novels and Maurice Schwartz's Yiddish Art Theater, which specialized in "new and improved" Shakespeare, I clung to crude pop for its seductive way of shaping my shapeless dreams. The soaring-sweet trumpet meister, Harry James, was my idea of art, Wee Bonnie Baker ("Oh, Johnny, Oh") my comfort zone. Classical music I first learned from Republic Studio's cowboy movies, where Comanche chases were often set to Liszt's *Les Preludes* or to Rossini because the old scores were free in the public domain.

It's possible I got stuck back there when the other Rockets were quietly evolving, behind my back, so to speak. How else explain that, as adults, Ike became a passionate opera buff or Julie Wax had enough math to become a B-17 navigator or Albie the Schtupper a serious Sunday painter in the Klee style? True, the teenage Rockets whipped my ass for reading "too many" books, but what were we holding out on each other?

Clancy's graduation photo from Howland elementary school in Chicago (second row, third from right). Age thirteen. Can you pick out his fellow Rockets?

Tom Sawyer in a Yarmulke

My Chicago in the 1930s and 40s was 95 percent Jewish and 115 percent Democrat. (Vote early, vote often.) Religion defined the neighborhood but not me. On Saturday mornings cantors' voices ululated through the Lawndale district, which supposedly held the highest concentration of Orthodox Jewry in the world outside of Poland. Some of the cantors were as famous to us as Enrico Caruso and Schaliapin were to opera lovers. There was a *schul* on almost every street corner, and sixty-five synagogues in a one-square-mile area, imposing citadels of faith that rivaled any Christian church brought over stone by stone to Chicago from the Old Country: Anshe Roumania, Anshe Makarov, Anshe Knesses Israel (Russische), K.J. Talmud Torah, Adas B'Nai Israel, Temple Judea. Sprinkled on any given block, as numerous as pubs in Dublin, were tiny informal front-porch schuls bearing the names of the *shtetls* from which their founders originated (Pinsk, Odessa, Wilno, etc.).

The twenty-fourth ward's main thoroughfares—Roosevelt Road, Sixteenth Street, Kedzie Avenue—were thronged with elderly Jews in ankle-length black frock coats and young *yeshivah bochim* in yarmulkes. Almost all shop windows had freshly white-painted signs in Yiddish, and on almost every counter inside you could find a blue and white slotted can for contributions to a Jewish homeland in Palestine or, if the proprietor was Communist, in Soviet Azerbaijan. The Midwest headquarters of the nation's most popular Jewish newspaper, the *Daily Forward*, was in a green-turreted building on Thirteenth and Kedzie a block from our laundry.

Yet I strolled around as if my ears were stuffed with cotton and my eyes half-blind to these obvious signs of the Old Country. There was an emotionality to the Jewish life around me—all that yelling, arguing, out-front loves and hates—that distanced me even as my life depended on it for sustenance and continuity. *Stop all this noise*, I wanted to scream at these vulgar, crude, cursing, pushing, elbowing crowds—before jumping in to add my own noise to the joyful and hurtful dissonance. A congregation's *kol nidre* sifting through the stained glass windows of the synagogues I never attended had a strange and unsettling effect on me. It was all mumbo jumbo I kept telling myself, while pausing on the corner to listen with all my heart.

On the Jewish new year, Rosh Hashanah, 25,000 Jews of all ages trudged down feeder streets to the Douglas Park lagoon to cast their accumulated sins into the mossy water, and on the other High Holidays boys my own age—including the Rockets Athletic Club except for Oscar Guttierez, Deaf Augie, and me—would suit up to play the chestnut game in front of the crowded synagogues. Approaching their thirteenth birthday, one by one my pals inconspicuously slipped away to study for their bar mitzvahs; and to my astonishment, on my own secular graduation day from Howland Elementary, the parents and *mispochah* in the school auditorium rose to their feet and stood to attention when we eighth-graders onstage sang the Jewish hymn "Hatikvah" in a medley of the world's national anthems. Even my mother, erect and proud, had tears in her eyes. What was that all about?

Jewishness was so taken for granted on the west side that up to then I'd believed that all of us, grown-ups and kids alike, were on the same assimilationist wavelength, that poverty and religion, which in my mind went hand in hand, would somehow disappear in the American Miracle. "Hatikvah" opened me up to Lawndale's beating Jewish heart. They were different from me, I realized. Up to then I'd successfully deluded myself, in a mental trick, that though my soul was Lawndale, a secret part of me lived along a Mississippi river bank with those honorary Rockets, Tom Sawyer and Huck Finn. I felt perfectly at ease absorbing the actual Lawndale into a rural fantasia of it. Everything that was the real Chicago around me—polyglot languages (Russian, Polish, Hungarian, German, Yiddish, Greek, Slovak, you name it), chicken-fat smells, the roaring iron rhythms of big-city life—somehow morphed into nineteenth-century Hannibal, Missouri, a boys' utopia, a lot like Chattanooga on its best warm summer day. Living this split existence was no strain. I was *here*, I was *there*, the two halves of my imagination in touch with both realities, my fantasy Hannibal and the actual Chicago. When MGM's *Tom Sawyer* movie came out, I was just sane enough to know that its rural Missouri was neither mine nor the real one but the studio's.

My private make-believe Hannibal had no Jews, real Lawndale nothing but. The psychic space between them licensed me, in my own view, to be a different self-invented Jew, unridiculed and unscorned, atheistic, unpersecuted, a Pimpernel spy in *goyishe* territory. For example, whenever I explored a new neighborhood, crossing forbidden ethnic lines, and was accosted by a gang of strange kids and they'd ask, "Hey, what religion are you?" (the Chicago version of "Who are you, alien?"), I'd glance around to spot the nearest church spire and, depending on its architecture, reply stoutly, "Lutheran" or "Catholic." I was quite good at this. Ma and I had pretended so often dowun sowuth to be other than what we were that it was second nature for me to lie plausibly. "Oh yeah?" a skeptical kid might demand, "do me a Hail Mary." And I'd drop to my knees and recite the Rosary like Father Lenihan, who operated St. Agatha's across Kedzie from the store, taught me.

About the only religion I never imagined myself to be was Jewish.

That's because I *was* Jewish. And *that's* because, encouraged by my mother's calculated lack of spiritual guidance, I felt I had a right to choose what kind of Jew I wanted to be. That is, to be a super-*American* Super-Jew who rode free on the backs of streetcars hanging by his fingertips from the rear window, thieved and burgled abandoned stores and apartments, built semilethal rubber guns, would gladly have died for a chance to be the Chicago Cubs' batboy—my second highest ambition—and fled guiltlessly from the Twenty-second Street Irish who were screaming "Christ killer!" Being Jewish had *nothing* to do with religion; it was a fighting creed or it was nothing. Both my parents, Jennie and Leo, were strong proud

Jews who rarely entered a schul, not even Knesses Israel Nusach Sfard or the "laundrymen's shul." Keep kosher? Ma loved ham, bacon, pork, shellfish—anything *trafe*. And Dad lived in an almost entirely gentile world of about-to-be-organized Italian barbers, German butchers, and Ukrainian meat packers where he—a small wiry man with a hair-trigger punch—relished "standing up" to real or imagined anti-Semites, the bigger the better.

I knew Jews *looked* different, just as towheaded Poles and fair-skinned Irish did. Many of my school chums—Moishe, Julie, Albie, Abe, Mendy—were small and dark and, yes, had "Jewish" noses: the immigrant look. (See my Patrick Henry and Howland school photos.) But along with Julie Wax and Legs Glasser I was one of the "American looking" Jews, who in any crowd could pass as Clarence Carmichael or Calvin Peterson or Clement Wood or any other Waspy name Ma invented for me. Being able to pass was useful "out there," in a world of Jew baiters and Hitler sympathizers; inside the Lawndale shtetl I felt deeply secure in my multiple Jew-who-is-a-non-Jew-but-a-certain-kind-of-Jew identity. Anyway, just as there was no gay option, what choice was there? Hitler and his American Nazi Bundists had defined me and my kind for all time as destined for *ausrotten*—extermination—so the judgment was in. We were the People Chosen to die. After 1933, when Hitler was voted into power, and NBC began radio hookups to Berlin, when the neighbors gathered to listen to translations of the Nazi rant, I had to move spiritually out of Hannibal back to where I felt safe and battle-ready. Everyone knew a war was coming; it became the Rockets' permanent anxiety and conversation piece. "Better now than later," we said, and our rough games became preparations for combat.

This left only the question of God.

There was no God. And I was angry with Him.

On warm summer evenings, while my mother and father were screaming at each other ("Leo, pay attention to the store" "Leave me alone, I wasn't born for this"), I'd slip out the Family Hand Laundry's back door through the alley onto Douglas Boulevard, a mile-long grassy strip, to lie on the dewy ground and stare up at the stars and shake my fist. "IF YOU ARE THERE," I cursed, "MAKE ME NOT BE." Especially on sultry thundery nights I'd call down lightning flashes to electrocute me like Bruno Richard Hauptman, the Lindberg baby kidnapper, staring God in the eye and calling His bluff. God the putz making my mother cry and ruining my Dad's bowels, and I was furious with Him for creating, or condoning, a profit system that had no profit for us. God was a Jew who probably owned a bankrupt garment sweatshop and squeezed, squeezed the workers until their tears ran dry.

This was not an abstract argument, nothing on the west side ever was. God was personal and immediate in His absence. My mother refused to intervene in my quarrel with the putz-god. Even though her dearest wish was that I grow up "more Jewish," she was totally unyielding that I find my own answer. "I'm an atheist," I protested. "So," she'd replied "at least be a *Jewish* atheist."

Case #1. Finally, when Jennie could stand it no longer she'd sigh, "Go ask Father Lenihan. He's closer to God than I am, for sure." He was the priest at St. Agatha's across the street, who let me use the church gym in the hope I carefully nourished, that I would convert. Also, I liked going to Easter Mass at St. Aggie's—it was safer inside than outside the church on the day Jews killed their Lord—and kneeling to make the sign of the cross with my fingers dipped into stone-urned holy water.

"Why is it, Clarence, I don't see you very often at services?"

"I'm sorry, Father. My mother's been sick." Lies in the sacristy.

"Oh, too bad. Would you like myself or one of the Sisters to call upon her?"

"We're not Catholics yet, Father."

"Ah, yes."

I had an exquisite sense of the mark.

Still, give it to him, Father Lenihan extended himself for a few more private sessions. Nodding sagely, grunting attentively, he'd listen to my God questions. Sincerity flowed from the man like communion wine. I was so sure he was sure he had me hooked that my tongue loosened. Jesus, I suggested one day, was the first socialist. Matthew, Mark, Luke, and John — I'd learned about them at Baptist primary school — were the first labor organizers, like John L. Lewis and Harry Bridges who were the Antichrists in the eyes of the *Chicago Tribune*, the most widely read newspaper in the Midwest. "Who?" Father Lenihan leaned forward to catch my drift until our heads were nearly touching. Suddenly he reached over, circled his big red hand around my ear, yanked me to my feet, and frogmarched me, my feet hardly touching the splendidly polished and waxed floor, to the side door, and with no particular violence but plenty of muscle kicked me out with a swift one in the keester.

What is it about men of the cloth and my ears?

Case #2. Ma dispatches me, age eight, to my first and only Hebrew school in Albany Park, Chicago, in an upstairs room leased from a dry goods store. The teacher is choleric Reb Barzalai, a large imposing man in a black frock coat. I survive a single day. Enraged by my unruly conduct, the Reb lunges at me, twists my ear, and throws me down a flight of stairs, where I tumble out onto busy Lawrence Avenue.

Case #3. Ma broods about my lack of *yiddishkeit*, a feel for the Jewish people. She sends me, age ten, to a pacifist-socialist *arbeitering schule* at the Workmen's Circle temple over by Ogden and Kedzie. The atmosphere is more radical and less pious. On the wall hangs a large tinted photograph of a World War I soldier with most of his face from chin to bridge of nose shot away. I am expelled for throwing spitballs. The teacher, a hitherto gentle man, walks down the classroom aisle, pulls me up by my ear, and takes me out into the street. When he releases me, he dusts off his hands and says, *"Feh."*

Last case. A sunny Saturday morning on Christiana Street, where my basement clubhouse also is located. On the sidewalk I am exercising my main talent, doing nothing. A little old man with cracked teeth summons me to him on the front porch of a two-story family house. *"Du kennst mir a bisselah helpf geben?"* I give him the classic west side response, "How much?" He holds out what turns out to be, on inspection, a nickel. He lures me inside a small dark apartment and gestures me to pull the string on a naked light bulb hanging from the ceiling. I yank it and find myself in the interior of a tiny schul, or "people's synagogue." Politely, he ushers me back outside to the stone porch. *"Boychik,"* he croaks, *"bis du nischt a Yid?"* "Sure I'm a Jew," I assure him. Whack! He slaps me across the face, grabs one ear and—yes—pushes me down the steps. *"Shabbish goy!"* he screams, meaning a non-Jew hired to do work prohibited to Jews, especially on the Sabbath. At the time, I have no idea what the crazy old bastard is yelling about. But I keep the nickel.

By now I am thinking that perhaps I am not destined for a religious vocation.

❊ ❊ ❊

Recently, I took Joe to his first Hebrew lesson at a local temple because my gentile wife insists on it . "He should know who he is," she says. "He already knows that," I argue, "and he has no identity crisis." "He's half Jewish," she persists, "and I don't want him having a problem about it later in life."

On Friday nights we have shabbat dinner, complete with chollah, candles, and a brief "Baruch atoi adenoi" blessing at table. Joe sports his yarmulke at a cocky angle like my father wore his Homburg hat. At Sunday dinner Janice says a brief blessing ("We give most humble thanks"), and that's it for theology. But as time goes by, more and more Yiddish street slang rolls unbidden off my tongue. I cannot pretend to a *Yiddishkeit* I have not earned, and not all precincts are in about God, as my mother would say, but perhaps through Joe I may regain a wholeness of what's left of that which Jennie devoutly wished for me to be, a Jewish mensch.

❊ ❊ ❊

In the *Midrash*, an ancient Hebrew commentary, there is a strange and gripping tale. Rabbi Meir, an Orthodox sage, is taking lessons from the Jewish heretic Akhar on a Sabbath. The heretic rides a donkey while Rabbi Meir walks beside him in deep argument. Suddenly the heretic says, "Look—we have reached the boundary [where no Jew is permitted on the Sabbath]. We must part now. You must not accompany me further. Go back!" Rabbi Meir returns to his Jewish community while the heretic Akhar—the Stranger—rides on, beyond the boundaries of Jewry.

This story has puzzled generations of Jews, including the Polish anti-Nazi poet and biographer, Isaac Deutscher, from whom I borrow it. But "beyond the boundaries" is where I live as a Jew. I was born a "Hitler Jew," just as today I am an Osama Jew: the real, personal threat gives me almost no wiggle room. Over the years I have, indeed, become "more Jewish," partly through having a half-Jewish son, partly in response to living so long in England with its closet anti-Semitism. That's my rational brain. But twice in my life, my soul—which the other marginal Jew, Freud, called an unconscious—commanded me. In the sixties, when I had a transformative moment (anxious witnesses called it a breakdown) in a schizophrenic halfway house in London, I suddenly leapt upon a communal supper table and pranced between the soup bowls with an imaginary *tallit* around my shoulder, singsonging Hebraic prayers that bubbled up from my repressed and long-denied Lawndale memory. And then in 1973, at the onset of the Yom Kippur War, when Syria and Egypt, backed by seven other Arab states, almost overwhelmed Israel, my feet surprised me by hurrying down to Trafalgar Square to mingle with thousands of perfect strangers, joining other Jewish men in solidarity.

Jennie probably would have rejected the notion of a "marginal" or non-Jewish Jew. "How can this be?" I hear her saying. So I argue with my mother, and the dialogue continues past death to the resurrection of the spirit we call a loving memory.

Small Expectations

There is something to be said for low expectations for children. On the Greater Vest Side, pressures to succeed or excel were almost nonexistent, and this lack of goals was perversely liberating. Since unemployment was a natural condition, home-work was as modest as our teachers' prospects for us and our horizons for ourselves. Our self-esteem came from one another.

How different from the way Joe Franklin is growing up! Despite my best efforts, our kid is *organized* in playdates, sleep-overs, Little League, Fall Ball, piano lessons, even something weirdly called "free play." All life in my universe is geared to kids, kids, kids, a heavy load to put on them. Whatever hap-pened to the healthy boredom of children for parents and vice versa, the benign disinterest that releases both of them into their legitimately separate worlds?

Fantastically, we Lawndale latchkey cadets grew up unim-peded by adult supervision and "time management," let alone academic stress. Little League, AYSO, and organized sports did not exist, at least that we knew of. A self-governing anarchy ruled our improvised games, which had no beginnings or ends or positive reinforcement ("Good eye, Kevin!" "Great cut, Justin!"), just peggy-move-up from sunup to sundown and taking your lumps if you screwed up on the base path. The notion that grown-up men should boss around (coach) chil-dren's games was bizarre; any adult male seen hanging around a boys' sandlot game would instantly have come under suspicion from the old grannies who were the neighborhood's informal police. Perverts and pedophiles were not unknown, but I don't remember anything like the current lynch-mob hysteria.

Take Stash, a new Rocket who was an immigrant from Lithuania, a bit older than us although in the same school grade, a gregarious if vaguely troubled guy. For a while we were tight as two clams. Later, while the rest of us were away in military service, he pulled prison time as a twice-convicted pedophile for molesting little girls in the neighborhood, and eventually was tackled after one of the fathers chased him down and nearly took off his head with a hatchet. Soon after his release from Joliet prison, he visited Jennie and me to weep repentance at our kitchen table. After he left, my mother sighed, "Those poor little girls," adding, "and poor Stash."

The Stash outrages created no vigilante panic, only a kind of stoic pity for both predator and victims. And no TV to broadcast the news region-wide and tell us what to think and how to feel. I doubt if even local rabbis and priests spoke about it from the pulpit, although his crimes were known to all. The Pulaski Avenue police were told to keep an eye on him and that was it. Too lenient? Perhaps.

Today, kids like my son are vastly more protected from felons like Stash. Convicted child abusers by law must register as sex offenders, and there are nightly news reports of angry, fearful residents rallying to harass these men-monsters out of town. In Whatcom County, Washington, two sex offenders were murdered by a stranger who accessed their names from the sheriff's sex offender database. A recent San Diego Web site that listed the names of local sex criminals had *one million* hits overnight. I'm sure all of these Internet inquirers were caring parents interested solely in the welfare of their children.

Yes, sure.

* * *

I do not believe in lost innocence. We Rockets were guilty as charged, free and lawless, afraid of a featureless future but without the vocabulary yet to fully install our terrors. The world outside might assault us but corporate Walt Disney hadn't yet gotten around to it. There was no TV, no car pools, no room of one's own; America was not yet obsessively child centered. In our Lawndale culture it was a given that children's things were of infinitely less interest than adult things. At the movies, aside from *Our Gang* shorts and Buck Rogers serials, all ages—seniors and seven year olds—watched the same adult fare: Myrna Loy in a silk chemise tossing off martinis with her alcoholic detective husband in *The Thin Man* or Joan Crawford trying on diaphonous slips in an endless series of working girl-gone-wrong weepies; even on Saturday children's matinees the triple features starred what today would be regarded as middle-aged actors, Tracy, Gable, Harlow, and Colbert. PG would have been laughed out of court.

In a time of economic terrorism—the Depression—we boys (but not the more family-protected girls) were let loose to fend for ourselves and each other. I suppose the long-term effects of our stressed-out parents' random wrath are still with us, and linger on in our children and their children, who may catch the anxiety virus without knowing quite where or why. But at the time, despite cockroaches in the bed, horseshit in the alley, and rats in the garbage, we boys, insulated by the cruel sweet narcissism of seedling adolescence, loved each other. For some of us, it was as close to love as we would ever know.

❄ ❄ ❄

A part of me never left Lawndale, not really. After I grew up and emigrated to England, I found excuses to visit Chicago on this or that pretext, before and after Martin Luther King was shot and GVS burned out in the '68 riots. Compulsively, I found myself wandering alone in a North Lawndale that was now almost entirely African-American and Soweto-like in devastation, and where neighborhood blacks were so flabber-gated at seeing a strolling white man that hardly anybody both-ered to hassle me. When Studs Terkel fixed me up with a friend of his, a black postal worker and his family who lived in one of my old buildings on Sawyer Avenue, I visited them several times, noting that the father kept a shotgun under the couch. Al, my host, would stand at his second-floor window speaking into his telephone to guide me from one phone kiosk to another as if I was landing on an aircraft carrier in a crosswind. ("Now walk a little faster, don't take the alley shortcut, see those guys on the stoop? just circle around and stop for nothing—") The Harrison District police, on whose blotter I was memorialized as a child, let me ride along with them as they night-patrolled the alleys of my youth, their hands gripping guns under their clipboards; most carried snub-nosed .38s taped to their ankles. Who could blame them? North Lawndale is the city's deadliest neighborhood.

I saw shootings, knifings, the aftermath of rape and murder. A street boy named "Dragon," age sixteen, died in my arms from a tiny, almost invisible hole in his chest as he lay half-seeing on Pulaski Avenue near a room where Jennie and I once rented. The detective filling out a form wrote DOA on it. I said, "He's still alive." The cop shoved Dragon with the toe of his shoe; the boy's eyes fluttered once and shut forever. "No he's not," the detective said.

Dragon was me with a black skin in a later time.

Rockets Forever

That same night, all adults now, we gathered in Heshie Wolinsky's living room in Morton Grove, a Chicago suburb where a number of the other Rockets had settled near one another. Julie Wax, Mendy, Legs Glasser, Deaf Augie, and Albie were at Heshie's along with Heshie's grim-lipped wife, who parked herself on a chair, arms folded, eyes fixed straight ahead, disapproving of something, everything. We chewed over old times, exchanged medical problems, perfectly amiable and genial for guys who never expected to live beyond twenty-one. I'd made the mistake of arriving in a Lincoln Town Car, to which Rent-a-Budget had upgraded me, but the boys seemed to have forgiven my rudeness.

Toward the end of a nostalgic evening, Heshie, ordinarily the most levelheaded Rocket, burst out: "Clarence, you son-ofabitch bastard, I begged you to stay in Chicago. Your mother practically got down on her knees and pleaded with me to argue you from going away. And you turned your backs on us all. Did it make you happy? Like fuck it did!"

I looked around at the other Rockets: the carpenter, the liquor store owner, the social worker, the phone company line installation foreman, the furniture salesman, and Heshie, who said he had worked as a metallurgist at the same steel-making company for thirty years.

I stammered something feeble about having to follow my own destiny.

Heshie leaned forward fiercely. *"And I went further with Faith Levin in Garfield Park than you ever did."*

What? He's kidding. We were fifteen. Faith Levin was one of the neighborhood girls who let you go that little inch lower or higher. I furtively glanced at Mrs. Wolinsky, who was staring cold fire at me.

Heshie's fury was uncontainable. The other Rockets looked on pleasantly.

"Faith told me everything! Everything you did!" Heshie

screamed. He got up so abruptly that for a moment I thought he was going to hit me. "I went *further!*"

My unwilled thought was, *That slut Faith Levin.* Then I made my second mistake. I laughed. "Heshie," I said, "that was years ago."

Heshie got up and ran past his dour, angry wife into the kitchen and slammed the swinging door, which made dying whooshing sounds. One by one, the Rockets rose, rather formally, shook my hand, and departed. Mrs. Wolinsky sat glued to her chair staring at me. Eventually I said good night and slipped out, too.

I'd been set up. But why? Was it the Lincoln Town Car? Or abandoning Chicago? What? My mind reached back to our basement clubhouse and to any possible sins I'd committed so mortal as to be unforgivable after all this time. Yes, I'd once made fun of Augie's deafness, tripped Mendy down a flight of school stairs, which had broken his wrist, cheated at cards with Alble—but surely the years had absolved me. Apparently not all the Rockets agreed. For the first time in my life I wished I had a "spiritual advisor" to help me atone for an unspecified crime I had committed by escaping from Chicago's tender strangle. Well, I'd have to work my way back to salvation. . . .

6

Ring Wise

For Dad, our Family Hand Laundry was turning out to be maybe an offer he should have refused. It was slow work organizing the comrades into a rival union to the Teamsters, and the store was running downhill fast. This was definitely not what he had bargained for when he first tipped his Homburg to the plump redheaded Jennie on the picket line in 1919. It's possible their role models were incompatible. She was keen on the romantic Greenwich Village lovers, John Reed and his freedom-seeking consort Louise Bryant; Dad's role model was more like the "Manassa Mauler," heavyweight champ Jack Dempsey.

Sharing angry scowls, bared teeth, panther's eyes, black brows, and unshaved chins, Dempsey and Dad might have been brothers. Dempsey, like my father, had been a "slacker" in World War I, unwilling to join up, and, also like Dad, had been an itinerant laborer who rode freights and camped in hobo

My Dad, Leo Sigal (at left, in bow tie), speaking to the Bronx Social Democratic Federation, circa 1950s. Note T(ough) L(ittle) J(ews) around table. They look mild, but appearances deceive.

jungles as a roustabout youth. The champ's trademark was brutal early-round knockouts, but he didn't become a popular favorite until he lost the title to Gene Tunney in the "long count" bout when the referee let Tunney recover from a knock-down and win the fight. Afterwards Dempsey told his wife, "Honey, I forgot to duck."

I forgot to duck, too.

When the mood was on him Dad tried to inject courage into me by teaching me the Dempsey style, crouched, stalking, crowding the opponent, and not pulling punches. Much to Jennie's disapproval, he'd improvise a boxing ring in the back of the laundry and show me how to bob, weave, feint, and, above all, throw a rifle-straight sockerino without hesitation. It's the closest we ever got together, me shuffling around him, terrified of body contact with hostile intent, backing off, pushing my hand out weakly for fear of retribution, my coward's eyes locked into his flashing glare, growing clumsier by the second. In school-yard brawls, I was famous for "fighting like a girl" by scratching, hairpulling, screaming, going absolutely nuts, which was my way of blanking out fear of close combat. But you couldn't do that with Dad, who insisted on strict ring etiquette and punches that really hurt. The one time I lost it and launched myself at him with a high-pitched feminine scream and clawlike fingers, he stopped, astonished, and simply knocked me down with a punch to my jaw. He stood over me, shaking his head. "Who teaches you this stuff?"

Of course he blamed Jennie.

My father did not gratuitously beat me up, ever. Instead, when discipline was called for, like so many men of his generation he took a leather shaving strap off a wall hook and whopped my ass with it despite, and I suspect because of, my mother's intervention. "Leo, *slaght niſt der kint. Mir ſind a haim,*" she'd cry. (Don't hit the child. We are a family.) My Dad would step back and raise his hands in mock surrender, with a smile that said to me, What kind of kid needs a skirt to save him?

I kept wanting to prove to Dad that I was who I pretended to be with my pals, a tough guy. So sometimes I'd swallow my fear and ask him to step into the "ring" to teach me how to box properly, and he'd say, "Not when your mother's around." Just once, when she was off at a meeting of her Riga-Baltic Progressive Ladies Society, he took me up, instructing me how to assume the Dempsey crouch, chin tucked into my left shoulder with my right hand cocked for an explosive haymaker, then he circled in front of me: "Okay hit me, sonny boy." The dread moment. I threw a punch as hard as I could without the banshee scream. It bounced off his arm. "Okay okay," he snorted a breath, shuffling in front of me, and whap! stars exploded and the hard wooden floor rushed up to my aching head. Dad said, "I forgot to tell you about the rabbit punch."

What did I have to do to win his approval?

If I couldn't beat up Leo Sigal, I could at least whip everyone else around me, so I tried Dad's rabbit punch on the back of Ike Lerman's head and he hit me with his shoe, so I shot him in the face with my rubber gun, which caused Julie Wax to pick up a half-eaten coconut custard pie from a garbage can and push it into my face and since Julie was a better fighter than me I made a scandal of myself by turning around to hurl acorns at ringleted *yeshiva bocchim* on their walk to temple. "Why do you *do* these things?" Ma asked. She'd never get it. In my misbegotten brain I thought if I beat up enough people Dad would love me more. But I explained to Ma, best I could, how I was two people, Kid Good who had no control over Kid Evil. Today my Joe gives me exactly the same reason for his disobedience.

Dad came and left us according to laws of his own nature and how badly our business was doing, vanishing without a word or a note and months later reappearing as if he'd just stepped out for a moment to the corner drugstore for a tin of Prince Albert tobacco. Yet even in his absences he was present in me, a living force, as I ascended a scale of delinquency that was sure to impress him. Shoplifting, hubcab-stealing, reasonless fistfights, baseball card scams, I was a one-man riot of petty crimes that *had* to get Dad's attention, even if from afar. One way or another, he'd be so proud of his son.

In the escalating quarrels between Jennie and Leo ("There *are no* jobs!" "Go out and look, you won't find them in a pinochle deck!"), her cold contempt locked into his self-defense where I instinctively sided with Dad, for whom I felt absolute love and awe. Why did Ma have to get at him so?

But it was Jennie who *owned* me and poured everything she had into me. Raised, suckled, fed, showed me how to tie my shoelaces, dressed me warm for the snow, knotted my tie the first day of school, was there when I came home, expressed outrage or sorrow at my behavior, received my lies, signed my report card, *was there*. I nearly hated her for it at times.

Because Dad was mostly gone he was a mythical figure in the shadows; Jennie was my reality, and I preferred living in the myth.

Until her string snapped.

Cook's Boy

"Ayeeee!"

I ignored her cry for help because my head was stuck in the small Bakelite Admiral desktop radio where *The Romance of Helen Trent* was blotting out the streetcar traffic outside.

"Ohhhhh—" A groan.

Aged eleven, I strolled out the back door of the Family Hand Laundry to see Jennie wrestling herself out of an open manhole cover in the narrow passageway that ran along the backs of the Kedzie Avenue shops. She had accidentally fallen in all the way up to her hip, the skirt of her housedress jammed against the pubics, one naked leg completely out of sight, the other askew on the pavement, as she used her elbows for leverage to keep from sinking further into the sewer below. The earth was about to swallow her up, my dream of orphanhood about to be realized; the Marks Nathan orphan home would *have* to take me now. She looked so absurd I laughed. As she sweated and struggled to extricate herself, she looked up at me in mute appeal, so I stepped over her truncated body and put my hands under her armpits to leverage her out of the open manhole, then let her lean on me as a crutch to limp into the store's back room. One of her legs already was purple and bruised. I sat her down, opened up a package of Pall Mall cigarettes she always carried in her housecoat pocket, lit it with a kitchen match, and gave the smoking life preserver to her. Her eyes welled with tears she refused to shed.

"Why did you laugh at me?"

My usual helpless shrug. How to explain the comic terror of the world turning on its head?

"It looked funny," I muttered.

She sprawled in the kitchen chair, her bruised leg straight out in front of her, staring at her prince.

"Sometimes," she observed, "I don't understand you."

There was no way for an eleven-year-old to explain the ambivalence of his feelings of being caught between a mother who was always there and a drop-in dad who wasn't. Leo might come on tough but Ma was the real *balabusta*, the undisputed boss; and bosses, in our worldview, were to be reviled. But what if your mother is your *balebos*, the woman who wears the pants as so many wives and mothers did in the Depression? There is a confusion of sexual identities, and, though the anxiety this causes may be useful to a future writer, it can tear a kid apart.

I like to pretend it's all behind me now. But there he is, Joe, the age I was then, in all his glory, acting out the emotions that I—and most of my soldiers' generation—covered up under penalty of going mad. Joe, too, is fighting a two-front war against my wife and me, for his viability and independence. Good luck to him.

❋ ❋ ❋

A few days after Ma dropped into in the manhole in the summer
of '37, with Dad temporarily back in the store, she simply lost
patience with things in general and took off with me in a Grey-
hound bus with a direct connection to South Haven, Michigan,
Chicago's major Jewish summer vacation colony, a borscht belt
without the mountains. Dad was left behind to manage the
unmanageable store. "Let's see how he likes it for a change,"
she said.

All the way to the Michigan state line I hummed Tommy
Dorsey's "Music, Maestro, Please" and when that didn't get her
attention crooned the words into her ear, *"Tonight we musn't
dream of love . . ."* She sighed contentedly, "My little Caruso."

Despite a reputation for anti-Semitism, fifty-five of the
local resorts and boarding houses around South Haven were
Jewish-owned. To escape Chicago's *mishegas,* the craziness of
her life, Jennie had hired on as a cook at a resort called
Fidelman's. The plan was to turn me loose while she had a holiday working a fifteen-hour day in the vast resort kitchen. Most
of the guests were from neighborhoods like Lawndale or
Rogers Park, people like us, except with a little vacation money
saved from the winter. The upper-class German Jews had their
own golden ghetto in a separate colony, Coloma, where many
owned their own cottages.

It worked out for Ma, and we hardly saw each other all that
summer. We didn't even sleep in the same cabin. I was put in
with a man, possibly a war veteran, who had a pink wooden leg
which utterly fascinated me as I watched him strap it on in the
morning, the thigh lace held on with a thigh cuff and shoulder
strap. One day he took his crutch instead of the prosthesis to go
to breakfast, and I tried fitting the flesh-colored leg with its
buckles and suction cup to my own healthy leg. Out of a rubber

band and a piece of black cloth I made an eye patch and went stumping around going "Har har har Jim boy" like Long John Silver, and of course he came back too soon and gave me exactly the same look as Jennie had given me as she was going down the manhole. The next day he was gone, and I had the cabin all to myself and my stack of *Astounding Tales* magazines.

Tall oaks, the lake, pleasant meadows, plenty of sunshine, no traffic noises: I'm a city kid and too much healthy fresh air insults my lungs. I got quickly bored at Fidelman's and began hanging around the kitchen swatting flies and pestering Jennie, who snapped, "I'm busy. Go make friends." She was sweating her guts out baking cookies in a huge hot oven. "Refrigerated air"—air conditioning—hardly existed. I tagged after the other guests, but even their kids from Lawndale snubbed me because I was the cook's boy. By taking their summer holiday at Fidelman's they had temporarily jumped up a class, and now I wasn't good enough for them. This puzzled me. One night when Jennie came to undress and tuck me in I asked her about it. "Forget them," she advised. "They're common Jews with two dollars in their pocket and think they're J. P. Morgan."

The upside was that I had time on my hands to ramble, poke, investigate, pry, sprawl on the grass to study dragonflies, pick my nose, practice my BingCrosbying on the nearby sand dunes (*"Imagination is funny / It makes a cloudy day sunny / Makes bees think of honey, just as I think of you. . . ."*), and reflect on the meaning of the popular ditties I sang to myself at full decibel when all other distractions failed (*"but sut rawlson on the rilleraw / And the brawla brawla soo-it—"*).

I simply did not know what to do with my cock and balls.

Puberty had erupted with a chemical rush. Banked up and uncomprehended sexual desire—for what? for whom?—easily turned to anger, spite, malice, resentment, and tasteless pranks, all directed at Jennie, who was carrying us both through the summer with her capable, sweat-slippery hands. I was getting high on pre-sex. Or something.

Fidelman's was rife with it. I spied on honeymoon couples, old marrieds, young girls. Stalking became my summer. If nobody wanted me, I'd *look* at them.

Guests complained. Who was this monster kid lurking in the bushes? They came to Fidelman's to get away from young animals like me. Jennie spoke to me about it several times, but what else could I do?

Toward summer's end, at the height of high season, she was terminated, I was pretty sure, because of me, but she refused to return to Chicago's heat. Instead, she found another job, in town, as cook in a lumberjacks' boarding house. These shanty boys, which is what tree cutters were called around there, were from UM, upper Michigan, and they proudly *hated* Jews. While Jennie cooked, I kept away from them, mainly by dancing along the railroad tracks near the boarding house and, almost my favorite thing, reciting the names of the railroad companies on the freight cars. Lackawanna, Soo, Burlington, Lake Erie & Western, Great Northern, Grand Trunk Western, Atchison Topeka & Santa Fe, Rock Island, Wabash rolling out a thunder of far horizons. Tracks are a wonderful world of found items. But Jennie got tired of the lumberjacks' lip, and we got fired from there too.

Summer was over, and for some reason Jennie decided to stay in South Haven, enrolling me in a public school while she went looking for a job. But before she could get hired again Dad showed up in a badly dented Hupmobile Aerosedan, a high-octane loaner from "the comrades," and soon the three of

us were rolling down the highway back to Chicago. By the time
we got back at night, Dad's arm was around Ma's shoulder and
her head rested on him.

Slumped in the backseat, arms folded, I sang my Lucky
Strike radio hits to nobody in particular:

". . . I never bother with people I hate
That's why the lady is a tramp . . ."

And the new Astaire-Rogers warble:

". . . the mem'ry of all that
No no they can't take that away from me!"

Dad was back, and I had to take a backseat, literally.

Da'

He was going to kill me for sure. Splatter my brains with a
single thrust of his piston-like fist or throw me under the Kedzie
Avenue streetcar thundering on iron rails past our laundry. Or
maybe he was determined on a two-fer, snuff Jennie and me
with a single Remington Bronze Point bullet. When he was out
of the place I crawled under their big four-poster looking for the
Colt .45 I saw him drop at the Slavic Hall, but there was nothing
except dust and an Orphan Annie secret-code ring I'd lost.

Murder had to be on his mind since it was on mine. If I was
outside playing and heard the distant siren of an ambulance or
fire engine, I'd race home swift as Erroll Flynn in *Robin Hood*,
knowing beyond certainty that both of their bodies would be
lying across each other in a blood-drenched heap on the wood-
slat floor beside the ceaselessly silent National cash register. I

was pretty sure he'd stab Ma with the same kitchen knife she sometimes threatened to kill herself with, and after that he'd carve me up and throw away the bloody chunks. RED COUPLE SLAIN, MOTIVE PUZZLES POLICE the Hearst *Examiner* headline would read. I gave imaginary interviews to the newspapers as the orphaned son of a mutually murdered couple or visualized myself in shackles at my trial on a frame-up charge of double slaying, like the actor Joseph Schildkraut as Captain Dreyfuss in the Warner Brothers biopic *Zola* shouting: "YOU ARE CONDEMNING AN INNOCENT MAN!" I killed and re-killed Jennie and Leo in a hundred creative ways, which would be my ticket of admission to the orphan home over by Albany Street where I was in the habit of swinging on the front gate dreaming up lies to get in, except the one time I really tried it they rejected me because, matron agreeably pointed out, my parents were still alive. (I was not the only west side boy clamoring to get in; successive matrons have reported it as a common occurrence.)

※　※　※

My father was a skilled craftsman in a trade that no longer exists: quality shirt ironing and finishing. I was extremely bigheaded about this and boasted, truthfully, to the other Rockets that he had been chief assistant shirt ironer and French cuff specialist at New York's famous Ritz-Carlton hotel, which most of the boys thought an odd thing to brag about. "So what? My Uncle Moe is a pimp and he makes a ton more money than your father," jeered my best friend Ike Lerman. Since I was incoherently proud of Dad's shirt-ironing talent, there was no option but to slug Ike into near insensibility to prove that Leo Sigal was, whatever he did, incomparably The Best.

Leo Sigal's other trade—his passion—was union organizing. Born in Kremenchug, Russia, he emigrated to America in 1906, at age sixteen, already a weapon-carrying radical. Like my mother, not yet on his horizon, he was an organizing prodigy at a time when all you needed was hard fists and a hot voice and your only public address system was a rolled-up cardboard shirt straightener. He'd been a rising star, two steps below immortals like John L. Lewis and William Z. Foster, when he made a bad career move by slugging his union boss at the Amalgamated Meat Cutters and Butcher Workmen of North America. He and my mother sometimes referred to this explosion of temper as "that time in St. Louis." Dad had an unfortunate habit of knocking down larger men whom he suspected, rightly or wrongly, of being Jew baiters or who were out to get him or just because he didn't like the cut of their jib.

Despite (or perhaps because of) his unpredictable temper, Leo Sigal was in demand as a mobile organizer and traveled by poor man's RV—riding the rods under freight cars—crisscrossing the country to sign up members. He'd been blacklisted, hauled off to jail, and ridden out of strange towns at midnight, taking his salary only when he stopped long enough to put together a "local" of five or more card signers who pitched in weekly dues of twenty or twenty-five cents. In Detroit, Cleveland, St Louis, all points of the industrial compass, he organized butchers, barbers, waiters, any man itching to improve his condition. During the Great War he might have been a conscientious objector pulling time in a federal prison; I'm still trying to locate the records, but the family legend is that he was in the same Atlanta federal penitentiary as Gene Debs, at that time American labor's living saint.

In 1919 Sigal played a pivotal role in a general strike of

meatpacking workers. By now an established "business agent" for the International Union, the only Jew among forty-six general organizers, with that one punch he killed his union career, or that's how he told it.

Then, at the peak of his self-confidence and belief in his own future, in a storm of lust and solidarity, he abducted my mother Jennie, a twenty-four-year-old virgin, from her loving, clannishly protective family. She was, or promised to be, or he saw her as, an untamable redhaired bohemian with whose support he would capture the heights, go to the mountaintop, except that later, when the baby, Kalman (me), came along, he saw his wild rebel girl mutate into a nursing mother and fretful bill-haggling wife. Where now was the flame of freedom they had promised to keep alive?

Some time in the 1920s, having survived the Palmer Raids of foreign-born radicals and meeting my mother Jennie—twin catastrophes, he later claimed—he attended night school and, improbably, opened an office as a chiropractor in Pittsburgh. (I've seen his chiropractic school graduation photo.) "His heart wasn't in it, and I had to go knocking on doors to squeeze money out of his patients," my mother testified. The very idea of my dad's angrily flailing hands manipulating a victim's sore back struck me as ridiculous. He had probably thought so, too, for he soon returned to the dubious comforts of night-riding the rails into the twilight zone of yard bulls, hobo camps, and catch-as-catch-can union work—always the unorganized, the illiterate, the immigrant—where he functioned at his fiercely stylish best.

My picture of Dad I have built up partly by digging through old letters, eavesdropping on my cousins Ida (daughter of my mother's brother Duvid) and Charlie (son of my mother's favorite brother Arkeh) recalling family history, and by piecing together stray bits of fact, memory's best guess, and overlapping Altmanesque dialogue. ("Let me tell you about your father, the *grosse knacker*—big shot." "Your mother, God bless her, a little *ongepotshket*, crazy.") In a family where secrets are typical behavior you listen hard and do your legwork, the perfect training for a journalist in short pants.

In this offhand way I was made aware of Dad's history— the part that was (in our terms) respectable and decent, the jails and beatings and gun battles, and alley brawls. He was proud of his achievements and wounds, but a lethal mix of his incendiary temperament and the lack of Depression-time union jobs forced him back to the ironing board where, in the steamy heat of a failing laundry, he tenaciously clung to an image of his younger boxcar-riding self, ever eager to answer the call but now hardly ever summoned.

All through my childhood Dad alternated brief periods with us and escape for a year at a time to freelance all over the country at the behest of the shoemakers, packinghouse workers, laundrymen, etc.—anyone who could handle his style and pay *per diem*. But, really and truly, he had lost his handhold. His wanderlust he passed on to me; for a long time, in my own drifting from city to city, here and abroad, I unconsciously duplicated his restless spirit, always finding new horizons as a means of escaping from myself in the service of a greater good.

Sometimes I anxiously study Joe for evidence that he inherited my dad's genes through me. Superficially, Leo and Joe don't look like each other at all; Dad was dark and small, Joe is a young Viking, a mixed breed descended from four separate streams bubbling out of the Carpathian mountains, the Alabama lumber forests, the plains of Proskurov, and that great source of so much American Jewry, Kiev. But there are early signs in Joe of Leo Sigal's stubborn, belligerent jaw and tender-tough eyes wary as a trapped wolf.

Dad Hits Bottom and It Hits Back

The time of the Slavic Hall near-riot was Leo Sigal's longest drop-in yet, but he probably wished he hadn't come when he had to apply for food stamps and federal relief.

By now he hated the store, my mother, his luck, and me in no particular order. Busted flat, he traveled way out to Chicago's north side to find a government WPA job digging sewers where none of his friends would see him. It was by pure chance that I spotted him from a streetcar on my way to Foster Avenue beach; there he was, neck-high in a muddy trench swinging a pick against a clay wall, his undershirt off revealing a frame so thin it's a wonder he could even lift the tool. His frailty shocked me; worse, I burned with embarrassment that maybe Ike and the other beach-bound Rockets might see him, too. Of course, most of their fathers were out of work, so where did I come off turning away from mine? Dad glimpsed me staring at him through the slat-bars of the streetcar window, and that's a thing you don't forgive easily, either way.

When the sewer job ended, Dad had more time for me, which wasn't a gift to either of us since obviously I wasn't his kind of guy, not since the time I'd fled from a bunch of bigger boys into his arms and he'd pushed me back into them with, "Stick it to them, boy!" After that, Dad kept giving me his Jack Dempsey snake-eye as if wondering, Who *is* this kid?

The ache of chronic idleness and Ma's silent judgment racked him so that his piles and hemorrhoids would keep him for hours on the toilet behind the half partition in the corner of the store. I competed madly by having my own brutal stomach aches and constipation and by puking on the floor when the tension between my parents became unbearable. Ma had her hands full cleaning up the angry spoor of the two men in her life.

And then Dad began stalking me.

Old Cyclops Eye, I called him to Ike. "My father hits me," Ike said, "so how come yours hardly ever gets around to it?" Dad did, and he didn't. Instead of the shaving strap, he'd slip off his trouser belt and wrap it around his hand and simply whale away. It was a sort of game. He'd let me dance away from the flailing buckle and wait for him to calm down and then he'd come after me again. It may sound odd but I felt *lucky* that he was at least noticing me.

Not just noticing but *seeing* me for what I was, Mister Fake American Boy. There was no fooling Leo Sigal. He *knew* that my every movement, tone, and gesture was so inauthentic I was forced to borrow my Self from movies and *Photoplay* magazine. My strut was pure James Cagney, wisecracks Clark Gable ("Frankly, baby, I don't give a damn"), my very thoughts second-hand from radio serials like *Jack Armstrong*. I, the real me, was a nothing, a transparency in a Halloween costume. He saw through the masquerade. Smart man.

Dad's baleful glare followed me all over the store, my every step, and he was even waiting for me, rocking back and forth on his heels, as if in training, when I came back from school with my pencil box strapped to my back. Jennie intervened only when his snake-eye burned into the red zone. She'd rap out low and controlled, *"Schloog ihm nischt."* ("Don't hit him"), handling Dad the way she dealt with hecklers, reading his moves for their explosive potential. West side women walked a thin line. Their men, humiliated by prolonged unemployment and failure to be good providers, were often dangerously close to physical violence, and then the blue flash would ignite and you could hear the screams a mile away.

I was dead meat.

❋ ❋ ❋

From the time the doors opened at 9:00 a.m. we'd been sitting on a hard bench in the government relief office on the south side and now it was nearly five, eight solid hours of humiliation for Dad. I was fascinated by his unshaven jaw grinding away in rage like a machine tool. The window clerk kept parroting, "You can't just walk in without an appointment, call back tomorrow, my supervisor isn't in, blah blah." Outside it was getting dark. "Let's go," Dad snapped, "they're taking us for suckers."

We followed him out to the cranky old Hupmobile parked in the cold slush. Without a word we climbed in to face the long drive home in the snow. Dad released the hand brake, rammed his foot on the gas pedal, revved up to speed, and roared straight at a steel pole on a cement streetcar island in the middle of Cottage Grove Avenue, drag racing against death. This was before seat belts, and we knew what was on his mind. Time stood still and my heart stopped as the steel pole loomed and a surprising bliss washed over me. *Finally, we were a family.* Not at all scared, I didn't mind dying if we were together. Seconds before a crash, Ma turned and gave Dad a calm, measured look.

"Leo, *the boy!*" was all she said.

Strange. That's what *he* always called me. The Boy, hardly ever used my name, any of them. She was trying to wake him up from a death dream.

At the last split-second Dad spun the steering wheel and swerved to run the Hupmobile up the snow-banked pavement, barreled along the sidewalk, hit no pedestrians with their scarved heads bent against the flurried wind, bounced back to the road, and straightened out to follow the streetcar tracks north to home. For the rest of the ride, and ever afterward, Leo Sigal's bid for immortality was never mentioned.

"Leo, *the boy!*" Now why did she have to go and make *me* responsible for our lives?

❋ ❋ ❋

Dad's brush with murder and suicide had the curious effect of restoring his morale, as if he'd died and been reborn without the crushing weight of the iron band that always seemed to be squeezing his head. Something had snapped; he relaxed. Maybe he felt he was already dead. His self-confidence returned, along with his old sense of sartorial style. Now, each morning he dressed himself with more than usual care in a Hart & Schaffner three-piece suit pressed and dry-cleaned by a comrade in the business, a steam-brushed Homburg set at a brash angle, a clean white-on-white shirt, and silk-pattern hand-stitched tie, ivory and gold monogrammed cuff links and, of course, those wonderful creamy spotless George Raft-style spats. Almost every day he'd slip next door to Mr. Riskin's barber shop to lean back in the swivel chair under the White Rock calendar girl and surrender to a hot towel and straight-razor shave and to be "cupped," an ancient practice of placing small heated glass cups like leeches on the customer's neck and naked shoulder to draw out the devils of stress. Then he'd amble back to our store and, as if clocking in, lean on the front counter all day long. He and Ma hardly spoke to each other anymore.

To my complete surprise, one day he said, "Snap it up, Boy—we're out of here," and jaunted out of the store with me trailing behind, Ma just standing there.

His near-death experience having released him, and with plenty of time on his hands, Dad began taking me all over Chicago with him, couldn't care less that we'd become truants, me from school and him from Jennie. It felt wonderful. At first we visited some of his old friends, the Tough Little Jews who operated small laundry stores like ours, where he let me hang out while he dealt pinochle in the back of the businesses that had no business. And if a wife complained, Dad would bow himself out with mock graciousness—"At your service, dear lady"—his contempt and self-contempt showing. He brought me for a visit to the vast Union Stockyards where he'd once commanded respect as a business agent for the Butchers International. The stink of newly slaughtered meat mixed with the frightened shit and piss of the slain animals disgusted and enchanted me. Dad introduced me to Alex, his former bodyguard, a colossal Ukrainian, with his massive chest bulging out from a blood-smeared leather apron. Alex's job was to patrol the two iron rails of the main conveyor belt of cattle hanging down from their twine-tied hooves and stun them with a bloody sledgehammer before slitting their throats. During a rest break Alex invited me with gestures to share his tin jug brimming with newly killed cow's blood, a widely used specific against tuberculosis. Dad took a nip of fresh blood and urged me to try it, which I did and gagged. Both Alex and Dad laughed. "You got a real kid there, Leo," Alex said.

Dad was visibly proud of me for taking a second slug of the blood just to prove I was a real kid.

Impatient and unable to be still, Dad moved on to penny ante gambling at pickup pinochle games and betting on himself at local pool halls, especially Weinstein's Billiard Parlor on Roosevelt Road and Independence. I believed there was *nobody* better than Leo Sigal—Homburg and spats and high-button high-shine shoes, a cigar cutter suspended on a thin silver chain across his ash-spattered vest—leaning at a crazy angle across the green baize Brunswick table, sighting along an August Jungbludt cue, taking his sweet time, losing almost every game against all comers, but not seeming to mind in the pure exhilaration of gambling against himself and not the capitalist system. My supreme pleasure was when he let me rack up the billiard balls. Even today the hollow click of an ivory ball caroming off the cushion into another ball, snick! is a sound that summons up the scent of blue tobacco smoke that fogged up Daddy's pool halls. I grew up in smoke that turned me on like nitrous oxide. (And gave me lifelong bronchitis.)

To be like, and to be liked by, Leo Sigal was all that mattered. As for school truancies, Jennie was my partner in crime; at home, in all sorts of subtle ways, she encouraged me in any misdemeanor that promised closeness between her man and her son. She lovingly reblocked one of Dad's old Homburgs so that I could wear it exactly at his jaunty angle, and somewhere she begged or borrowed a second-hand topcoat like his with velvet lapels and "English dandy" drape, and she stuck a white handkerchief in the breast pocket, just like his. I even copied Dad's peculiar shooting style, leaning almost parallel across an unoccupied pool table, my right leg lifted like a stork's. An old pair of his spats found themselves on my feet. I was completely unaware of the absurd picture I made—Buster Brown shoes with spats, knee-length knickers, topcoat, and fedora, until Ike

Lerman pushed me over in the snow. "You look like a fat pimp," Ike jeered. That word again.

My heart practically burst as I sat alongside Dad dressed like him when he took me to see Willie Hoppe, the world's reigning three-cushion billiard king, play an exhibition in the Holy Vatican of American pool, Bensinger's on Randolph Street, with its velvet curtains and original oil paintings on the walls, and wrought iron open cage that brought you up three floors to the cathedral-like hush of high-stakes snooker. It forever imprinted on me the idea that a poolroom, a poker table, a bookie joint was not a haven for felons but a modern *agora* where stylish men conducted the real business of life. Dad, a Greco-Roman wrestling buff, also brought me to watch the "monster of the midway," football star Bronko Nagurski, wrestle Jim Londos, the "Golden Greek," at the Chicago Stadium; and where the newly retired welterweight champ and west side hero, Barney Ross, climbed out of the ring as a featured guest and shook hands with everybody in our row, including Dad and me. Barney Ross! Dad was initiating me into a manhood ritual and I grew taller in his company.

He was growing me up his way, and I flourished in his sight. One Sunday night he even took me to my first play, a revival at the Blackstone Theater of Sinclair Lewis's antifascist *It Can't Happen Here*, in which the actors playing American Nazis burst into the theater to seize the stage and threaten the audience. When we got home, Dad switched on my tabletop green-eyed Admiral radio until he found Father Coughlin, the anti-Semitic priest, ranting about Jewish control of the banks and press. *"There will be a reckoning. A day will come when the money lenders will be whipped out of the People's Temple and Christians will rejoice in the redemptive power of Judgement Day,"* Coughlin ranted.

Dad switched off the radio and said, "Remember that man's voice. Now what's the Boy Scout oath?" Not waiting for an answer but curling a fist under my nose: "You're a Jew. *Be prepared.*"

A Killing in Gary or Wherever It Was

A writer named Rick Cohen recently wrote a book *Tough Jews*, about his heroes, including Killer Lepke, Bugsy Siegel, Meyer Lansky, and Kid Twist Reles, who were psychotic neighborhood thugs, professional strikebreakers, wimps with guns. The author clearly knows little of really tough Jews, the kind of people I grew up with.

Men such as my father and his friends.

My memory of the following incident is misty, as it tends to be when I am confronted by, or participating in, traumatic violence. For years I assumed this all happened in a dream my unconscious had constructed from the Hitler terror and fragments of old crime movies. Gradually, it kept coming back to me, always in the same meticulous detail even though I know it's possible to hold onto a false memory that is so vivid it clings like a leech. But when I finally located my father, he mentioned it in an offhand remark without prompting and then, when he saw he had my attention, he changed the subject. (Me: "But it did happen?" Leo: "In your dreams, boy." Me: "But you said—") For reasons best known to himself, he, like Jennie, had gone from keeping secrets in order to survive to holding back out of habit.

One snow-driven Saturday moment in Chicago when Dad was eking out a non-living with a collar-starching route— among his last moments with us—he offered to take me along to a picket line in Gary, Indiana. We didn't tell Ma. It took him forever to crank up the ice-solid engine of his used Plymouth, a step down from the old Hup. I was thirteen and thrilled to be invited. He bundled me into the old car and drove out to South Chicago where he picked up some more union guys and rolled past the Indiana state line to a packinghouse worker picket around an Armour or Swift plant, I forget which. I had a grand time squashed in the backseat between guys I wanted to be like, including Dad's old bodyguard Alex, the blood-guzzling Ukrainian. On the actual picket line nothing much happened, just the usual, hands warming over upturned oil drum fires, jokes, Hey Leo that your kid where's his union button?

On the way back to Chicago we—I felt so proud to be one of them—stopped at a greasy spoon diner off the highway where I ordered a chocolate malt and spun around and around on a revolving high stool at the end of the counter, in pure heaven. With an earsplitting crash, the diner's front window collapsed, somebody picked me up by my coat collar and flung me over the counter, where my head hit a coffee urn and I blacked out. I never heard, or remember hearing, shots. Or ever got a straight story about it. Dad hustled me into the Plymouth and when we got home to the store Ma was furious. "Are you out of your mind, Leo? Completely *mishuga?*" Jennie never got it about Dad and me, that I would have died—*preferred* dying—for him. A few days later there was one of those big Chicago labor funerals for Dad's friend Carmichael, who apparently had been hit by the slugs in the diner. Jennie, Leo, and I marched down Ashland Avenue hand in hand among hundreds of mourners. Banners, songs, and a band from the plumbers' union.

I've gone in vain through old Chicago newspapers in an attempt to find the incident. There are lots of gangland murder stories—Schemer Drucci is the only hoodlum ever killed by the police rather than by other mobsters—but I guess labor violence was too routine to make it into print. Dad had wanted me to witness that part of his life, to understand something about it, but it only made Ma want to reclaim me again and to keep me safe and sissy. Clearly, what excited me about being with Dad only filled her with dread. For a long time afterward, whenever I got into any kind of trouble, petty or not, and pleaded "Nothing happened, Ma" she'd say, "Carmichael happened."

Spring was on us, and playing hooky as usual, I lounged around the melting snows in my ridiculous topcoat with muddy spats, wondering what new escapade Dad was cooking up for us. I bounced into the store, and Jennie, at her sewing machine by the front window, said without a tremor, as if talking about the weather, "We'll have early supper. Set the table. For two."

The next time I saw Dad was twenty-three years later.

7

Bum Heaven

1937–38—Cubs lose World Series to Yankees in four straight. Shirley Temple tops box office. Hindenberg zeppelin crashes. Japan invades China. Gas masks issued to British civilians in Munich crisis.

". . . Don't tune me out! Hang on—this is a big story, and you're part of it . . . It feels as if the lights are all out everywhere— except in America. (Up chorus Star Spangled Banner) Keep those lights burning! . . . Hello, America! Hang onto your lights! They're the only lights left in the world!"

—reporter Joel McRae into a London BBC microphone as Nazi bombs drop in Hitchock's *Foreign Correspondent*

You had to be a Deaf Augie not to hear the Nazi war drums in the Berlin radio broadcasts and screaming newspaper headlines and in Leni Riefenstahl's propaganda film *Triumph of the Will*, a Nazi *coup de theatre* widely shown all over Chicago. We Rockets had no doubt our turn was coming. The Devil in Europe had us in his sights. After all, were we not the Chosen People?

The Devil came to Chicago, too. His name was Tom Girdler, chairman of Republic Steel works over by a high grass prairie on 113th street on the southeast side. On Memorial Day 1937, in a picnic atmosphere, massed ranks of Chicago police, sweating in their blue wool uniforms under a hot May sun, shot forty unarmed striking steelworkers in the back, killing ten, as they waved American flags. Women and children were beaten, clubbed and gassed, all of it caught on a Paramount newsreel. The *Chicago Tribune* headlined the massacre RED MOB LUSTING FOR BLOOD.

Chicago police beating up unarmed strikers outside a steel plant on Memorial Day 1937. Our laundry store was an improvised hospital for the wounded.

Some of the wounded, bandaged, and dazed made their way to our Family Hand Laundry miles away from the killing field. The victims did not want to go to a normal hospital because the cops had fanned out all over Chicago picking up troublemakers, and the Sigals were known as safe harbor.

When the first damaged strikers wandered into the store, Jennie sprang into action, making sandwiches and coffee and acting as traffic cop to the toilet in the corner; my job was to crouch on the store's roof overlooking Kedzie Avenue and peer over the parapet and if I saw any approaching cops to kick on our ceiling as hard as I could.

Ma and me, a team again.

Venus Among the Hoboes

Wherever and whenever Jennie and I moved, even into the pokiest rooming house, she used a nail file or kitchen knife to scratch on our door lintel the signs below. They were a secret code, meaning, respectively,

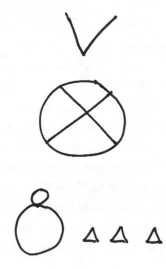

"OK good people"
"Easy handout" and
"Kind lady."
Any place we lived was a stop on the Hoboes' Highway.

During the Depression, tramps—who might be ex-cons, battered women, wild kids of the road, fugitive jailbirds, IWW roving agitators (Wobblies), or just plain homeless vagrants— drew symbols of a new language to help fellow "bums" find their way during hard times. The signs, known as hoboglyphics, were scrawled with chalk or coal chunks on sidewalks, trees, walls, doors, trestles, and fences, a secret code that gave information and warnings to their fellow knights of the road.

At 1404 South Kedzie, it was an established part of our routine to open up the store in the morning and find a homeless man huddled inside our doorway waiting for a handout. Whatever our circumstance, Jennie never let him go without a baloney sandwich and coffee or a Nehi orange drink, of which she kept a plentiful supply for emergencies. She was never afraid of these unkempt strangers who kept tramping in and out. Especially after the Republic Steel massacre, the word spread on the bush telegraph that the Sigals were a soft touch, and hoboes came in droves. Our back room soon filled up with unwashed unshaven hungry strangers who smelled really bad and looked worse. Without any cash customers in the front to distract her, Jennie piled up Wonder Bread-and-baloney-with-French's mustard sandwiches; fussed over the men; let them shave and hose down in the fifteen-gallon galvanized iron washtub that was the family bath. Occasionally a guy wandered in who Jennie had known in better days, but there was none of this "Jim, what happened to you?" crap because hard luck was the common coin. Ma was very careful not to violate the guys' dignity; there was no shame about being on the skids. Anyway, a number of our visiting hoboes wore their poverty as a badge of honor, a freemasonry of the road.

I was an awful snob about the bums who took Jennie's attention away from me now that I had her all to myself from absent Dad. Their stink, their dark jaws and dirty handkerchiefs, their very presence in our house, put me off. I was going through a conformist phase I blame on MGM's *Andy Hardy* series of movies; from the balcony of the Central Park Theatre we jeered and threw empty Milk Duds boxes at teenage Mickey Rooney playing Andy, but secretly I envied his Ford roadster, his white picket-fenced house, and his saintly parents— the wise old Judge and the eternally tolerant Mrs. Hardy— everyone, including Andy's pucker-lipped straight-nosed girlfriend, Polly Benedict, so *goyishe clean*. In Andy's hometown of Carvel, Middle USA, there was a verifiable absence of street fighting and horse turds on the streets and old men blowing snot on the sidewalk.

Our hoboes didn't belong in an Andy Hardy movie. What studio in its right mind would want to dolly up to a polyglot bunch of ragged-trousered philosophers, boxcar willies, rabble-rousers, Wobbly lumberjacks, chronic radicals, self-taught Reds, Trotskyists, socialists, De Leonists, Schachtmanites, Cannonites, conscientious objectors left over from the Great War, bohemian anarchists, labor heroes and small time hoodlums, Preacher Caseys of every political stripe or no stripe at all? Where did they fit into a Busby Berkeley musical? They were *outside* the frame, but inside my house.

To them, I was merely "Jennie's kid," to be casually ignored, looked through, and talked past, there but not there, no offense young man. That was the culture then. So I crawled under my collapsible card table to eavesdrop or do my school homework and let it all wash over me, the torrent of argument, gossip, debate in these nonstop seminars on revolutionary "theory and practice." The utopian stars—Kropotkin, Durruti, Bakunin, Malatesta, Henry George—ricocheted like bullets around me in fierce disagreements between the Communists and the anarchists. Much of what the bums were talking about was way above my head, but it didn't matter; it was great having noise again in the store. It's said that if you play Mozart to an infant in its crib it will grow up with an instinctive feel for great music. Same with me, only the music was these intense, passionate debates over what kind of world I was about to inherit.

Jennie was happier, too. She climbed out of her drab, husbandless housecoat into her low-bosom, Boston Store "styles for the stout" dress—her Sunday-promenade frock—and her step seemed lighter, her face more animated. She smiled a lot more easily. She didn't exactly flirt with the strangers or cocktease them, that wasn't her style, but male animals prowling about visibly warmed her blood.

She presided over our constant turnover the same way she ran union meetings, with a light but firm hand. Her only rules were: no bad language in front of "the boy" (me) and no weapons. Like Tombstone's Wyatt Earp, she required all guests —the word she insisted on—to deposit their clasp knives and knuckle-dusters in the Tampa Prince Invincible five-cent cigar box Dad had left behind.

This was her element, her world—men going about their business. It didn't matter that they had no jobs and wore ragged clothes and had cardboard in the soles of their shoes. To Jennie these tramps, bums, and hoboes were *somebodies* who required attention, *her* attention, and, if handled tactfully, her management. She did not pretend to be Florence Nightingale or Mother Cabrini, Chicago's own saint, nor did she fake being one of the gang. She was, in every sense of the word, a comrade.

Since nobody paid me no never mind, I felt impelled to assert my own identity to these scrungy intruders. So one day I rolled out from under my folding card table to boldly announce, for God knows what reason, that from now on I was changing my name to "Lance" Sigal. Lance, got it? The name of the son of Woolworth heiress Barbara Hutton, the pampered kid who newsreels showed tooling around in a fully motorized streamlined go-kart.

Chatter in the back room stopped briefly, then a guy at the kitchen table broke the silence. "Sure, kid. Why not? It's a free country." One of the others chimed in, "Hell it is—" and they were off again.

The guy who told me it was a free country was a square-built, hard-muscled traveling fruit picker named Swede Hammeros, who looked a little like "fighting Marine" Gene Tunney—Jack Dempsey's ring nemesis—only blond. Hard jaw, intelligent eyes, thick but carefully combed hair, the sleeves of his blue work shirt rolled high up, knotted arms, a certain look in his eye. Dad had that same look. Except that the Swede didn't seem as consumed by his own hot-wired anger, maybe because he was so big and imposing and didn't have to go around proving himself as did "the little Jew," Leo Sigal.

The change in Jennie was startling when Swede was around. After Dad took off, a victim of his restlessness and her disappointment in him, her freckles had faded into deep worry lines, she smoked more if that was possible, and she spent whole days without bothering to get out of her housecoat. Most alarming, weeks would go by without her visiting Betty the manicurist at Riskin's barbershop next door. But when Swede showed up, all he had to do was walk in, toss his leather billed cap on the counter, and give my mother a certain look, and she lit up like a Christmas tree. Soon she was back in a proper dress all the time, with makeup, nails polished with fifty-cent-a-bottle Revlon enamel "Chinese red" (none of your ten-cent transparent Cutex crud), hair set, permed and hennaed—on show. Unlike most other guys who came around during Dad's absences, the Swede didn't court me, too, none of this mussing my hair or giving my hand a manly shake. Swede was like Jennie that way. He kept his distance without actually pushing me away; I had to come to him.

His visits became routine. In the mornings she put out a breakfast plate of Heinz baked beans and fried sunnyside eggs the way he liked them; and he'd drop by after I left for school and he was there when I came back.

Around this time, the laundry business got so bad that on afternoons and weekends I developed a stage act—by climbing inside the store's front window to tennis-bang a Hi-Li paddle— designed to attract the business of potential customers, a kind of freak show that bankrupt businesses indulged in then, like flagpole sitting, dance-athons, six-day bicycle races, Cannonball Kelly with ten guys standing on his stomach, etc. A Hi-Li was a small wooden paddle with a rubber ball attached by a long elastic string that let you keep hitting it over and over again without missing a beat. I had won a set of roller skates (which we pawned) on the stage of the Central Park Theatre by whacking the ball with my paddle over a thousand times while blowing huge bubbles from wads of pink powdery Fleers bubble-gum in my chipmunk cheeks, beating the competition into the ground.

Inside the store window I quite enjoyed posing as a laundry-store mannequin and showing off in front of passing non-customers even if my tired arm felt like falling off.

When my Hi-Li vaudeville flopped as a crowd pleaser, Jennie asked me if I'd parade up and down Kedzie Avenue with a homemade sandwich board proclaiming the lower prices of Family Hand Laundry (a lie, the local Chinese did shirts cheaper). On vanity grounds I refused, so Jennie and I negotiated a compromise where I'd write and hand-distribute all over Lawndale an advertising flier which Harry the Printer over by Thirteenth Street would cyclostyle for us in return for laundering his ink-stained aprons. Here is my very first real writing effort.

FAMILY HAND LAUNDRY
We Do It All!
Wet or dry, shirt iron, collar turn, Grade A finish
Your Wash Is Our Command
Prop. J. Sigal   1404 S. Kedzie

No phone listed because it had been cut off long ago.

Nothing doing. The 1937–38 "depression-within-a-depression" kicked hell out of the laundry business. For us, as for millions of others, FDR's New Deal was No Deal.

❊ ❊ ❊

About Swede. I didn't know if I wanted him to stick around or not, but impromptu he began taking me places just as Dad had.

"Let's head into town and stir things up," he'd say, and together we'd ride a Roosevelt Road streetcar into the Loop and stroll under the Wabash Avenue L tracks, winter sunlight shafting through the struts, until he ran into one of his friends panhandling or mooching outside a bar. "That your kid?" they'd ask. "For now," Swede replied. He said it so casually that I began to think *Hey, maybe there's a future for me there*, and immediately felt disloyal about Dad.

Sometimes we'd wander up to the offices of *The People*, an old-time radical weekly newspaper, where Swede would pick up a bundle to distribute in coin-operated metal boxes along State Street. Gradually, he let me take over his newspaper route while he stayed in the office gabbing with the editor, then we'd ride home, side by side on the streetcar's reversible wicker seat, not speaking much and not having to. He had such a lazy offhand style, the very opposite of my intense Dad, or so it seemed. Back in the store, I went around idly crooning into a broomstick end, *"You're getting to be a habit with me. . . ."*

All that spring of '38 we were a threesome. Swede would take Ma and me rowing in Douglas Park lagoon, or down to the Grant Park bandstand for a concert, and a couple of times to the Oak Street beach, just like any other family. I'd catch him looking at Jennie in this appraising, lazy way—later I'd learn to call it sensuous—and stop thinking about it.

What happened then was this: I'd just come out of the gym of St. Agatha's church across the tracks from the store— this was before Father Lenihan threw me out, his one and only Jewish catch—when a larger boy, probably an Irisher from up by Twenty-second Street, walked past the church across from the store and, for no reason except that I was there, slammed a fist into my stomach while observing, "Your mother's a hoor." Ooof! I crumpled over and exhaled, "So what if she is." Now why did I say that? Astounded that this strange Irish kid knew so much about us, I fled across the streetcar tracks into the store, where both Swede and Jennie had witnessed the episode. My father would have poured silent scorn on me for running away from an insult. How would Swede vote?

He took me by the hand and walked me out of the store north on Kedzie Avenue past the Midwest headquarters of the Jewish *Forward* on Thirteenth Street, with its white plaster Moroccan turret, until we caught up with the ambling Irish kid. "Hold up there, boy!" Swede said. The kid kept walking, strolling really, insolent. "Stay here," Swede ordered me and caught up with the kid and spoke in a low tone to him. The kid shook his head, but Swede kept right on talking, soft, unthreatening, until the kid made as if to walk away. Swede touched him. It didn't look like much of a punch, but the kid hurled himself backward against the brick wall between two stores and fell down. Unhurried, Swede dragged him by his torn sweater into an alley and I trailed after them. All the time, Swede kept chatting, like he was discussing philosophy. In the alley the kid got up and then his head snapped back. I hadn't even seen Swede hit him. The kid collapsed again and Swede stood over him for a moment, thoughtfully gave him a single hard kick, then came back to me and Ma (her fist in her mouth) standing in the alley. She looked at him with new eyes. Swede said, "Hey, Jennie, no sweat."

All my life I'd been waiting for somebody to take my part, but, now that Swede had done it, it felt as if something had been taken away from me.

Soon afterward, Jennie stopped leaving a breakfast plate

out for Swede, and now when he came calling and sailed his leather cap onto the counter she politely picked it up and handed it back to him.

I didn't know how to ask Ma what was going wrong between them so I just said, "You know, Swede is a really nice guy." All she said was, "On Sundays when it isn't raining." What did that mean?

Then, like Dad, he simply wasn't there anymore.

I didn't realize until Swede left that the other hoboes hadn't come around as often when he was with us, but as soon as he was gone they flocked back like birds on a tree branch after the hawk has flown. Same as before, Jennie fed them and presided over their quarrels, but it wasn't the same at all; something was gone. Jennie never said she missed Swede. He'd made her laugh, she came alive around him, and he hadn't exactly been the daddy I longed for, he was no Judge Hardy dishing out "life guidance," (maybe it was against Swede's syndicalist principles).

But he'd been good enough.

So there we were, Jennie and me together again, running a customerless store, me in the front window again banging my Hi-Li paddle and chewing Fleers like a madman, Ma slumped in her frayed old housecoat at the sewing machine fiddling with pieces of fabric, both of us waiting for somebody to walk back through the front door, setting off the tinkle bell above it and ripping open our lives and making us better for it.

Only the hoboglyphics changed. One morning soon after Swede disappeared, Jennie went outside with a piece of sandpaper. She stared hard at the symbols carved on the lintel, then forcefully sanded out

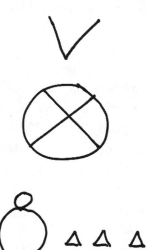

Stepping back inside the store, she had a second thought, reached for a pair of scissors by the sewing machine, came out again, and stabbed the door wood with

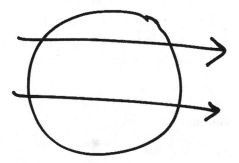

Translated: "Hit the road."

Swede Hammeros was not coming back, I guessed.

＊ ＊ ＊

Several years later, while a part-time baker's assistant at the National Biscuit Company over by Racine, I bumped into Swede as he was piling boxes in the Nabisco loading yard. We had a friendly chat without mentioning Jennie. And even later, in crossing the country by car on my way overseas, I tracked him down running a farm with a widow woman in Ohio. More mellow and self-protective of his new contentment, he didn't seem the same man. *Is this what happens to aging rebels*, I wondered? He didn't ask me to stick around, but when I was about to drive off he leaned in through the car window and asked, "Did your pa ever come back?" I said no, and he said, "Well, life makes fools of us all," and bade me good-bye.

＊ ＊ ＊

Men such as Swede and my father are like human magnets drawing me to them. Ever after, I've searched for a father in men as close to the original as possible, guys on a volcano's edge of violence, fighters against themselves or the world or both at the same time.

Why couldn't Jennie *hold* her men?

And why couldn't I?

8

Jennie and the Women

On June 22, 1938, sixty-eight million people—the highest number ever for a radio broadcast—tuned in to the second heavyweight fight between Hitler's champion, the "Teutonic Titan," Max Schmeling, and African-American "Joltin' Joe" Louis. Joe whips Max in two amazing minutes and four seconds of the first round, his fists the opening salvo of the American counteroffensive against fascism in our imaginations. The night of the fight in Yankee Stadium, the hearts of American Jewry seem to stop until Schmeling crashes to the canvas a beaten pulp. Then you can hear it all over Chicago, deafening on the west side, a tidal wave of emotion exploding in every household that had a radio. Jennie, who hates boxing, has tears of joy in her eyes as she listens to the referee Arthur Donovan count Schmeling out, and the ringside announcer almost bursts an artery screaming, "Schmeling is DOWN! He's OUT!"

Joe Louis's crushing right hook to the kishkes is an omen.

We can win.

Later that year, 100,000 Jews march in an anti-Nazi rally in New York in response to the mass arrest of German Jewry and their banishment to concentration camps.

After Swede and Leo Sigal delivered a one-two punch to her heart, Ma shut down on men. Even now, it's hard for me to know if she sent them away or they took off on their own, but they seemed to confirm in her a deepening disgust with the species, who spelt more trouble than they were worth. Right now, she needed another kind of love.

My Mom the Dealer

"Two pair showing, Surkah. Keep an eye on Sadie's possible flush."

"Minnie, you're folding with three of a kind? Go ahead, be brave, raise Bea a nickel."

"Nothing, nothing, nothing, ace high bets. Tuva, you can check, Nonie has a pair on the table."

"Leah, you got eye trouble? Look at Essie's hand. Essie, touch your nose to warn Leah."

My mother The Dealer.

A lone woman on Chicago's west side was a life at risk. The neighborhood social structure held little status for a widow, divorcée or, most culpably, a spinster. Without men in their lives, and soon to lose sons to war, such women constituted a potentially subversive sexual subculture in the heart of one of the most conservative neighborhoods in America.

The umbrella under which my mother and her friends chose to come together, or camouflage themselves, was the Riga-Baltic Progressive Ladies Society, a gentle fiction since none of the ladies hailed from the Baltic nations; most, like Jennie, were Great Russian emigrants, but they needed a respectable cover to fit snugly within the community's cat's cradle of benevolent organizations. I was cover, too; after all, how dangerous could a coven of single not so young women be if they dragged along a bored twelve-year-old?

The Riga-Baltic met four times a month, with a ceremonial poker game on alternate weekends. Ma and I would go, say, to Surkah Ginsberg's place, where a blazing white lace tablecloth on a large dark mahogany dining table, brought over from the Old Country as part of Surkah's dowry, awaited players. The table smelled of furniture polish, and on the tablecloth sat a nearly full cut-glass decanter and six or seven empty clear shot glasses with thick bottoms. The hostess, Surkah, waited for everyone to show up and then ceremonially filled the glasses with Four Roses or Old Grandad from the decanter. The women would raise their glasses — *L'chaim!* — and battle commenced.

"A pair of queens bets. Sadie, I can see your cards, hold them closer. Essie, put money in the pot, don't be a four-flusher."

The poker games Jennie ran usually were on Friday nights when more Orthodox, and orthodox, women were at home preparing a Sabbath meal for their menfolk. But the Riga-Baltic ladies were manless, either through death, departure, or the disappearance-in-place Essie described as "He's not there even when he's there." These were women on their own leaning on each other. Every player came out even at the end of Ma's poker games. If anything later ruined me as a poker player it was being taught how to "read" the table by a bunch of lonely working-class women for whom the loss of even fifty cents at the end of a social evening was a financial and moral disaster.

The game was always seven-card stud, nothing wild. If someone was dealt an indisputably winning hand—say, two face-down aces and a third showing—it was mandatory for her to loudly clear her throat or wink to signal her luck so the other players could fold with honor. And if, say, Essie Rabinowitz rashly bet against the aces with only a low pair, Ma wildly grimaced or whistled in an attempt to persuade her to fold. The Mosaic sin was sandbagging or raising after checking.

Surkah, as tonight's hostess, would hover obligingly from a wheeled gurney which she maneuvered with her toes or hands, pushing herself this way or that against a solid object like a wall or table. She suffered from a crippling form of arthritis that made her spend most of her time lying on her back or side, and from this awkward position she was capable of remarkable feats of housewifery. If she had to leave the game, she'd roll around the flat, dusting and cleaning and loudly humming "Little Sir Echo," and the Baltic Ladies made sure to include her in as many activities as possible.

Warmed by the Four Roses, the women gossiped while Jennie shuffled and dealt. "Did you hear Chava Roth changed her name to Eve?" "Pearl Berkowitz's daughter, the cockeyed one, is seeing a guy who works in a Sheridan Drive butcher shop. Social climber." As the night wore on, the ladies, infused by gambling fever, played faster and looser, racy even, raising bets, going for it, and if, by some mishap, Tuva (now Toni) or Polly Nudleman or Aviva Zaretsky came out winners by as much as a dollar, there would be a fast and furious last round in which Jennie dealt intentionally winning hands to losing players to keep things healthy. Afterwards, at home, I'd protest that playing to lose was idiot's poker. "We're gentlemen," Jennie said firmly, "and we play like gentlemen. You want to be a killer at the table like your father—little good it does him—I'll show you how," and she'd sit me down at the kitchen table with a clean uncut pack of Bicycle playing cards to teach me with a swift and merciless eye the permutations and odds. I swear she'd give Texas Dolly Doyle Brunson a run for his money.

Some men have Oedipal trauma; I have a seven-card stud complex.

P.S. Jennie's poker playing genes skipped a generation and landed squarely on Joe Franklin. Five card draw is his game, and Cincinnati Kid is his name. He could be the next Texas hold 'em champ like Amarillo Slim. Joe bluffs like a demon and has no "tells" as far I can see. He keeps this same diabolical grin on his face if he's holding a straight flush or zip. "Who else do you play cards with?" I ask. "Oh," he replies casually, "a few kids at school." Any moment I expect a police raid.

The other preferred Riga-Baltic venue was a center table at Carl's Restaurant, a popular deli on the main drag, Roosevelt Road. Again I was a largely silent partner, a "beard," for these widowed or otherwise unaccompanied ladies who had largely given up on the possibility of another man to replace the dead, "divorced," or deserting one. Something about Carl's busy festive air gave gossip a harder, wilder edge when the ladies' ribald laughter drew disapproving stares from other customers who included, I now realize, the men—tonight dining with their families—whom the ladies knew on the side and who were the subject of some of their coded jokes. Unlike the poker chitchat, the tittle-tattle at Carl's had a defiantly sexual tinge. For example, Rosalie Levin's visit to a back-alley doctor, Sol Schecter's marital unhappiness, Dorothy's non-appearance at

Riga-Baltic gatherings due to facial disfigurement from her husband Max's beating, Manny Solow's vacations in the Wisconsin Dells without his wife—

The thing about these Saturday night meals—sweet and sour *tzimis*, tongue sandwiches on dark pumpernickel, *kasha mit varnishkes*, schmaltz herring, "book steak," *matza brie*—was that my presence seemed not in the slightest to inhibit the women. Either they felt confident a twelve-year-old didn't catch the double entendres or, on this their special evening, they simply didn't give a damn.

❊ ❊ ❊

Entering my teens, I was catching on to something the other Rockets probably grasped from the cradle as part of west side ecology: prostitution was a workingwoman's second job. I felt stupid not having realized that part-time hookerdom was apparently taken for granted by everyone but me. Putting the puzzle together from the hints dropped at Carl's restaurant, I deduced that most local whores did it mainly on a barter basis, that is, goods, not cash, for services. This was distinct from the full-time professional prostitutes in established brothels who had their own peculiar arrangements with the local police which, like all systems, occasionally broke down. We Howland school kids knew all about that, because in the middle of one school day, Mr. Kelly, the math teacher, was busted in a vice raid probably triggered by a missed payment to the police watch commander. In full view of us at recess he was led out, sheepishly, in a file of johns to the paddy wagon, a subject of adolescent jokes but not of community censure. And he kept his teaching job.

The raid was exceptional because if the routine was working correctly nobody messed with cribs which operated under the protection of Capone's west side Cicero mob composed of marquee names like Johnny Torrio, Frank Nitti, Machine Gun McGurn, Greasy Thumb Guzik, Schemer Drucci, and Hymie Weiss, who were as recognizable to us as Babe Ruth and Clark Gable. As familiar, say, as the legend of the Jewish mobster "Nails" Morton, who, adopting the social manners of the city's WASP aristocracy, took up horsemanship but was killed when his mount threw him on the bridle path, causing his "boys" the next day to go to the stable and assassinate the offending horse in classic gangland style.

Sex and the City

Love, oh love, oh careless love
You worried my mother until she died
You caused my father to lose his mind. . . .

— old blues song

The Riga-Baltic Progressive Ladies Society was rooted in a sisterhood of pride, but also of shame. In some measure, Jennie and her ladies accepted that each had done something less than honorable in losing her man, and that life was forcing them to walk alone, each to make her her own arrangements for pleasure and survival.

I looked around the table at Carl's Restaurant with the eyes of an adolescent whose idea of sexual beauty was Rita Hayworth and B-movie cheesecake queens, most of them slim and blond. Was it even remotely possible to a twelve-year-old that the Riga-Baltic's high-busted low-hemlined stoutish women with their corsets and girdles were in the same league as

Hollywood starlets? Was it conceivable that they ever "did it," that is, opened their legs for a bunch of radishes? Absurd. Even entertaining the thought that women my mother's age had sex, or that men found them available and attractive, was so foreign as to be almost un-American.

Yet once I heard the rumors, I couldn't take my eyes off these Baltic ladies.

* * *

Jennie enforced the same rule at Riga-Baltic meetings as for herself and me: no crying, no outward expression of inner anguish. Grief, sorrow, or anger was impermissible past a certain point; after that it was self-indulgent. Self-pity left you weak and victimized; self-control was the ultimate—perhaps the only—virtue. An example: a few weeks after Aviva Zaretzy's husband died, she began without preliminaries to weep in the middle of the *gedempte fleesh* at Carl's, great pendulous tears soundlessly splashing down her rouged cheeks, making a sad clown effect. The other women quietly put down their forks and knives to look to Jennie for guidance, and when Mrs. Zaretsky's tears continued to roll without letup, Jennie, in a voice like God's, split through the uncomfortable silence, *"Sadie!"* Her tone implied, You will *not* break now after all you've been through, you will *not* let yourself down, you will *not* make a spectacle of yourself. Immediately Mrs. Z's hand darted at her eyes with a lace-bordered hankie and she made a successful effort to pull herself together, furtively glancing at the Baltic Ladies in apology that she had, even for a moment, opened the floodgate of heartache.

Ma did her job as emotional policeman perhaps too well.

When Joe Franklin expresses his feelings, by sobbing or laughing too loudly, despite myself I sometimes command him, "Tone it down, kid." And he gives me this look that says, What's wrong with you, Dad?

Well, what is?

* * *

Dark, Spanish-looking Aviva Zaretsky was—I realize now—a very attractive woman. She was in her mid-forties, with a high smooth forehead, brown, oval, almost Egyptian eyes, jet-black hair tied tightly in a bun, and a body that, unlike Jennie's, did not look as if she wore too many girdles and corsets. Until her husband Eddie fell dead on a beach outing, she had been the Riga-Baltic lady most full of pure fun and off-color jokes. She and my mother were bonded also by self interest; Aviva's apartment over a mom-and-pop pickle factory on the same block as our store had its own private bathroom with a full-size bathtub which she let me use from time to time, an unparalleled luxury for someone used to squatting in a fifteen-gallon galvanized zinc tub. So, on hot summer days, with Aviva Zaretsky's permission, I'd tuck my towel and toy wooden boat under my arm and scamper upstairs to her place while she was out, let myself in without a key, and loll about in the bathwater, finger-flipping my boat around the tub pretending I was the admiral of the USS *Dreadnought*.

One glorious afternoon, alone in the Zaretsky's tub, I let the boat nudge my penis, which sprang erect. As Basil Rathbone's Sherlock Holmes might say, "Hmmm, and what do we have here?" Wow, I had *invented* something. Every week from then on I looked forward to getting into the tub for my boat hard-on. Edison didn't stop with the incandescent light, and

soon I devised a wind sail out of a toy balloon for my penis bat-
tleship. If I blew up the balloon and tied it with a string to the
mast with a certain twist, the boat moved by itself as the air
slowly whooshed out of the balloon. Science proceeds by acci-
dents, and on a fateful day, as auspicious for me as Samuel F.B.
Morse's first telegraph message ("What hath God wrought?"),
the balloon-powered boat brushed against my penis, which
exploded into a flower of sperm. My first ejaculation. The sheer
awfulness and grandeur of its scattered milky-white tentacles in
the dirty water stunned me, and I lay back and imagined Mar-
cella Goldberg's breasts touching my cock and poff! it went off
again—and again. I was dying, exhausted, pale, and sapped,
but couldn't stop. Scared, full of dread and joy, I had embarked
on a lifelong sex trip.

Then, like the poor schmuck in David's painting, "The
Death of Marat," I got trapped in the bathtub.

It happened like this: I was coming to a climax, spouting
like a sperm whale, when I heard a noise. I couldn't stop
exploding but hastily covered up when the sound turned into
voices from the front of Mrs. Z's long narrow apartment. Panic.
My clothes were a mile away on a nearby chair. I stood up in the
bath and tried pushing open the grimy bathroom window but it
stuck. In the middle of my exertions, Aviva Zaretsky stuck her
head in. "Pssst, Kalman!" she hissed, gesturing for me to get out
of the tub and follow her quietly. I hesitated. Jennie and the
Cook County visiting nurse were the only women who had ever
seen me naked, and I still had my erection. Past embarrassment
into total terror, I climbed out of the tub and gathered my clothes
in front of me as a shield. "In here," she whispered and pushed
me into a dark hall closet and flung my towel in after me before
shutting the door. "Aviva!" the man's voice called from the front

room. As I was quickly dressing, the closet door opened again. Mrs. Zaretsky whispered. "Don't be scared. I know him. It won't take five minutes." She shut me in again.

Even though the closet was hot and stuffy, I was shivering. I kept thinking of my slimy sin that I had no time to scrub from the tub.

I had to get out of there. Carrying my gym shoes and wet towel wrapped around the wooden boat, I crept out into the long hallway and headed for the back door when I stumbled over a grocery bag, spilling the contents onto the kitchen lino. Just then I heard the front door open and shut and Mrs. Z, calmly fixing her hair, entered to find me frantically scooping stuff back into the grocery bag. "Here," she said, "sit, I'll do it. Glass of milk?" I shook my head. She got up from the floor and stacked the items neatly on the table. They were mainly lending library books authored by best sellers Fannie Hurst, Pearl Buck, Sholem Asch, and John Marquand. There was also a large blue tin of ex-lax and a package of Feenamint ("for constipation") gum, and also a bottle of Lydia Pinkham's Compound. The label read, "For Female Discomfort—40 proof." Sherlock Sigal deduced the things probably came from Berman's drug store on our corner. Mr. Berman? Whose only joy in life was chasing me away from his magazine rack of "naturist" and health magazines with naked ladies posing on seaside rocks?

Aviva Zaretsky sat across the table and weighed me with her eyes. I said, "I take that, too." Her eyes opened wide, "Lydia Pinkham?" I blushed. ex-lax, I said. "Does the job," she said, "though personally I like the Feenamint. Care for a stick?" I shook my head again.

She didn't seem ill at ease or awkward as she reached for my hand then thought better of it. "Take it easy, Kalman. It's nothing. You saw nothing." I gathered my toy boat and towel, and she opened the back door to the porch for me, suggesting, "Maybe this one time you go out the back way." As I was easing out she added, "Come for a bath any time." I understood she was making a west side deal to buy my silence.

But I was wrong. A few nights later, at supper in the store, Jennie said, "Aviva tells me there was a traffic problem the other day." What else had Mrs. Zaretsky told Ma? I was afraid to ask. Jennie drew out a Pall Mall cigarette, lit it, and slowly blew the smoke out in a ring. "She didn't touch you, did she?" Absotively no, I said. "You'd tell me?" she persisted. I cried, "For chrissake, Ma—what do you think I am, Mister Berman?" And could have bit my tongue, but it didn't bother Ma in the least. She said, "Aviva is a wonderful person. She lost her man, you know," as if that explained anything.

Nothing much changed after that except that I was marginally less welcome at Friday night meetings of the Riga-Baltic Progressive Ladies Society, Jennie tactfully suggesting, "Tonight you feel like the movies, take a dime from the register." Eleven cents with federal tax now, I said. "Smart guy," she said and handed over the coins.

I should have felt relieved of the obligation to spend my Friday nights with a bunch of chattering ladies, but I'd come to like being "one of the girls." They had privileged me to see something—I wasn't sure what—that I was eager to know more about. For example, Aviva Zaretsky and Mr. Berman. What was that really about and who was there to explain it?

Oh, yes, one other thing. Jennie did stop me going for my weekly bath to Mrs. Z and instead, on most Sunday mornings, before our promenade along Roosevelt Road, hauled our zinc tub to the middle of the room at the back of the store and ordered me to undress and scrunch down in the water—I hardly fit any more—to hose me down from the kitchen sink. That first time, wielding a bar of P and G White Naptha Soap and a stiff-bristle brush, she furiously rubbed my naked body until the flesh was raw-red. "Go easy, Ma!" I yelled. Timing her remarks to her movements, she applied more elbow grease to my already gleaming flesh.

"*Schmootzik*—in—this—family—is—not—acceptable. We—are—not—dirty—people."

And that was that.

Protection Racket

Before Joe Franklin was born my wife told me that everything "below the belt," meaning the penis, was my province, which of course in due time has led to the Dreaded Talk.

"Dad!" he protests in acute embarrassment, "I know all that."

Okay, I retreat, I'll try again at the next solar eclipse.

Protect yourself at all times, Dad used to warn before knocking me flat in our sparring sessions. Ma now came up with her own version.

When I was just a little older than Joe is now, instead of a bar mitzvah my mother delivered the long-delayed Dread Talk.

First came out the Pall Malls, a match struck, curling blue puffs of smoke over the oilclothed kitchen table. Then Ma reached into her apron pocket and placed an object on the table between us.

A small blue and white tin of Trojan brand condoms. Rubbers.

My neck felt hot enough to melt, Ma's face was so red her freckles vanished.

She used her fingernail to flip open the small box and withdraw a single wrapped rubber. It lay, like a Capone-murdered corpse, in its distinctive figure-eight shape on the table. I could not believe my mother knew about "protection," a subject of smashmouth hearsay among us Rockets, let alone she was about to demonstrate it to me.

Our eyes refused to lock.

The condom stared up at us. The guys and I had horsed around with new and used Trojans and Sheikhs for years, fitting them on each other's hard-ons, masturbating in them, and swinging the sperm-filled transclucent bags around like shillelaghs. But this was different. This was about *sex*.

I jumped up, "I got a ball game—"

"Sit," she said. I sat.

"Ma," I whined.

"Embarrassed?"

"C'mon, I know all that."

A tone like tempered steel. "From who may I ask do you know "all that"? From Albie or Chaim or Isaac? I'll run tell their mothers."

This was heading where I didn't want to go.

"Syphilis," she declared. Yipes.

All over our neighborhood you still saw ex-World War I soldiers who had come back from France with untreated venereal disease and progressed into paresis, the "stumblebum" syndrome of blindness and motor dislocation. Kids knew about it because sometimes we'd help them cross the street.

"Pregnancy," she followed up. "Knocking somebody up," she added as if I didn't understand simple English.

"Jesus, Ma."

"You're old enough to father a child," she insisted.

"I am not," I declared. The idea was absurd.

Ma lit another cigarette and looked affectionately at me. "Tell that to your bedsheet, comrade."

Oh no. She knew.

"Don't interrupt," she commanded. Then it poured out of her, the lecture she'd been saving up, a virtual medical history of the twentieth century: Margaret Sanger, Dr. Ehrlich's magic bullet, planned parenthood, Emma Goldman, free love, contraceptives, fallen women and contaminated men, heartbreak, anguish, indescribable wounds, amputated limbs, white slavery, prostitution, shame, regret, abuse, surgical wards, wayward girls—a history, too, of herself if I'd had the wit to really listen.

She drew a big breath.

"It only needs one," she said.

"What?" I blinked.

"One sperm," she said flatly. "Below your belt. Half a million each time. Five hundred thousand. It only needs one."

I didn't know that and began to do the math.

"You know how to use this?"

I glanced away. "Yeah."

"*How* do you know?" she persisted.

"Ma, let it be."

"Have you used one?"

I looked her square in the eye.

"Fuck," I said defiantly, using that word for the first time to my mother.

She sat back, stubbed out the ciggie in an ash tray, and folded her arms thoughtfully.

Then, quite deliberately, she reached out to unwrap the Trojan in a practiced gesture and grasp it, rolling it down her two upraised fingers then holding her now joined fingers for me to inspect.

She wiggled her fingers inside the sheath. I laughed. She pushed the Trojan tin over to me.

"Protect yourself at all times, Kalman."

I took my shot. "Did Dad ever use one?"

"No, never." Her eyes misted over slightly as she reached out to take my hand in hers. "You were my gift to myself."

One out of five hundred thousand. I figured the odds were on my side, and went out to play ball.

The Shandeh Gives a Dinner Party

I am going on thirteen. Jennie, in exile from her New York-based family because she ran off with a married man, rarely speaks of her brothers, sisters, and cousins because the memory of them makes her eyes mist up. So I have a poor sense of "family," which I define as my mother and whatever is happening on the street. But one day, Persily relations descend on us for a surprise visit. She is surprised and delighted, and determined to do right by them.

The visitors are the two grown sons and teenage daughter of her most beloved brother, Arkeh Persily, the brother who most stood by her when the other brothers vowed terrible revenge on "the animal Sigal" for hijacking their sister, whom they feel they lost to a predator. I don't yet know all the ins and outs of this powerful tale of blood and intrigue, but tonight it's important that Jennie put up a reputable front despite the glaring absence of a man in the house.

Just as she is serving dinner in our living quarters in the Family Hand Laundry, her dream of a quiet family reconciliation shatters along with the store's plate glass window.

"Come out, you damn whore!"

A woman's shriek is followed by the loud crash of a second brick through the other front window.

My mother sits like a stone at the head of the table she has meticulously laid in the back room.

Her nephews, Arkeh's children, Charlie and Joe-Davie and teenage niece Esther, sit immobile and speechless.

Somebody has to break the silence. I get up from the table and, seemingly unconcerned, stroll out to the front of the store to inspect the busted windows. A bareheaded woman in a cloth coat stands under the street light. We meet each other's gaze. She shouts:

"Tell your mother the *kourvah* to come out!"

When I go back to the table Charlie—on his way to join the Abraham Lincoln Battalion to fight for the Loyalists in the Spanish Civil War—gives an almost invisible shake of his head to me. I know that gesture, a Persily trademark; Jennie does it all the time to signal me to keep my mouth zipped.

Cousin Charlie, seventeen, soon to fight in Spain with the Lincoln Battalion against the fascists, in his U.S. National Guard uniform. Charlie joined the Guard to persuade troopers not to be strikebreakers.

A cold draught from the splintered windows whistles into the back of the store which Jennie so lovingly transformed into a family dining room.

Charlie's older brother, Joe-Davie, a CIO regional director, says gently to no one in particular, "Shall we, uh, begin?" Jennie doesn't like their politics but loves her cousins dearly. Until now, I've hardly been aware I *had* relatives but now I'm to find out that Joe was bayoneted in the shoulder by a National Guardsman in an Indiana strike, and has a bandage to show for it, and that Charlie is a warrior on his way to the antifascist front. Other than breaking bread with Pretty Boy Floyd and John Dillinger, what more could I ask?

Cousin Esther gives a strangled cough and says, "It's fine brisket, Jennie."

(Courtesy of Harold, Christy, and Fred Persily)

Cousin Esther, Charlie's sister, in Womens Army Corps WWII.

Practiced at pretending, I slip back into my chair with an Ipana smile for all. Charlie puts on his charm, "So, Carl, how you doing at school?"

Who is Carl? Oh, me.

I steal a look at Ma. We're all waiting for the woman outside to make her next move, but she's gone away into the night.

Joe-Davie says to Charlie, "Let's have a look at that window."

Jennie speaks for the first time. Eyes down, hands flat on the table, she sits as if in prayer for a long moment. Then raises her eyes and coolly meets everybody's gaze. "Eat," she commands.

And we do.

Later, the angry lady, or her neighborhood clone, will try to kill us.

Who Put the Red Diaper on the Baby?

A word of explanation to readers unfamiliar with radical families. Several of Ma's dearest nephews and her most beloved brother were Communists; my mother was a socialist. In their day, that was all you had to say about the epic quarrels that estranged such families.

To care about something outside yourself is even riskier than fighting oil fires or being a cop in Chicago's Harrison District, because the thing that makes you human can also wreck your life.

For Jennie and Leo, the Stalinsts were gangsters who betrayed the American union movement with their slippery shenanigans and secretive agendas; both my parents carried scars, not only from police thumpings but from run-ins with Red musclemen on the other side of the Great Family Quarrel.

Jennie's rebel heart belonged not to the Bolsheviks and Lenin, but to hellraisers like Upton Sinclair, Clarence Darrow, Emma Goldman, and Red Emma's lover, Alexander Berkman (who shot Carnegie Steel boss Henry Frick three times and stabbed him twice, so much for pacifism).

There is hardly a Jewish immigrant clan of their generation that was not bitterly split between the "ists"—socialists versus Communists or both against the Trotskyists who didn't like the de Leonists who loathed the Cannonites who despised the Schactmanites who—and on and on. In the best circles—that is, the American labor aristocracy into which I was born—it was uncool not to be an "ist" of some kind, and an "ist" is genetically coded to engage in fierce factional disputes over the most profound of human questions or the tiniest of procedural points. You argued for your "position" as for your own life.

Warren Beatty's film *Reds* makes a good stab at portraying the white-hot passions involved in families like mine. *Reds* is also useful for identifying the exact modern moment when brother and sister, mother and son, turned against one another in one of the great classic debates about whether the working class should go to war against itself. My whole life before I was born was shaped by bearded disputatious men in smoky halls passing resolutions in foreign languages about countries I only knew about from my stamp album.

In 1912, the influential Socialist International, including the Americans, met in Switzerland and pledged to oppose the coming butchery in the First World War. They called on workers to lay down their weapons or turn them against the generals. The word socialism had heft then; in America, fifty-six socialists were mayors of U.S. cities, Oklahoma had a "red" legislature, Kansas was a hotbed of radical publishing, and the party published 262 English-language weeklies and five daily papers. Overseas in France and Germany, socialists had near majorities in their parliaments. Yet in a single moment, when war broke out in 1914, it all collapsed at the first sound of the regimental bugles in Serbia, Austria, Germany, France, Russia, and Britain, when the socialists saluted, clicked their heels, and voted for "war credits," that is, to back their respective governments in sending workers to slaughter each other in the trenches. Hitler, who served bravely on the western front, and I are direct descendants of the moral disintegration of socialist pacifism in that war.

That night at dinner in the back of the store, when a woman in the snow cursed my mother as a dirty whore, we all, consciously or not, carried the burden of that quarrelsome history, acting out in our own lives the insults and shoving matches of a noisy night in 1912 in Basle and Zimmerwald. The "personal is political" is a tired cliché, but in our family the political really *was* personal.

The other cliché is that politically minded people don't have personal lives or, if they do, they self-destruct because their ideals take priority over their families. Whole books have been written about how the "struggle" wrecks relationships. Look at the mess Karl Marx made of his daughters; how Engels snobbishly refused to marry his factory-girl mistress, Mary Burns; Lenin's hotsy-totsy adultery with the haut-bourgeois Inessa Armand; Stalin murdering his wife; the storm that was Louise Bryant and John Reed's marriage; and the long list of complaining children I know who blame their personal problems on their parents' social dedication.

Yet I cannot imagine being the child of anyone other than Jennie and Leo, whose lives were a constant toss-up between high ideals and messy reality. Of course, they could have done this or that better—there's this whole question of an absent dad—but in the end I've come round to loving them, not only for who they were but also for who I am and who my son Joe is. Joe wouldn't be alive if Leo hadn't ambled past this sparkling redhead on a cigarette-makers' picket line in 1919 with a corny line of flapdoodle, "Anymore like you at home, honey?"

The emotional lives of radicals often strike me as muddled, complex, tangled, tormented by unresolvable contradictions, failed relationships, unfulfilled dreams, neurotic betrayals, and just all-round shittiness. But is this so *very* different from "mainstream" families? Check out from the library John Cheever and John Updike, or look around at your next-door neighbors in Scarsdale, Winnetka, or Pasadena. Anyway, in my world, my culture, my parents *were* mainstream, as I define it.

They're with me still, Jennie and Leo, when I'm putting Joe to bed at night or choose this word over that on the typing keys or wonder in the middle of a domestic crisis how my folks might handle it differently?

Especially Jennie.

1939—Nazi-Soviet pact frees Hitler to invade Poland and start WWII. Judy Garland in The Wizard of Oz.

Jennie and the Women (II)

In Chicago, arsonists-for-hire were a neighborhood institution on a par with accident fraudsters who professionally hurled themselves in front of oncoming streetcars for a cleanly broken leg and the insurance settlement. To set a good commercial fire you had to be careful to hire an experienced man, or else somebody could get really hurt. It was how desperate people lived then.

At about the time when Jennie was negotiating with a two-man firebug team to burn down our Family Hand Laundry, a landlord's eviction notice arrived followed by a bailiff's papers. Jennie thought *To hell with torching the place, it's too much trouble,* and in a single night moved us out of the only home I'd known for three years. None of the "comrades" helped because most of them were flat broke, or they may have held it against Dad for ducking out of his commitment to organize them against the Teamster goons.

I hated leaving the store, its pink and green sign sighing in the wind, the gold and black National cash register that rarely registered anything but "No Sale," the Chinese down the street who had cut our throats, the ornate crown molding on the ceiling I stared at by the hour to zone out my parents' fiery quarrels, the back alley window barred from robbers moronic enough to break into our bankruptcy, the damp comforting smell of drying laundry. Our three years there had been a purgatory for Jennie and Leo, but it had given me a life, plus a license to my own name even if I hated it.

Jennie moved us in with a family on the "Polack" side of the Pulaski streetcar tracks, but they weren't any more welcoming than the Jews who had taken us in as paying boarders. The Poles came into our room whenever they felt like it to turn off the lights day or night; and of course their sons began beating on me, but now that I was bigger and stronger I won as many bouts as I lost.

As if we didn't have enough troubles, one day, as Jennie was coming back from job hunting, she was drawn down the hall by a great sobbing from inside the room next to ours. I peeked out to see Ma listening through the other door. Seeing me, she jerked a thumb, meaning "Follow me into trouble," and grudgingly I followed as she marched in without bothering to knock. There was a girl in the room, maybe sixteen, rocking back and forth on a threadbare couch, alternately weeping and moaning to herself. Jennie plunked herself down beside her, smoothed her straggly blond hair, and got the story: Charlotte was unmarried and pregnant by a Great Lakes Training Station sailor who had walked out on her. My heart sank, knowing from experience how this would galvanize Jennie, and so it happened. In the next weeks Ma took charge of this perfect stranger's predicament, forbade her a back-alley abortion, the only kind available then to a single girl, saw her through the birth of the child, located a Catholic adoption agency, wrote a letter to the sailor's commanding officer (we never heard back), and gave Charlotte enough bus fare to get her home to Naperville, Illinois. All this time, I grumbled that Ma was meddling, who did she think she was, God? "What planet are you living on, son? She would do the same for me," Ma shut me up. Life in Naperville turned out to be unbearable for Charlotte, who came back to Chicago where Jennie spread her freckled arms over this lost child and found her a waitress job at a Thompson's cafeteria and in no time Charlotte, a church-going Catholic, became a member ex officio of the Riga-Baltic Ladies Progressive Society. I attended her first, and my last, sit-down dinner with the ladies at Carl's Restaurant. Charlotte took one look at all the food dishes laden with brains, calves liver, tongue, gefilte fish, and all manner of *forshpie* entrails and almost plotzed. Jennie smiled, "Welcome to the Jews, sweetheart. The Alka-Seltzer is on the house."

My mother the saint, except with other women's husbands, or on a picket line.

Jennie the Chicagorilla

After nearly putting a match to our store, and back to our old pattern of tiptoeing down the back stairs for a midnight flit from rooms we couldn't pay the rent on, by luck my mother was thrown a life preserver of a part-time piecework job at Regal Frocks, a Loop sweatshop. She was a skilled overlock machine operator gifted with the holographic three-dimensional mind of an industrial engineer who at a glance could take in an entire factory floor and spot the production logjams and how to fix them. Since Regal was nonunion, she put in a call to the Amalgamated Clothing Workers, which assigned a full-time organizer, and, as night follows day, the boss fired Jennie and a strike was on.

I was thirteen and just entering Marshall High and transferring my libido from the Rockets to girls when one afternoon my supper wasn't on the table, and something told me to grab a streetcar downtown to look for Ma. The picket line in front of Regal Frocks was just dispersing under the watchful eye of one of Chicago's finest smacking his billy club into the palm of his hand in time-honored style. "Where's my mom?" I asked. A woman striker put down her placard and pointed up to the sky—at the L (elevated) train that circled the Loop and ran out to the neighborhoods. "Better hurry and catch her," the woman said ominously, "or somebody's getting killed'."

I raced up the L stairs and caught the train just before the doors shut and bounced down the aisle toward Jennie, who waggled that very familiar warning with her eyebrows to go past and ignore her.

Way out beyond Comiskey Park on the south side, another passenger, a large rawboned white woman carrying a straw carryall, got off at Forty-seventh with Jennie trailing her. I

143

followed down the station steps to the street. When the big woman passed an empty lot Jennie caught up with her and began chatting, then talking, then arguing with her. The woman's hand darted into the carryall and came out with a pair of mean-looking cloth-cutting shears that Jennie pushed away, whereupon she knocked the woman down with a haymaker punch to the jaw that Jack Dempsey or Dad would have admired. Then, scanning to see if there were any witnesses, she dragged the yelping woman by her hair into scrub bushes and, while I watched in astonishment, slugged her a couple of times and kicked her in the ribs for good measure, just like Swede had done to the Irish kid. I couldn't believe this was my pacifist mother who wouldn't even let me join the Boy Scouts because they wore military-style uniforms. I ran over. "Ma, are you nuts? What are you doing?" She straightened up, not even breathing hard, briskly took my arm, and walked me away. "You saw nothing, you heard nothing. Oh look, there's our streetcar."

Later, I got the full story from Dinah Farrar, the Regal Frocks dress designer who had seen the whole thing from her office window. "The woman, a scab, day after day she threatens the pickets with those scissors. Jennie tried everything—you know how she is. 'Please put away the knife.' 'Come, let's have a cup of coffee and talk about this.' 'We're not your enemies.' 'I'm a mother, are you a mother?' I don't have to tell you, Jennie's a talker, appealing to the woman's better nature. But, nothing. The woman wouldn't listen. So nature took its course."

I asked Dinah what happened to the scab.

She said, "Oh, she never came back to Regal. What, she's got a death wish?"

Much later, I mentioned the Regal incident to Ma. She replied that her memory wasn't too good anymore.

Her exact words were: "Who remembers everything? Thank God."

※ ※ ※

Like Joe is with my writing profession, I tried to know as little as possible about Ma's work. But after the Scissors Woman incident I began slipping down to Regal Frocks after school to escort her home in case of trouble. Waiting outside the factory for the closing whistle, I'd climb up an alley window to peek in and it wasn't at all like photos I'd seen of sweatshops with grimly silent, oppressed women bent over their machines. At her overlock, it was another Jennie, perky and alive, chattering animatedly, one of the girls. True, Regal Frocks was a sea of whirring machines, regimentation, repetitive work, all that, but it was something else, too, a place for Jennie to show what she was worth, what she knew, her skills—and above all to enjoy the company of women.

This changed as she got older and slower. Years later she wrote me that with the influx of Spanish-speaking workers and language a barrier to floor gossip—in the old days she would have picked up "Spanglish" in a day—her mind sometimes overtook her fingers as the past threatened to overwhelm her. "Occasionally at work, when the power machine is running, the more I think about all the yesterdays the faster I drive the machine, until I wake up and I know that it is all in the past and I was part of it—"

The work that killed her saved my mother's life.

145

You're the Pop
You're the baby's father
You're the Pop
But you needn't bother
I won't make a claim to your ancient name at all
The day you made me you promised you'd take me to City
Hall . . .
My mistake
Was in getting plastered.
What a break
For the little bastard.

—improvised unpublished Cole Porter lyric
recalled by Elaine Stritch

MGM's Truth Serum

I was born out of Jennie's movie-loving rib. The closest either of us had to a religious life was a shared, almost insane passion for sprocket-hole fantasies. Despite different tastes—mine Flash Gordon, hers Garbo and Mae West—we'd have odd truces of going together, arm in arm, alternately to the other person's pick-of-the-week at a local theater. In a rough neighborhood like Lawndale, attending a matinee with one's mother was not a cowardly thing to do.

One bright Sunday afternoon I took Jennie to the Central Park Theatre on Roosevelt Road to see her matinee choice, an MGM weepie, *Blossoms in the Dust*, starring Greer Garson as a Texas unwed mother who builds an orphanage for thrown-away children. Garson, dignified, noble and self-sacrificing, was my mom's special favorite because she almost never lost her temper on screen; even Myrna Loy threw vases at her husband, William Powell, and as for Jean Harlow, well, what can you expect from a *common* blonde? I said nothing to Jennie about Garson's openmouthed kiss with Laurence Olivier in *Pride and Prejudice* which profoundly reorganized my feelings about sex.

After watching *Blossoms in the Dust*, we strolled back to our little room, with kitchen privileges, in the apartment of a no-neck local family, the Orkins: Betty the pinch-faced mother, and a Depression-faded father who was part of the wallpaper, and two sons about my age, skinny bucktoothed Harold and nasty little roughneck Sidney. I could outbox and outfox Harold but his peewee sibling had a fist like a piece of flying concrete and, although smaller, Sidney walloped me almost daily.

The room we rented overlooked a garbage-strewn alley that was handy for leaning out the window to chat with passing kids. Which may explain how easy it was, in our absence that Sunday, for somebody to toss a grenade — a cherry bomb packed with extra gunpowder loaded with three-inch nails taped to it — through the half open window and land squarely on the bed Jennie and I slept in. It blew apart the coverlet, scorched the top sheet, which had a big hole burned in it, and sent nails flying into the wall. One nail had buried itself flatwise just above my headboard.

Jennie sat down on the ruined bed to survey the damage. Then out came the usual Pall Mall to clear her mind.

I was surprised at how *un*surprised she was. My mind raced through a list of my potential assassins but there were too many to count, topped by Melvin Abrams whom I'd tripped and sent sprawling down the stairs at Howland Elementary and who now wore his broken wrist in a plaster cast which he swung at me in the playground like a medieval mace.

Jennie chain-smoked and was figuring how to tell the Orkins, to whom we owed back rent.

She decided: "Forget it, it's just one of those things."

Not to me, it wasn't. Fists and chunks of coal inside ice-snowballs were legit but bombs were not.

"Why would anyone do this to us?" I asked.

At first, she dodged my questions, then said, "It wasn't *us* they were after."

"Who then?"

She was silent.

Light bulb flashes on. *She* was the target.

Jennie sighed, "We'll move again. It's a bad neighborhood." That was crazy, the neighborhood was all I had.

"We calling the cops?" I asked. She gave me her patented are-you-out-of-your-mind? look and stubbed out her cigarette.

"I'll take care of it," was all she said, gathering up the burned bedsheets.

I'll take care of it. Kids' minds are like Enigma decoding machines, and suddenly, in that bomb-seared room, I flashed on a picture of Jennie not as my mother but as a woman with a separate secret life independent of me. She was Greer Garson, who had a dark secret. It made sense. I blurted:

"I'm a bastard like those kids in the movie, right?"

Her back to me, Ma's reply came as quick and trite as Garson's dialogue: "There are no illegitimate children, only illegitimate parents!"

Bull's-eye! Somehow *Blossoms in the Dust* and the blast in our bed had temporarily shaken Jennie loose from her impulse to cover up.

I parked myself on the scorched bed. "Ma, honest, double cross my heart and hope to die, it's *great* to be illegitimate." The words tumbled out before my brain thought them.

And then, because I believed it was a cute and obliging

thing to do, I quoted lines from the poet Ogden Nash, whose doggerel was to me the height of sophistication:

> . . . *our parents forgot to get married*
> *Our parents forgot to get wed*
> *Did a wedding bell chime*
> *Our parents were always somewhere in bed* . . .

Completely out of character, Jennie burst into tears, her shoulders convulsively shaking with the effort to hold them in. She held onto the edge of the bed to steady herself, then got up and went to the busted window to look out, and I went to stand next to her. We made no move to clean up. For the longest time she simply stared out.

I slipped between her and the window to shield her from whatever it was outside. The person who had done this had to be female, I knew, because the previous week, on my own, I'd gone to Hitchcock's *Rebecca* and found out all about a woman's twisted heart. Somewhere out there was a wronged wife with a vengeance lust, just like Max de Winter's jealous housekeeper, Mrs. Danvers.

I came into Jennie's arms, a rare event between us, and for once said the right thing.

"Whatever happened, Ma, we didn't do anything wrong." We. Her and me.

I went into a boxer's crouch just like Dad taught me, feinting a mock slo-mo uppercut to her chin, my body language saying, *Hey it doesn't matter nor anything else you're doing on the q.t., it's all jake with me.*

And that was that. Nothing more that day or ever afterward was said about it. Flame-haired Greer Garson, her hair the exact color of Jennie's at the age she gave birth to me, gently shut the door on the secret Ma had borne so heavily for so long, so alone.

On the following Monday after school, I went to the Douglas Park branch library and requested a dictionary at the reference desk. I looked up "illegitimate," which said "against the law; illegal; born out of wedlock." How satisfying. Wedlock certainly was how you'd describe what Jennie and Leo had going; the word itself suggested a jail. And "against the law" and "illegal" were nothing new since we'd lived so much of our lives on the other side of the penal code. It took a few days for me to completely register my new status, but the more I thought about it the better I liked it. Indeed, I began to look around at the other Rockets with a certain pitying condescension because—unless I was wrong— none of them bore the mark of my distinctive bastardy. I loved new words and looked this one up in other languages. *Bastardo, batarde, salaud, cabron, mamzer, wang ba дan . . .* and walked around the neighborhood talking quietly to myself, *cabron, wang ba дan . . .*

A perfect fit.

And I vowed that, whatever other sins I might commit against Jennie, that's one she wouldn't have to suffer. This we'd do together.

Before Karl Marx There Was Billy Jurges

I was six, nine, and twelve when the Chicago Cubs, the city's stellar team until the White Sox broke an eighty-eight-year curse by winning the 2005 World Series, won their last three National League pennants, long before a fan (Steve Bartman, may God protect him) tipped the ball out of Moises Alou's glove causing the mentally shaken team to lose a 2003 World Series chance to the Florida Marlins. That's when the Cubs rocked, and I drew the natural conclusion that hard times bred hard men who could swing a bat somewhere other than on a picket line. My passion for the big red C inside the blue circle was nearly pathological. I memorized the lineup and batting averages (nobody, in an era when players drank in the dugout, bothered to count fielding stats), and talked myself to sleep mumbling a slow poetic reading of the Cubs' team roster. Gabby Hartnett, Babe Herman, Hack Wilson, Phil Cavaretta, Stan Hack, Woody English, KiKi Cuyler, Big Bill Lee, Lon Warneke — In time, I was absolutely certain to replace Cuyler as the Cubs' center fielder. I had the chatter, the pepper and the right moves; all I needed was a decent mitt and talent.

Most other Rockets were White Sox fans, but what other team than the Cubs could boast an infielder like iron man Billy Jurges, shot twice by his mistress Violet and then returns to the lineup *in three weeks*?

I lived for spring Opening Day, as a fan and as a sandlot pickup player. None of this Little League shit, no grown-ups admitted. At summer's dusk, I'd stroll out to an empty lot, which was grown over with the most amazing variety of exotic weeds and city-flowers, stand alone on a nonexistent pitcher's mound, in my hand a beaten-up Wilson softball with the horse-hide half torn off showing the core of packed rubber bands, and mimic the windup-and-delivery moves I'd heard described on Pat Flanagan's tickertape radio commentaries. (Flanagan, like his downstate colleague "Dutch" Reagan, had a genius for faking the action on games played hundreds of miles away from his broadcast booth.) I had a beautiful follow-through kick.

I don't remember my father or mother or anyone else's parents ever attending a Rockets ball game: an adult hanging around a kids' playground would have drawn the attention of a policeman or prying *bubbeh*. Benign neglect by grownups—better yet, being bored by us—was a liberating force. Today, Little League, with us caring parents, supportive coaches, hired umpires, bat bags, masks, shin guards, and uniforms, strikes me as an absurdity. Yet, despite all, I have become a Little League dad of the worst sort. If Joe strikes out looking, it's a knife in my heart; he makes a nifty force-out at second, my soul sings. I'm in seventh heaven when he's up there pitching. Such cool control! My little Roger Clemens. But when Coach removes Joe to give other kids a chance on the mound and puts him in right field—the daydreamer's position, my favorite—I find myself in such a (silent) rage that it's easy to sympathize with the Texas "cheerleader mom" who plotted to murder her daughter's main rival at high school. As usual, baseball is a mirror of my true character.

This season, Joe and I have been pitching and catching a lot of ball together, fielding webjams (line drives he has to stretch for like Willie Mays), everything but sliding, which we both hate. At dusk when the light isn't so good—that's my story—I drop the ball now and then. "Let's face it, Clancy," he comes up to plop the ball into my Derek Jeter-signed glove. "You're not much good at anything except being a Dad."

＊ ＊ ＊

War in Europe broke out on September 3, 1939. The Cincinnati Reds whipped the Cubs five nil in the series.

Overnight, Billy Jurges faded in favor of "Peter Wimpole,"

a name I wholly invented for an English boy my age in an imaginary gas mask who cowered in an air raid shelter. My Peter, a mental composite of newsreel images of children evacuated from about-to-be-blitzed London, became my very personal responsibility. I'd talk to him about the war, his favorite Royal Air Force planes, his family, is the gas mask sweaty? and was farm life hard on a city boy? Of all my pretend friends, from Tarzan to Prince Valiant, Peter Wimpole became the best because I had created him myself.

The 1939 baseball season was a bust anyway. The Cubs came in fourth in the pennant race, which I blamed on manager/catcher Gabby Hartnett's purchase of the pitcher Dizzy Dean from our archrivals, the St. Louis Cardinals. It was obvious that Dean was a spy sent in from the German-filled town of St. Louis to destroy the Cubs' World Series chances.

To hell with baseball, anyway. Well, almost.

9

Die, Yankee Dog!

Let's remember Pearl Harbor
As we go to fight the foe
And remember Pearl Harbor
As we do the Alamo . . .

—jukebox favorite

7:55 A.M. Honolulu time. In Chicago it's a cold bright Sunday noon. People look up at the clear blue sky only rarely when they hear the engine drone of an overhead plane or the strange feathery rustle that sparrows and finches make when they impulsively dart around in packs. THWACK! I strong-armed the thread-trailing softball over the roofs of parked cars, over the heads of the Horowitz brothers on base, and it sailed up the street to land on the stoop of our latest home at 4104 Grenshaw by the Sears railroad siding on Chicago's west side. It was the longest hit I'd made in pickup baseball all year.

Finally, at fifteen I was getting into my stride as the next "Hammerin' Hank" Greenberg, the Detroit Tigers' first baseman.

Jennie, in a flapping flowered housedress exposing her naked thigh, instantly shattered my Hall of Fame dream when she came stumbling down the stone steps of the two-family graystone residence screaming, "The Japanese! Bombing Hawaii!" Rounding second base between manhole covers, I was mortified by another one of her lies; lately she'd been doing it a lot. "Ma," I yelled, "g'wan home, okay, you're embarrassing me." What would she think of next?

Jennie's cry of havoc in her housedress shamed me on the street. Normally she never left the house in anything but full Lane Bryant-and-Max Factor armor, so either she'd blown a gasket or the unthinkable had happened, the Japanese had actually torpedoed my winter baseball schedule. Soon there would be snow on the streets and I'd have no chance to practice my up-from-the-knees swing, the SuperJew swat. And, as neighbors came running into the street and Ma's tale was confirmed, I was totally pissed because the Pearl Harbor attack simply didn't fit in with my carefully constructed analysis of world events. How could I be so wrong?

❀ ❀ ❀

In the 1940s you were not considered off-the-planet weird if you were into hard-core politics as well as street corner gangsterism. It was a sort of white ethnic pre-Blackstone P Rangers thing. (Later the Rangers would rule Lawndale.) Some boys coped with the "threat of world fascism" by invoking comic book fantasies—Captain Marvel zaps Adolph Hitler—others by denying it, but a few of us adopted a coping strategy of trying to *understand* as a way of saving our sanity.

* * *

For Midwesterners, certain truths were inalienable. First and foremost, "war is a racket," in the immortal words of Major General Smedley Butler of the Marine Corps. The Pacific ocean was an unconquerable American lake, Europe the source of all our troubles. War profited only the "merchants of death," the profit-greedy weapons makers who fanned the fires of brainless nationalism. Simple. America should stay out of other people's fights. Or, as the popular radio comic, Eddie Cantor, sang every Sunday night, "*Let them keep it over there.*" Jennie and I argued about it at the time, she the pacifist claiming that Jews had no choice but to fight Hitlerism and I, a lover of military paraphernalia but raised in an antiwar anti-imperialist atmosphere, thinking *Why not make common cause with German workers?* My feelings about the coming war were all tangled up in other tensions between Ma and me. We fought out our personal and sexual conflicts on a world map, Oedipus at the kitchen table arguing his heart out.

Our quarrels had gotten more intense after September 15, 1940, a few days after my fourteenth birthday, when three hundred Spitfires rose in the skies over southern England to fling themselves against five hundred Nazi Dornier bombers and their Messerschmitt 109 fighter escorts. It tore me up to betray my imaginary friend Peter Wimpole, but you had to hold the line somewhere, right? In vain, Jennie pointed to the contradiction between my hatred of war and my consuming, obsessive identification with Movietone newsreels of the London children with their brave tearful smiles and gas masks. "Just like your father," she said. "Right hand a stranger to your left hand." So? If it was good enough for Leo Sigal, it was excellent for me, I brayed.

＊ ＊ ＊

4104 West Grenshaw was only a couple of streets away from Rocket territory, but by the mere act of moving across the Pulaski Road streetcar line I'd exiled myself from our home turf. I was lonely for the boys and kept looking for a substitute Rocket, only to find him in a pale-faced, four-eyed geek with a heart murmur, the kind of kid no self-respecting Rocket ever normally associated with. Never before had I chosen a friend for his brain power, an ultimate betrayal of the Rocket code.

The new companion of my fears was Barney (Baruch) Herzog, who had a fiercely engaged mind locked inside his shiny high-domed forehead, and a suicidally depressed older sister locked in a dark back room of the family apartment over a butcher's on Sixteenth Street. Back in the old neighborhood, I would not have given Barney a second glance; but ever since Jennie moved us to the hinterland west of Pulaski, coincident with the first blitz attacks on London, Barney and I had struck up a strange, mismatched friendship. I felt hugely protective toward him because I was his only friend in high school.

The qualities that put other kids off Barney, his stubbornly belligerent integrity and fierce mode of arguing, were the things that attracted me to him. We'd debate over anything, the shape of postage stamps from Chad, how to spell chlorophyll, but most especially, and bitterly, over American intervention in the coming war. After several fist fights in which I pulled punches because of his heart condition—he hated me for this ("Hit me! Hit me! I'm normal!" he'd cry)—we finally shook hands on a mutually acceptable compromise. Despite a successful fascist uprising in Spain when we were eleven, despite Hitler's march into Austria and Czechoslavakia, despite the Nazi invasion of Poland and the German bombs rained on London's children, the war in Europe, we kept telling ourselves, was essentially an "imperialist adventure" dreamed up by DuPont, Vickers, Krupp, and all the other death merchants. Therefore, the only sane response to the war makers was something like the ill-fated Ludlow Referendum, a Congressional proposal requiring a nationally held election before the country could go to war.

"Don't you go back on it," Barney warned.

"Don't *you*," I said more strongly than I felt.

Essentially, our radical critique was rooted in a mainstream mind-set that was an almost perfect fit with the established radical pacifism I was born into. From the earliest possible age, I hated war, no doubt partly from a desire to wipe out the war between my parents, but also as a kid's response to a world collapsing around his ears. The whole "isolationist" popular culture of the Midwest—against involvement in foreign wars—was especially prevalent among ex-soldiers denied their promised World War I bonus by both a Republican (Herbert Hoover) and a Democratic president (Franklin D. Roosevelt). A sizeable fraction of the heartland's population, much of it German immigrant stock, in Wisconsin, Minnesota, North and South Dakota, and Illinois, was opposed to, or lukewarm about, this new "Good War." "Pulling England's chestnuts out of the fire" was a commonly heard phrase, trumpeted by the region's most widely read newspaper, the *Chicago Tribune*. An often radical pacifism was the conventional wisdom in prairie states like Illinois. Once, in a failed experiment at giving me "culture," my mother briefly pushed me into a Workmen's Circle school on Ogden Avenue, where on the classroom wall hung a grisly photograph of a living soldier with his face blown away from forehead to chin. For me, this faceless guy became a central image of any war—a warning, a nightmare.

❊ ❊ ❊

That Sunday evening, December 7, after my ball game, Barney Herzog and I met as usual over a Monopoly board in his family's gloomy flat. "Roosevelt got us into this war," Barney asserted, moving to Park Avenue, and for the first time I wavered. "Maybe," I replied feebly, going to Jail, "it's all a misunderstanding,"—like the U.S. navy vessel *Panay* that the Japanese "mistakenly" bombed in the Yangtse river. Barney angrily scooped up much of my real estate. "Why were our sailors guarding Standard Oil barges? Any fool can see the Rockefellers are behind it!" He shook a stack of toy currency at me, his eyes piercing me through his thick bottle lenses. "Don't give up the ship. Fire when ready, Ridley. Horatius at the bridge. Defend the Alamo, Clarence."

But our united front was crumbling under the pressure of the war itself. Even though my imaginary English pal, Peter Wimpole, was pressing me to have a rethink, I couldn't bear letting Barney go, the only boy I'd found on the west side to share my mind with. I had a premonition, the seed of a tremendous guilt, that the attack on Pearl Harbor was going to make Barney lonelier for the rest of his life because I, his only friend, might abandon him to the jocks and yahoos. Unlike me, he was powerless against loneliness and the world's scorn; at school, nobody chose him for anything, he stank at P. E., was too good at books, and refused to tell dirty jokes. His clever mind and stricken heart, the angry cerebral look of him, put off the other kids. I was his island of safety, he was my braver unconforming self.

I, Roland, bravest of Charlemagne's twelve paladins, was betraying Oliver, who had saved my life against the Saracens.

I tossed out a face-saver, "Hey, Barn. War is rotten, but maybe let's win this one only."

Barney glared at me. "We *shook* on it."

There it was, blood calling against blood. Voices raised, insults exchanged, and suddenly Barney and I had challenged each other out to a snowy alley downstairs where at first I pulled my punches again. This enraged him. He hit me hard, and I knocked him to the ground. I pleaded, "Don't get up, Barn, I don't want to hurt you." This drove him wild with humiliation and as he struggled to rise I had to keep pushing him down. "Please," I begged almost in tears, "stay the fuck down! I can hurt you!" This reminder of his disability drove him completely crazy and he grabbed my legs and sent me sprawling in the snow and all I could do was cross my arms and fend off his hysterical, tearful blows. Finally, I rolled over and ran away, followed by his great cry: "Come back, you coward, and try to kill me! I dare you. You never can, you never can . . . !"

❊ ❊ ❊

Monday, December 8, at Marshall High, in Miss Ballard's glee club class, we boys sat at our cafeteria-style desk tables as the school p.a. system piped in President Roosevelt's Day of Infamy speech. *"And therefore I ask the Congress to declare that a state of war exists between . . ."* At long long last, the moment we'd been dreading and waiting for, the thing that movies like *Wings*, *Road to Glory*, and *Hell's Angels*, Fleers bubblegum cards ("Die, Yankee dogs!" screech the Nipponese soldiers as they plunge bayonets into the breasts of U.S. Marines) had been preparing us for—exploded. I looked around at the faces of the other boys. A few giggled out of fear or maybe they didn't get it yet. I got it. My life, our lives, were changed forever. We were sitting atop a treacherous tectonic plate that was shifting massively, convulsively, and you felt the jolt, the displacement, the world sliding away under your feet.

The catastrophe was not catastrophic for everybody.

I had grown up into a world where you did not expect a job. Now I had a job. A future.

Jack Perry, the pale jokester who sat next to me in glee club, whispered: "I'm joining up. Twenty-one bucks a month." "Schmuck," I said, "you're only fifteen." "You'll see," he vowed. And Jack kept the faith: he fell as a Marine on Okinawa three years later.

Only last week I'd swung along Roosevelt Road crooning,

Franklin Roosevelt
Told the people how he felt

And we damn near believed what he said—
He said 'I hate war, and so does Eleanor
But we won't be safe till everybody's dead—'
Plow 'em under
Plow 'em under
Plow 'em under
Every fourth American boy.

But suddenly, war delirium hit me like malaria or flu, fevering my brain and heating my blood. Those damn Japs! And Hitler any day now. I had a lot of wimpy pacifism to live down. A blinding surge of naked patriotism struggled with my antiwar genes, and, by jingo, won. Pearl Harbor sent me back to the streets and to Flukey's joint where I drooped like a vine over the rising-bubble Wurlitzer juke box, snapping my fingers to:

Praise the Lord
And pass the ammunition
And we'll all be free

I regressed to a childish fascination with all things military. As real-life soldiers, sailors, and marines filled the sidewalks of west-side Chicago in their khaki and blue uniforms—Fort Sheridan and the Great Lakes naval base were nearby—my eyes tracked them as if they were gods on earth. I idolized men in uniform, tagging along after any ordinary soldier for blocks rather than let him out of my sight, on the principle that he was fighting for *my* life, defending *me*. All men in khaki were the big brother I didn't have.

Clancy, age fourteen, in Marshall High School ROTC uniform.
Joined ROTC to cut gym class, and thus avoid showing his
body, and learn weaponry for the coming war.

For the next four war years, I played a scorecard in my
mind; a private was one point, Pfc two, corporal three, and so
on. Once, late in the war, I glimpsed an officer with oak-leaf
clusters on his epaulettes, and got so excited I fell off the Kedzie
Avenue streetcar I'd been hanging onto at the back-end cow-
catcher so as not to pay my fare.

War became my frenzy.

Now, when Barney Herzog and I brushed past in the halls
of Marshall High, we avoided each other, I in embarrassment,
he in anger. But his unfaltering gaze followed me everywhere.
We'd bump shoulders, sidestep, or pretend not to notice, and
when we had to go to the same room in Miss Saunders' American history class there was an agony of awkwardness. Boys
break up, but I keenly felt the loss of Barney, the only one my

age who came near understanding my need to locate myself in a world of destruction. One day, a whole year after Pearl Harbor, I opened my wall locker at school to find a single sheet of three-hole notepaper impaled on the coat hook. On it was

SELLOUT

in his familiar loopily slanted scrawl.

Barney didn't have to worry, he'd never have to serve, but I was 1-A meat. So why did I feel he was the hero and I the coward?

✿ ✿ ✿

Barney and I lost touch after I was expelled from Marshall High. But one way or another, I managed to keep coming back to Chicago, at first to roam what was left of Lawndale after the '68 riots and then to track down the remaining Rockets. I kept Barney Herzog almost till the last; he wasn't a member of the club. Also, he reminded me painfully of myself at my defiant best, the self I'd lost track of. Forty years later after the fistfight in the snow I found him in a small apartment in Evanston, Illinois, and we spent an afternoon together while his wife—a clone of Heshie Wolinsky's frowning frau—glowered from a corner of the dining room.

Classified 4-F in the war and undrafted because of his health, Barney had become a copy editor at R.R. Donnelly, the commercial printer, and, like almost all the Lawndale boys, married a local girl. He had not "done well" despite the jump he had on those of us who lost time in service. Our visit was awkward, possibly because he was unsure why I was there in the first place. It wasn't easy to explain to him, or perhaps even to myself, that the search for Jennie took me on roundabout routes but always seemed to come back to Lawndale and its long-held family secrets. He might have sensed and resented that I was doing this for myself, to clarify my own life and not his, but Barney put himself out as much as he could under the stern, unyielding gaze of his wife. Oh, those wives!

I remembered Barney as an angry vulnerable boy fluent of speech and bristling with beliefs, feelings, ideas. But now, confronted by our mutual past he may have recalled only in vague outline, he haltingly searched for the words, backtracking, pausing for long stretches while he narrated a personal history of tragedy involving family suicides, madness, and violent tricks of fate. He was convinced his career had been stunted by McCarthyism, because a distant relative had been a Communist. Now, as a sixty-two-year-old man, he still carried his high-domed head with a certain sidelong arrogance, but the eyes which used to glisten with a keen intelligence refused to meet mine. The blank unseeing stare, like that of a blind man, fixed to one side of me as we spoke softly together that afternoon. He kept moving his head as if to hear something in my voice: was he, like me, trying to remember? Or did he have glaucoma? Was he, like some of the Rockets I was visiting, suspicious of the visiting writer from Hollywood with the rented Lincoln Town Car on the street below?

I'd made the same mistake once before, in crossing the country in a red De Soto convertible on my way anywhere but the United States. That's when I'd deliberately hunted down old friends and comrades, only to find them "selling out," as Barney had accused me in high school of being disloyal to my most closely held values. Or they were somehow lacking in what I wanted to preserve in myself, a fighting spirit. In the Red Scare days it had been all too easy to find people whose spines had bent or broken under pressure. At the time, I discounted something as ordinary as the sheer grind of normal life, the thing that Jennie had in so many ways tried vainly to tell me about. "Sometimes . . .," she'd reply to my high-minded demands on her never to grow old or tired but to keep on organizing, ". . . sometimes, it's . . . a little *too much.*"

And of course I didn't bring up the war thing that had broken up Barney and me.

But *he* did, in his way. Out of nowhere he nodded gravely, "We played Monopoly. And argue, oh my, all the time. Nothing else but whose turn it was to throw the dice. Nothing else but the dice." He studied the wallpaper behind me. "But we never really had fights, did we? Not once." He was speaking in code to me.

Mrs. Herzog coughed, moved restlessly, coughed again. Time to go.

Barney and his wife did not get up when I said good-bye. But as I turned the knob of the front door to go he called out, quite strongly, not in the quaver he'd used all afternoon, *"We can still be friends."*

So he remembered!

❀ ❀ ❀

I left Barney Herzog's building in Evanston with a keen sense of a job undone. Downstairs, in the Lincoln, I laid my head back on the leathery-smelling headrest and fought an urge to run back upstairs and physically pull him back into the same time warp I'd fallen into on these Chicago trips. If *only* I had stuck by my convictions and not gone sick with war flu—if only I'd taken my chances on a federal prison rap of conscientious objection—if only I hadn't let myself be swept along with the flag-waving crowd, Barney would have married a better-dispositioned woman, been richer, happier, all-seeing—and I would look like Robert Redford. I laughed, and headed the car toward Morton Grove, a suburb where so many of the guys had moved with their west-side wives.

"NEED I SAY MORE": A Soldier's Story

I saved Ike Lerman for the last because we had been the closest, two lonely kids pretending otherwise, chasing each other in the alleys, tighter than brothers, two halves of a single personality. He, too, had been an "unwanted" child by at least one parent, like me a dreamer, a blotter to absorb the world's troubles. The moment I walked into Ike's place—a middle-income condo—I knew it was a home blessed by a happy marriage. Maybe I judge these things by how the wife treats me. After a usual round of street insults—"You used to be so fat. Now look at you. *Oysgedart*—a skeleton. She's not feeding you, what?"—it's curbstone bullshit time again.

"What did we do all day as boys? What a question. Walked around the streets doing nothing and it took us all day to do it. We were both worriers. I am still. How about you?"

Today Ike, a big tall handsome guy, is a retired truck driver and opera afficionado who has raised a large family and guided them through every possible trouble. Quietly, he is most proud of two things, his time with the 103d ("Cactus") Infantry Division in Europe in WWII, and "I paid my bills. That's not bad for a kid who never expected to live beyond twenty."

Despite the long distances that separate us, I constantly

think about Ike, not just because we were practically joined at the hip as kids but because he was a kind of moral ideal for me, a notion that might give him a heart attack laughing. Of warm heart, he seems to see life clearly and quite coldly and dislikes my habit of romanticizing our past. "You always leave out the dead rats in the alley, the epidemics of diphteria and scarlet fever, the big red quarantine signs. Remember when you had 105 fever and Jennie had to stick cotton swabs up your nose to keep you breathing? And the old men blowing snot through their noses on the sidewalk. That was part of it, too."

Like me he loved Lawndale—and its multiplying anxieties. "We were concerned about food, the family unit, and being Jews. We *had* to be worriers. It's osmosis, picked up from our parents. Where was the rent coming from. Hitler. War and fascism. We thought that's the way things were always going to be. Nazis and death camps. We were kids, we didn't know, *but we did*. Of course, we knew! Big west-side families with relatives in eastern Europe. Herschel Grynspan, remember him? The Jew who murdered that Nazi diplomat in Paris, which brought on Krystallnacht. That's when we *really* knew. Talk about dread. The rabbis would sermonize. Homilies. I can remember our rabbi saying they were being slaughtered in Europe years before anyone else knew. Or would admit they knew. Or didn't want to know.

"Even as a kid you couldn't face reality. You go into denial." He laughs. "I'm *still* in denial.

"Back then, the only person making a living was a postman and he got his job from the precinct captain who knew the ward committeeman who kept Jake Arvey in cigars who fixed the ballot boxes for Roosevelt. What's wrong with today's Democrats, they don't know how to fix elections any more? I would have liked to be a postman, only they weren't hiring the day I stepped off the train after the army discharged me. I needed a quiet life. To keep from blowing my own brains out."

Half the Rockets had had a medical condition that technically made them 4-F, unfit to serve, but they went in anyway. Despite a heart murmur, Ike was assigned to the infantry, where he ran into barefaced anti-Semitism from other GIs and his officers. "All through the war they called me Jake, which is short form for kike. I couldn't fight everybody, so I selected. In the worst combat, I kept two bullets polished for my sergeant who kept sending "kikey Ikey," me, up to the point day after day, to get my ass shot off. And, you know? I put cellulose nitro, the stuff they drop down mortars to give them a bigger bang, under the latrine seat of my captain, likewise a Jew hater. In the army it wasn't easy to be the only Jewish guy in the company."

(Courtesy of Mr. Lerman)

"Ike Lerman," my best Rockets friend. A gentle warrior.

Ike spent 112 days in frontline combat with the 103d, "forty-eight of them bad. You don't know what darkness is until you're in the dark in Alsace-Lorraine. Tree bursts, ground so hard you can't dig a foxhole." He says he knew something was wrong in a rest area "when they gave us fruit cocktail. Uh-oh. Here we go. We dug into Alsace for six solid weeks under fire. Retreating most of the time. Nazi SS had a few of us trapped one day in the upper floor of a house, one of our buddies rushes in and says 'We're surrounded!' and I say 'How do you know?' and at that moment a mortar shell flies down the chimney and he says 'Need I say more?' and we dive out the back window and land in a pile of horseshit, the more horseshit a farmer has the richer he is, this guy must have been the J. P. Morgan of manure, we're shitting in our pants and run into the woods with the SS yelling at us, 'Come back, you fucking Yank!' "

Ike took cover in a shell hole with a German soldier aiming his rifle at him, but Ike got the jump, "and I blew his head off, but it was raining shells so I had to stay all night and most of the next day in the rain in a hole with this headless corpse. Not appetizing.

"How did I keep my sanity? I didn't. Same way we did as kids. Two phrases kept me going, 'Nobody lives forever' and 'Better you than me.'

"Look, you live on many levels at the same time. You have to be different things to different people—and different things to yourself, or you couldn't survive. You can be up with your family and an hour later by yourself you nose-dive. The 'secret' Ike is all of them, us, you, who knows?

"We took the Brenner pass. I saw the concentration camps. I liked getting into Nazi girls' pants by telling them Fritz Kuhn [U.S. Nazi leader] was my father and as I was pulling up my pants telling them I was a Jew. I fucked German women on potato bins. In combat you had a license to do anything you want—to kill."

Combat, Ike says, "was the adventure of my life. You go into this dreamlike state exactly like when things got really bad in the old neighborhood. When you're there, you don't believe you're there, and when you're out of it, you still don't believe you're out of it."

After the war, like almost all Rockets, Ike married a local girl who had written to him in service and, with the help of a GI loan, began long-distance truck hauling as an owner-operator. "I'm at this truck stop in Moline with this load of frozen fish. Not diamonds, just fish. This creep climbs in and sticks a gun in my face and tries to hijack me, and I tell him, "Hey do me a favor and shoot. It's all a dream anyway. *Gay en ∂rart* (go to hell), prick!' and he was so surprised he freaks and runs away, the schmuck."

Although he had free tuition on the GI Bill, Ike did not go to college. "I don't know, I was blocked. I wanted to live, not take tests. I'm self-educated by WFMT, classical radio, and going to concerts. When the other truckers were tuned into Elvis and Johnny Cash and that "Convoy" shit, I had my earphones on to Koussevitsy and Callas.

"They call us guys the Greatest Generation. So much crap. Your mother Jennie spent more time on a combat line than anybody, only it was the undeclared war in our homes. You and me, too, we've been at war all our lives."

❀ ❀ ❀

Practically all the others except Deaf Augie—Oscar, Albie, Jules, Mendy, Legs, Nate—had seen front line fighting, an unusually high percentage considering the normal ratio of rear echelon to combat troops. They'd all turned down college on the GI Bill. After the Battle of the Bulge, Leyte, the Aleutians, and the Siegfried Line, life was too short to sit around a classroom. You wanted to earn, get married, make babies, move on up. In my round of visits and dinners, it became clear that Pearl Harbor had boosted us all toward a life we could hardly imagine before December 7. That is, all of us who survived the war except little Nate Manoff, who dreamed of playing concert clarinet and lost two fingers on D-plus-One at Omaha Beach and ended up in a psych ward and some say a suicide.

For us, the attack on Pearl Harbor was an extension of FDR's New Deal, a vast works project. The bomb that tore into the ammo room of the USS *Arizona* lifted a huge load of anxiety from the poor. Emperor Hirohito's bombing of Hickham Field, catching all our planes on the ground, did for the American economy what even the most utopian New Dealers could only fantasize. The rush of patriotic adrenalin, not to mention federal money flowing into factories, offices, and farms for war orders, primed the pump as no government works project ever could.

We on the bottom of the pile could breathe again.

But the suspicion never quite left me that World War II, the "good war," was anything but good, and that it was a continuation of the demolition job on our morale and militance that the Depression had begun. I did not know at the time that legions of grown-ups were grappling with the same dilemma as two Lawndale boys who had loved each other in the winter that changed all our lives.

❊ ❊ ❊

While Barney and I were still brothers-in-dissent, we had an American history class together from a teacher named Miss Saunders, who was the sand in my oyster.

She was a small, disputatious woman with distressed hair and a kyphosis-shaped back, who spouted crabby "isolationist" opinions and was a troubling, provocative, superb classroom educator at Marshall High. I owe her. She and I spent the semester screaming at each other, boring everyone else in the room but ourselves. She called it "Mister Roosevelt's war," her code phrase for Jewish-instigated, and kept dropping heavy references to "Warburg" and "Rothschild." If I leaped from my seat to protest, her typically manic flushed face would pull a violent rictus and she'd jump up from her desk to stamp her feet. "Pulling England's chestnuts out of the fire!" she'd snarl in fury, and froth white foam at the corners of her mouth, which she did in moments of excitement. I was up and down in my seat like a jumpin' jack, supposedly to debate with her but really to pull her chain, when one day she lost it and hurled herself from her desk and ran at me with a wooden ruler in her upraised fist.

"You little Communist bastard!" she shrieked, waking up the half of the class that was asleep. She was trembling from the top of her nearly bald head to her brown Oxford shoes as she launched herself straight at me. *She's going to hit me*, I thought, *and I'll be the talk of Marshall High*. Some miracle of self-control stopped her at the last second, and she stood over me glowering and frothing so heavily I thought she was going to have an apoplectic fit. At last she drew a deep breath to keep her voice steady. "GET OUT! Out! Out this instant! Go to the Communists where you and your kind belong!"

Your kind. Anti-Semitic bitch, I thought cheerfully.

The hall bell rang. As we students tumbled out of Miss Saunders' room, one of the boys from the class was hanging around outside waiting for me. Max Weinstock, gauntly tall, awkward, and intense, put his hand on my arm. "Some performance you put on there," he said. "If you're interested, I can show you some *real* Communists."

Thus began my next life.

But it was without Barney Herzog. No more beloved friends. Now I had comrades.

✾ ✾ ✾

My Joe resists any hint from me that I want him to believe as I do. But sometimes blood will tell, and he'll surprise me, like the other day as we're coming back from Little League practice, he bursts into song:

Oh, Franklin Roosevelt/
Told the people how he felt/
And we damn near believed what he said . . .

I look over and ask, "Do you know what that song means?" He glances at me derisively and seems to channel Jennie through one of her favorite responses, "You think I'm stupid?"

10

Old Folks at Home

Jennie, an aspiring entrepeneur who hated the profit motive, started up yet another doomed business at about the time Hitler goose-stepped into Paris and in Mexico City a Stalinist hit man stabbed Leon Trotsky in the head with an ice pick. Nowadays, this new enterprise might be called an "assisted living residence" in our apartment in a cheap floor-through at 4104 West Grenshaw. The entire building smelled richly of tobacco because Mr. Ginsberg, who lived upstairs, was a cigar maker hand rolling leaves on his dining room table.

Ma and I had but one client, a senile, dribbling, apple-cheeked diabetic named Mr. Haroldson, who sat on his bed all day in a ratty bathrobe and made halfhearted passes at me. ("Here's a nickel. Come be a nice boy.") If he followed me out into the hallway with malice aforethought, I body slammed him but he liked it a little too much. Unperturbed, Jennie advised, "Be broad-minded, son. All he needs is a little human contact."

I sure gave him that. The bar for child or elder abuse was set rather high at the Grenshaw Home for the Aged, as Ma called us, because we needed the money the grown Haroldson children gave us for his upkeep.

A whole different mind-set operated in Lawndale when it came to child endangerment. There was no elaborate social service and police apparatus sensitive to, or set up to deal with, crimes like rape or incest, and this fairly low level of awareness may have licensed some family crimes. The neighborhood dealt rough justice to troublemakers or let it pass, but only in rare instances took it to the law, which was universally seen as hostile to poor people.

We did our best for Mr. Haroldson, feeding him regularly and giving him his daily insulin injections (I got good at this) and being gracious to his mistress, who arrived by taxi twice a week. She wore enough lipstick and rouge to start a cosmetics factory, weighed about two hundred pounds and swept in like the Queen of England, reeking of White Lies perfume. She locked Mr. Haroldson's bedroom door behind her. "What do they do in there?" I asked Ma. She shrugged. "It keeps him occupied." Then her peculiar sense of humor kicked in. "Finally, a man in the house."

Two men, actually.

Out of the night mist, again without explanation or excuse, Dad turned up for his final appearance in our lives. He'd been gone a year, four months and nine days. (I kept a calendar.) Our apartment seemed to come alive when he was in it. To keep him happy and at home I went for boxing lessons at the local club—the American Boys Commonwealth (ABC). The red-brick building had been a gift to the underprivileged from the parents of Bobby Frank, the rich Chicago lad murdered by the "thrill killers," Loeb and Leopold, in the 1920s. I also practiced deepening my voice and throwing short right hooks in the mirror the way Dad had taught me. He had left me a boy, but now I was a man qualified for him to stay.

With Chinese laundries spreading like fungi all over Chicago, there was even less likelihood of his making a living as a shirt ironer. So Dad, like Jennie, invented yet another hopeless business, delivering starched and finished collars on a waxed string all over town, which gave him an excuse to stay out of the house most days. Mercifully, he let me tag along. I helped him run the enterprise from the lay-down rear door of a $25 much-used Plymouth business sedan. It was like the old days when he took me to Bensinger's Pool Emporium to see the two Willies, Hoppe, and Mosconi cue it out for the world title. Dad's few collar customers were the same old guys, the "comrades," who'd invited him out to Chicago in the first place and who played cards all day in the back of their bankrupt stores. And who adjusted their trousers as if to compensate for the guns they no longer carried in a waistband. They seemed to hold no grudges against him for taking a powder on organizing the anti-Teamster drive.

Please God make him stay, I prayed to the God I didn't believe in.

One afternoon I cut class and came home early and walked into a side bedroom of the Grenshaw flat where Jennie was on her knees in a housedress blowing Dad. The shades were down, putting them in semidarkness. His naked back arched like a cobra's, glazed eyes unseeing at the ceiling. Dad was out of it. His glistening penis, wet with Mom's saliva and his sperm, struck me with an ecstasy of malice, envy, and joy. In my mind, as I fumbled to escape, I magnified his cock to the length of what I fantasized belonged to Doc Savage, Man of Bronze. I was experiencing something like the same morbid thrill as when the rusty old Colt automatic dropped out of his pocket at Slavic Hall. What a man. Ma glanced up and without dropping a stitch, so to speak, spat, and said, "Your father has a rash I'm helping him with."

Oh, right. A rash. Sure, absolutely.

I backpedalled from the dark room, thinking: *How clever of Ma.* I saw through her scheme. She didn't really *like* what she was doing. But it gave Dad such pleasure that she was forcing herself as a trick to get him to stick around with us. She was doing it all for me. Ah, brilliant Jennie!

Out in the hallway, Mr. Haroldson shuffled by with his usual feeble touchie-touchie stuff, and absentmindedly I slapped his hand away. Animals, this apartment was full of them. I felt cold and hot at the same time and went outside to sit on the stone steps. Why had this unwanted knowledge come my way, at this particular moment, just after Pearl Harbor, as if that wasn't enough to think about? Ma looked so undignified on her knees, her standard I'll-kill-myself posture in front of the gas stove back at the Family Hand Laundry; and Dad getting his rocks off from Ma doing something I associated with suicide-by-gas and strangulation. There had been an expression of pure agony on his gaunt face. This would take time to figure out for sure.

I looked up and down the street, but for once there was little comfort there. Cold now with curiosity and an odd fury, I flew out of myself, soaring high up into the sky to look down on me from a great height like a circling falcon, on a kid on a stoop feeling pretty much as he had when Ma was arrested by the state's attorney's cops and he was sure he'd never see her again, a sort of death. Nobody was taking her away this time except Dad, and that's what I wanted, wasn't it?

❁ ❁ ❁

On or off her knees, Jennie was smart but not quite smart enough to keep her man.

Bye-bye Daddy. So much for cocksureness. This time, he took off for good and all. Phffft, gone. Jennie was strangely unmoved, as if she knew all along the rash cure wasn't going to work. She didn't even seem surprised when a letter from Dad arrived from off the road. We sat down at the dining room table to read it together. Postmarked Pittsburgh, but headed New York, it was all about his trouble making job contacts, the poor employment market for laundrymen, etc. As a scribbled p.s. he added a note disowning me, bingobongo just like that, declaring he wanted nothing further to do with a son who associated with "red scum." Ma looked a question at me, and I threw it right back at her. But I knew why he wrote the p.s. Just before he left us, and in a childish burst of euphoria when I believed he might hang around, I bragged that when I grew up I was going to fill his shoes as a labor organizer, my preferred union being the CIO, the young breakaway from his own (more conservative) American Federation of Labor (AFofL), to which he'd given his life. At the time, he'd let it pass as mere chatter, but in this last letter he said he hated a " 'splitter'—rimes with quitter."

My chin trembled without my meaning it to.

I asked Ma why Dad didn't want to speak to me again.

Nothing betrayed in her voice. "It's just an excuse. Probably been carrying that letter around with him for years."

I went crazy. Crazier.

❁ ❁ ❁

In the film *Dead End* there's a scene where Humprey Bogart as fugitive criminal startles his old mother by suddenly reappearing in the old slum neighborhood. "Don't you recognize me, Ma?" he pleads. She stuns him with a hard slap across the face, snarling. "YOU AIN'T NO SON OF MINE!" His morale broken, Bogart commits suicide by shooting it out with the cops. From the moment the Rockets saw *Dead End*, we slapped each other around mercilessly while screaming "You ain't no son of mine!" enacting and re-enacting a ritual drama of parental rejection that, in one form or another, we had all encountered.

I wasn't any son of Leo Sigal's. But his saying it didn't make it so. I wrote him letter after letter to a P.O. box without result. After a few months, I figured it all out. To hell with him, his union, his cigar. He was going to have a tough time getting rid of *me*.

❊ ❊ ❊

When a father abandons a son, the son takes on the role of guilty party. If you have admired your father, then you must see his wisdom in ditching you. You deserve punishing because he knows you for the piece of shit you know yourself to be. He's a *man*, and men know things. You don't cut it for him. If only you were more compliant, less of a flincher, or more loving in some unspecific way, he would still be here. Better yet, if you had not been born. That's it. *He left because you exist.*

So you do your best to self-destruct.

A Kiss to Build a Dream On

A cultural feature of Lawndale life was the prevalence of pre-teenage kissing games when few, if any, of us even knew what a vagina was, let alone *where* it was. From about twelve on, spin the bottle, post office, truth and dare and freeze tag were established parts of my Friday-to-Sunday nights. We'd use any excuse for a weekend party, in some empty building or an apartment where the parents were away and then . . . kiss away like sixteen inch guns. We called it smooching, and the girls seemed as eager to play—is the word indulge?—as the Rockets.

Technically, there was a lot of body rubbing and face rolling, except that we absolutely did not do "Frenchie." The first time a girl tried to slip her tongue between my lips I leaped back in disgust. Eww! The point was to *play* at dread or anti-cipation . . . peck here and there . . . dodge from unattractive girls . . . but also steer clear of the most beautiful girls because we wanted them so . . . and try not to lose status when, in post office, we were chosen by a girl we liked too little or too much.

Kissing games could be risky. If you were seen deriving too much pleasure from kissing a girl, you lost macho points in the playground on the following Monday. And if you kissed the "wrong" girl—for example, sent her a "special delivery" (long kiss in dark closet)—and she had a larger boyfriend or, God forbid, someone like Angie Lombardo from ethnic-enemy turf, you could call upon your head all the devils of passionate revenge. And then, of course, there was always Father Lenihan's warning that your fingers and toes could drop off if you caught VD from an unclean girl's touch. But how could one tell who washed?

Kissing was like playing baseball. You had to concentrate if you wanted to succeed . . . though "succeed" at what I had no idea. So far, girls were simply odd collections of hips, breasts and eyes, and I hadn't yet learned to puzzle the jigsaw pieces together into a human something connected in any way with the serious sexual activity I suspected Ma got up to either with Dad, or whomsoever when he wasn't around. In other words, I wanted the kissing—like the neighborhood—to go on forever without much change.

It could also be confusing. The prettiest girls were not always the "best" kissers. Irene Wukowski, a quite overweight young lady of my age, took a shine to me, much to the Rockets' merriment, and sent me special deliveries every time we collided at a party. She'd wrap me in her big fleshy arms and press me to her woman's bosom and plant one on me that . . . was terrific. I fought clear the first time, but when she really went after me I gave in and let her swallow me up practically on top of her Matisse-like body. Something wrong here. Kissing pretty girls was fine, in its way, but Irene gave me a boner every time. I was beginning to suspect that there was something very complicated about this kissing thing.

And that was my mind set when Cenza Dominici entered my life at fifteen.

❊ ❊ ❊

With Dad gone, It was ridiculously easy to mess up. Leo Sigal was tough? I'd be tougher. There was no risk I imagined he took that I could not do double.

To get right to the heart of the matter, I hooked up with Innocenza Dominici, the most dangerous girl on the west side. "Cenza" was sixteen, black-eyed, and the girlfriend of "Crazy Angie" Lombardo, a slim dark Sicilian-American teenager with a ferocious rep as a knife fighter and implacable avenger of slights nobody but he noticed. One moonless night, I took Cenza out to Douglas Park for my, but not her, first sex experience. Actually, the night was so cold and we did it so fast on a bench I'm not sure it happened. She did something, I did something, the moon came out of the clouds, and I clearly saw

Cenza's face looking up at me more in curiosity than passion. "I love mockies," she said.

Mocky, sheeny, nickel nose, Ikey-mo, Hebe, clip tip (for circumcised), Hymie, Abie, Crikey (Christ Killer), Morta Cristo (same thing, in Italian), bagel dog—all anti-Jewish slurs commonly used by the Eye-talians or Irish against us on the street or at school. Often passed casually in conversation, like "Who's the Abie broad?" Cenza made "mocky" sound like a word of endearment.

I'd done it (if I had) with Cenza because I knew she was sure to snitch to Angie and he would kill me. A glorious death in Rocket terms: my legend would live on. Except that it didn't quite happen that way. In due stomach-churning time, Angie and several of his brothers, cousins, and friends led a squadron of cars down the middle of Roosevelt Road shouting anti-Semitic insults and flinging empty beer bottles and bricks at our make-out joint, Flukey's Hot Dogs, and fled the scene laughing. Within the hour, older Jewish guys from Davy Miller's bookie joint, swinging tire chains and sticks, had put together a retaliatory caravan that struck deep into Italian territory, and I jumped on the running board of one of the Jewish cars. The newspapers later reported it as a "race riot," but really it was just a few punches thrown, no knives or guns, before we got back into our cars and retreated to our side of the racial frontier. As usual, the reporters got there before the police. Maybe a year later Angie passed me on the street and I thought, *Sicilians will wait forever for revenge*, and I got set for my execution by throat slitting. He just breezed by without a glance. I felt bitterly disappointed, because I'd spent so long gearing up for this confrontation and he was letting me off his hook with total indifference. What a put-down!

Nobody got killed in the so-called riot, though it wasn't for want of trying. I think the mayor appointed a "racial harmony" committee, the boys' clubs got an extra donation, and even the senior gangsters stepped in to enforce a truce, because too many cops were coming around. All from the simple act of slipping my hand inside Cenza Dominici's blouse on a black, frigid night and praying for my extinction one way or the other.

A pity Dad hadn't been there to see it. Next time I'd have to go one better.

In the War

1942—110,000 Japanese-Americans "relocated" to concentration camps. Sugar and gas rationing.

That first summer of the war, life for us was much better. Jennie got a real full-time job sewing olive drab sweaters for the multiplying U.S. army, and then—all hail to the "national preparedness drive"—her paycheck allowed us to rent a virtual mansion all to ourselves, no sharing of the bathroom down the hall, no landlords sneaking in to check if a light was on. A second-floor back at 3451 Douglas Boulevard, our most respectable address ever—and, blissfully, once again in Rockets territory—was a one-and-a-half room apartment with a Murphy pull-down bed that came out of the wall on its spring hinge. Jennie now could afford new clothes and I had a little pocket change from working in a grocery store when the owner's son got drafted. It looked like the end of the endless summer of the Depression.

War began to seem as natural as breathing. You could almost hear a huge sigh of relief go up from the neighborhood as jobs seemed to sprout on trees and the old rules relaxed.

The Rockets now had a proper basement clubhouse, and I was so glad to be in the club again that I threw myself at them with a manic, almost erotic, ferocity. Although the youngest by a few months, I was the nuttiest: from now on, there was no dare I refused. One blizzardy winter day, on a bet, I balanced myself on the ice-glazed, ruler-thin stone parapet outside the Adler Planetarium, leaning way over roiling Lake Michigan holding onto nothing and letting the blasting wind keep me upright at a wobbly angle as I inched all the way around the observatory to safety. *Hey Dad, top of the world!* I was no *feigelah!*

A Mainbocher creation. It drove
Jennie wild when she found me
playing with flanged cut-out
dolls.

This issue of homosexuality had lain between Jennie and me ever since she walked in on me, at perhaps six or seven, scissoring "Wee Winnie Winkle" paper cut-out dresses from the Sunday cartoon section of the Chicago *Herald-Examiner* and arranging the panelled skirts and blouses on Winnie's softly modelled shoulders and hips. I loved nothing better than playing with the splendid full-color, full-page dolls of working girls like Winnie, "Tillie the Toile," and "Ella Cinders"; they might not be Charlie's Angels but they still had a lot of spit and fire. The miniature dresses had paper flanges that you hooked onto the chemise-draped ladies and let you experiment with fashion. I felt absolutely safe and free to do this until the Sunday morning, when I was about twelve, that Jennie came through the beaded curtain separating the Family Hand Laundry business from our one-room home in back and stopped dead when she found me happily fitting patterns to a whole show of newspaper cartoon women. To my astonishment, she grabbed the fabric shears out of my hand and demanded, "Why aren't you playing with Tarzan?" to which I replied that the Sunday dress-up section had only girls. "You can't put a skirt on the Ape Man," I said reasonably.

"I don't care." She stormed back into the store. "From now on, no more dressing up your sweeties. Put clothes on Smiling Jack!" I was amazed she even knew the name of the daredevil cartoon-strip pilot. Did she know any of my other secrets?

Out front, she banged down hard on the keys of the old and black National cash register, making an exclamation point of sorts. If Ma was such an ace labor negotiator, how come she wasn't negotiating this?

Okay, I was a fat kid, growing breasts like a girl, maybe caused by twice-a-week hormone injections (for an undescended testicle) in my ass from the visiting county nurse, and, yes, I swanned about crooning "Music, Maestro, Please" at the top of my breaking tenor and was addicted to daytime radio soap operas like *Our Gal Sunday*. ("Can a simple mining girl from the West find happiness with a British aristocrat?") Jennie suffered me through it all, but now that I was approaching puberty her antennae convulsed over my infatuation with fashion accessories. Indeed, she seemed more comfortable with my bloody noses given and taken in alley fights and my position as South Kedzie Avenue's chief armorer and supplier of hand-crafted (for five cents) rubber guns, than with my "feminine" hobby. In her eyes, pure male was an absolute good. For all her troubles with Dad, she'd never lost her admiration for his macho swagger, and though she often disapproved of my behavior, she also signaled that she was proud of the cocky style I'd inherited and copied from him.

Statistically, there must have been queers in my neighborhood, but it wasn't an option for boys then. Our idea of gay was a kid who practiced piano or was named Sherwin . . . or Clarence, which probably is why I got into so many fights about it. To be overweight with a name as easy to ridicule with "Clare" or "Clarice" was an intolerable insult to the part of me that wanted to be most manly, like Leo Sigal.

Some time in early 1942, after Pearl Harbor, with the laundry sold before Jennie could torch it, and when we Rockets got into the habit of thinking of ourselves as dead men, our school principal at Marshall High called a special assembly, not to hear the usual retired ROTC officer prattling a patriotic pep talk but to welcome the school's most famous alumnus. As was our custom, my thugs monopolized the entire back row in the auditorium balcony, feet hanging over the backs of the seats, elbowing, and kicking, normal behavior. The girls in the balcony front row shot us dirty looks, but the Rockets were so totally outside the student pecking order that we were noninsultable. Somewhere, perhaps, boys in checkerboard-pattern Hart, Schaffner & Marx sports jackets jitterbugged on a polished gym floor with scrubbed-clean girls in pressed dirndle skirts who were the yearbook editor and got A's in civics class; somewhere brawny young Jews—Marines in the making—took Marshall High to yet another All-City basketball championship. Not us. We weren't even tough guys. Just young petty criminals without any sense at all except of ourselves, our basement clubhouse, and the certainty that Hitler meant it when he promised to kill all the Chicago Jews. In today's jargon, we were latchkey children who rode free on the iron-grated cowcatchers of the huge roaring red and green electric streetcars, snored in class or pretended to, and dreamed of absolutely nothing.

The featured speaker down on the stage turned out to be a tubby, neatly dressed little man in a white shantung silk Palm Beach double-breasted suit and two-tone wingtip shoes. What had we done to deserve *him?*

"And now," announced Mr. Beer, the principal, "Mister Mainbocher . . ."

Who?

Mainbocher—one name only please—was, it turned out, a *couturier,* the world-famous dressmaker who had designed the wedding gown of King Edward's bride, the Duchess of Windsor. I cannot remember a thing he said, partly because we were all in shock. This was the best Marshall High was capable of—a fag dressmaker? The other Rockets may have felt something like it, too, because an incoherent sense of disbelief swept over the back row. This went *way* beyond deadly insult to our brittle identities. Hell of a way to prepare us for war.

After the assembly, we went a little mad, viciously shoving people around, loudly banging lockers to make our presences felt, snapping the bras of girls whom we hadn't dared approach before, and tripping each other down the school stairs. In some unspeakable way, we had been dissed and needed to strike back.

Outside the school we got into a terrific fight, only in this case we put up our local champion, Abe Goldman, to challenge slim and smooth Davie Dolin, who always wore a sports jacket and knife-creased trousers to school, danced like a dream, attracted girls without even trying, and was in every known school activity. Our exact opposite. Big Abe was a monster, with naturally buffed biceps and a giant's gentle disposition. Reluctantly, he let us push him forward into the fighting circle formed by a crowd of students. That was our second big shock. Davie Dolin broke his nose with one punch. Life was so unfair.

It also turned out that Mainbocher — the name transliterates from the Jewish — had escaped from Paris only one step ahead of the Nazis. He wasn't just a *feigelah* but a kind of war hero. Too damn much.

Between my mother denying me Wee Winnie Winkle's off-the-shoulder blouse and Mainbocher speaking at our school, and Big Abe's failure to deck Davie Dolin, I suddenly felt a little shaky about what a man was, anyway. My moral failures mounted. I failed to confront Jennie about my comic-strip dresses, I didn't step in to help Abe knock Davie Dolin on his ass, and I didn't become homosexual. Fortunately, my masculine future was soon to be written in military jargon — "Asgd/MOS 745/inf rflmn."

Fish on a Bicycle

A woman without a man is like a fish without a bicycle, feminists used to say. They'd have a hard time convincing Jennie. Her attitude to men, though laced with equal parts admiration and contempt, had a strong measure of pure biological desire.

As time went on and my father's absences grew into total separation, Jennie's attitude to herself and to men, including me, changed. At first, she suffered a kind of shock of abandonment, anxious depression, a collapse of the sexual ego for which there appeared to be no remedy, not even the sacred company of women friends. But gradually, her sexual clock reset as she gave up her dream of an enduring love in favor of a more hedonistic, cheerful, selfish, and personal satisfaction. That's about when she gave me up as a lost cause and began dialing — we had a phone now — for "professional help" for me.

What she gained in sensual pleasure in making a new life she lost in sexual idealism, emerging as a harder, shrewder, wilder, and more devil-may-care person, somebody I hardly recognized. From her old mantra, "There's nobody for us but your father," it became, about any new guy, "Oh, I suppose he's all right. Treat him nice. Do I want him to stick around? Check with me tomorrow after I sleep on it."

The most startling change was that she no longer bothered to be secretive around me, almost as if she *wanted* me to know. Psychoanalyzing your own mother is a mug's game, but let's guess that we were back to our old game of multiple identities and I had become my father, on whom she was taking a kind of revenge by exposing him (me) to her intimacies. So there, Leo Kalman!

Masquerading as my father, in her eyes, was easier now

that adolescent hormones had seized my body to lengthen and strengthen it. Jennie's eyes shone with admiration at the sheer manliness of what was happening to me. She was proud of, not to say relieved about, my descending ball, my flattening tummy, widening shoulders, and, for the first time, the muscle to back up my swagger. I might be an ill-mannered, self-centered, disrespectful, zoot-suited ruffian — but I carried the Sigal seed.

She worried a great deal that I was like my father in treating women badly. "I hear what you're up to on Roosevelt Road. Don't you dare *use* women," she implored. Like a lawyer, I laid out the defense case: girls weren't women; they liked being "hondled"; they gave as good as they got; the existence of their older brothers set limits on the Rockets' misbehavior; and who got hurt? "You're exactly like him," she said in an observational rather than accusatory tone. "Him" was in the air all around us. I wished he'd come back, drop dead, or take one of Angie Lombardo's knives and decisively cut the knot that bound us all even in his absence.

What Lies Beneath

Ma was right to be anxious about me since I exhibited "symptoms" that today you find listed in the P.D.D., Pervasive Developmental Disorders, a.k.a. the psychologists' bible. Aside from almost every conceivable alimentary, bowel, and intestinal complaint — cramps, constipation, vomiting, nausea — I had an early speech defect that embraced both stutter and stammer, a lisp (later noted in my FBI file as "probably homosexual") and a failure to pronounce "sh," "ch," "j," "z," "zh" or much of anything else without stumbling. ("Bullsit maketh the grath grow greener, thmuck"). Then there was always that "low normal

IQ" taint that caused Jennie to demand a second intelligence test which came back exactly like the first.

I *was* slow. Slow-thinking. The other Rockets thought I was with malice aforethought slacking off my school lessons, hence the poor grades, which was fine by them, but the truth was I worked hard to learn almost nothing. Algebra, science (all that chlorophyll!), penmanship—even trying with all my might, they came very s.l.o.w.l.y. For a while Jennie thought I was doing marvelously at Howland Elementary because my report card had so many "A's; I lied that "A" was the highest grade. Actually, "A" stood for Average, the dummies' mark.

As any secret illiterate knows, it's amazing how much you can get away with if you have balls to bluff. What helped me cover up my s.l.o.w.n.e.s.s. was hiding out in the local Douglas Park (now Stephen Douglass) public library. Ma had taught me how to read, working with me on wooden ABC blocks practically from infancy. So, in the ordinary give and take of street life, I'd randomly throw in sentence structures and unrelated facts acquired on my precious library card—from "The Little Shepherd of Kingdom Come," "Three Musketeers," "Stover at Yale," Paul de Kruif medical biographies, Flying Aces tales and John Gunther's "Inside Europe"—and slot it into our gang repartee with lots of big words, and then walk away a smart guy. To this day my school chums remember me as a top scholar. See how easy it is when you have no options?

After a neighbor woman told Ma what an "A" grade really stood for, she became less enchanted with my throwing around random facts and figures. She threatened to go down to talk to my teacher, Mrs. Johnson, a fearsome disciplinarian, about why I couldn't use my big brain to get higher grades.

"What big brain?" I said proudly, citing my IQ test results.
"You faked the tests so you wouldn't have to work hard,"
she insisted.

I hadn't faked them, but it gave me a warm feeling to know
that Ma believed I had.

"I'll do better," I promised. "Just don't talk to the teacher."
She looked at me almost pleadingly. "Be normal. Not low
normal or high just normal, all right?"

It would have been easier if she had asked me to strap on
Buck Rogers's rocket belt and fly solo to the moon.

Stu

I had a dozen nicknames, but the one that most painfully stuck
was "Stu" for stupid, which Oscar Gutierrez translated into
Mexican-Spanish as "estupido" which evolved into Dodo and
occasionally Doodoo.

Although the other guys knew I had periods of seclusion in
the public library, they also knew I was, with the possible
exception of Deaf Augie, mentally and intellectually, the
s l o w e s t. Their general assessment, made without rancor,
was that I was estupido.

"You are *not* stupid," Ma angrily claimed. "They're just
paśkudnyaks, small-time Charlies pretending they're big men.
What do kids know?"

They know *me,* I thought. They'd pinned the tail on my
donkey and, since there was nothing to be done about it, I'd
wear it with pride. You say I'm a stupe, I *will* be one. So I went
around the neighborhood posing as a *dybbuk,* a dislocated ghost,
more accurately a *golem,* an ignorant mud person, acting out the
part as a juvenile Frankenstein-monster, dragging my feet and
pushing my hands in front of me as joke claws. "Arrggghhh."

Some joke. Ma hated my spaz act. She complained that her friends were reporting to her that I was on the verge of seizures on the sidewalk.

"Are you sick, Kalman?" she demanded. "Or just plain stupid?"

I smiled. "There . . . you see," I said triumphantly.

Child Abuse

Remedial teaching, of a certain sort, may have saved my life. When the s.l.o.w.n.e.s.s. and stammering and tongue tics became flagrant, I was removed from my home room and placed in what was called the subnormal class along with a couple of half blind albino twins, a few deafies, undiagnosed mental cases and bone lazies. Once a week a special teacher, Mrs. O'Brien, came to Howland Elementary to help me with my speech disability. Her method was clear and simple. In an empty room she sat across a small table from me and every time I mispronounced a word or stuttered she slugged me sharply on the wrist with a twelve inch wooden ruler. In any given session she might strike me a dozen or two dozen times. It did not occur to me to protest because, at some level, I felt that she was a kindly person doing her best to cure me. She was giving me the attention I needed. I looked forward to her visits if not necessarily to the stinging blows.

Nearly a year in subnormal class (which vastly improved my status among the Rockets), and many visits by Mrs O'Brien, significantly improved my speech habits. Ma, who saw the progress, didn't object to the corporal discipline, either. We felt gratitude more than bitterness. "It's child abuse!" friends tell me today. "You should have sued." I'm aware of how much damage was done in the past to patients, for example, by "kindly" administration of electro-shock therapy or surgical lobotomy. I was lucky. The worst injury I received from Mrs. O'Brien was a skinned knuckle when her swinging ruler missed my wrist. But I felt then, and feel now, that this big steadfast patient woman and I were working together to help me.

"Say "sh," " urged Mrs O'Brien.

"Th . . ."

Whack!

"Sh . . ."

"Tsh . . ."

Whack!

"S . . . h . . . h . . ."

Just a great big Irish smile.

"Now let's move on to "J" . . ."

            ❀ ❀ ❀

Ma and I were like two erotic locomotives heading toward each other on a collision course. I was sixteen and inventing myself as a man, she was forty-seven and struggling to liberate herself from the trauma, just setting in, of Dad's exit. Sparks flew whenever we were in the same room. Our passions ignited in quarrels over food, politics, and my "delinquent" behavior. Whatever was going on, neither of us had a vocabulary for. I recoiled when we brushed past each other in the small apartment; she sternly abstained from touching me. Yet, my pubescent body, with a will of its own, seemed to involuntarily lean into hers at the slightest opportunity. Something had to give.

11

Among the Amazons

*1942–43—Warsaw ghetto uprising. "Bataan death march" in
Philippines kills many GIs, some from Chicago. Nazis plot
"Final Solution" (mass murder) of Jews at Wansee Conference.
Stalingrad epic battle. Bogart in* Casablanca.

They couldn't break a hard case like Bugsy Sigal.

An assault-and-battery of Jewish Social Service Bureau
caseworkers (Mrs. Adler, Mrs. Strauss, and Miss Loeb), a probation officer (Mr. Watkins of the juvenile court system), and
Jennie faced me across a bare wooden table on which lay a
Devil's bargain.

Due to "behavioral problems," I would be sent for my
junior high school year to incarceration at the inner-city reformatory, Montefiore Special School for Boys, with its high
yellow-brick walls and prison population of Jew-hating
polacks, micks, hunkies, and cabbage heads—or I could choose

to enroll at a trade tech like Crane, Lane, or Flower High where, if I applied myself diligently (their words), I might learn wood shop along with polacks, micks, hunkies, and cabbage heads who hadn't yet ended up in Montefiore.

Mrs. Strauss raised a third, dubious alternative. Since my IQ and general aptitude tests slotted me as "low normal" but with a faint trace of numeracy, "in your own best interests" I could be placed in Jones Commercial, Chicago's only public high school specializing in business skills. No more options, no further leniency.

In my ever-growing experience with them, caseworkers named Strauss, Adler, and Loeb were usually high-German Jews from Lake Shore Drive, Chicago's Park Avenue, who looked upon us street yids as inferior and barely salvageable beasts.

Mrs. Strauss stared at me with concern and loathing. I was the nightmare that justified her charity avocation, an unredeemed Jewish bum, *ah yunge stain* in an orange satin shirt I wore specially for my trial.

I looked over at Jennie. She gave away nothing.

The fix was in. My sins were listed in the file folder that lay open on the table. Riot and affray (the Angie Lombardo fiasco); shoplifting (accomplice to stealing a Raleigh bicycle piece by piece from the Sears and Roebuck basement display); disturbing the peace and defacing religious property ("BANISH GODS FROM THE SKIES AND CAPITALISTS FROM THE EARTH" scrawled in Crayola crayon on synagogue steps); assault, along with Julie Weinberg and other Rockets beating up an older guy who had taken Julie's sister into the park bushes; leaving a dead rat in the desk drawer of the algebra teacher (Miss Busby) at school; etc., etc. Compared to Bed-Stuy or Compton today, nothing.

Across the social workers' table I gave Jennie my Jimmy Cagney stare and she gave me back her Barbara Stanwyck glare, both of us full of guilt and self-justification.

"I'll take Jones," I muttered. Business school. That meant I wouldn't get my hands dirty.

"How's that? Speak up, young man," said Mr. Watkins.

I sold my soul. "Jones," I repeated.

Mrs. Strauss stood up. The Jewish Social Service Bureau and the Probation Department would be "monitoring my conduct" and any serious infraction would necessitate—their language—a "reassessment of my educational opportunities." Meaning, juvie detention at Montefiore.

But I wasn't a criminal, just an ordinary west side boy who had come to somebody's attention.

Mrs. Strauss smiled and reached over in a maternal gesture to gently muss my helmet of thick black hair, combed straight back like Dad's, and shrank back as if touching dog turd. She stared down at her hand, gooey with my soft perfumed varnish of Wildroot Crème Oil. I beamed. It looked just like jizzem.

Jennie and I rode home on the streetcar in silence.

"Ma," I said.

"Not a word," she snapped.

"But *why?*"

She turned to look right into my eyes.

"Your father isn't here anymore. I am. Get used to it."

❊ ❊ ❊

Jennie and I were approaching critical mass. In the house, I'd sway my hips and hold out my arms for her to dance with me while I crooned the Peggy Lee hit, "Why Don't You Do Right?", or idly toyed with her red, slightly graying hair at the dinner table ("Stop it, you know I hate that!"), or blow down the back of her neck as I zipped up her dress before she went out, all the while mimicking my current idol, the Glenn Miller saxophonist, ape-jawed Tex Beneke, fingering his instrument and wailing my heart out in tuneless howling songs of hunger and temptation. We had gone beyond incest to something too electric to touch.

After lights out, sleeping close together on separate beds, our habit was to call out softly to each other in the darkness across the oceanic space that separated us, a good night consisting of words I picked up in Miss Adamson's Spanish class. We would reach out and caress each other's hand.

"Buenaſ nocheſ," I'd murmur.

I could not fall asleep without receiving my mother's benediction in return.

"Buenaſ nocheſ," with a Yiddish-Jewish-Ukrainian lilt.

Inevitably, one night, pretending to be asleep, I crawled off the couch and into her Murphy bed, snuggling up against her bare arm, my hand on her hip. It felt warm and cozy, a blissful return to childhood.

Her body grew rigid. Pretending to sleepwalk, I retreated to my couch and began to snore.

That's when a frightened Jennie blew the whistle for the social workers to come blasting in like SWAT cops.

❀ ❀ ❀

On a snowy Monday morning, on a side street called Plymouth Court in Chicago's Loop a block away from the burlesque district, like a bank robber I cased Jones Commercial's old building to figure what gang of guys went there. I waited, and waited. At last, among the crowd of girls, two or three boys filed in, silent and carrying briefcases, heads down as if following an invisible track, to be swallowed up by the chattering crowd.

Nobody had told me.

Jones was a girls' school.

Besieged, Bothered, and Bewildered

(Courtesy of Peg Pinaglia, James College Prep)

Never before or since have I felt under such sustained assault on my sexual ego as at Jones. My self-image as a Lawndale lover and carnal know-all collapsed overnight. One or two girls on a streetcorner, even a giggling clique, I could *hondle* or outmaneuver. But all these Amazons-in-being at Jones? Their very existence—their *femaleness*—threatened my existence. There were too many of them to single out for fantasy—almost. On top of which I was sweet on one girl, Beatrice Podolnyi, a sexually fully developed classmate in typing and steno class. The awful thing was, she was *friendly*, charming, tactful, lovely. *Nice.* And she treated me like a . . . pal.

In my first Jones Commercial semester I got into a fight in the neighborhood with a gang of "goy boys" outside a Madison Street bowling alley. They jumped me on a Jewish holiday. (Them: "Hey, kid, what church you go to?" Me (quickly looking around for spires): "Um, St Barrabas . . ." Them: "There ain't no such church." Bam! Right in my mouth.) I spent that weekend anxious about what I would look like on Monday with a puffed split lip and a cut over my eye. I needn't have worried because at school *nobody noticed*. Like Jesus I could have spilled my blood right in front of them and they would have walked on past. Suddenly I was aware of my acne, mismatched socks, oversize ears and gargoyle presentation-of-self. *They didn't notice.* Beatrice most painfully of all.

I'd show them.

But they showed me.

Frances, or Frankie, Lebedeff, known as "Slugger," was the only one of Jones Commercial's four hundred girls who came from my own Lawndale neighborhood. Most of the other girls were Wasp or Catholic from high schools way out across the racial divides, in enemy country, from schools like Sullivan, Gage Park, and Maria Assumpta. The girls looked like they all had meathead brothers who drank beer in taverns called Policek's or Hruba's or O'Reilly's. You could tell by the virginal way they fixed their hair, not a perfect follicle out of place, no eye shadow, the merest trace of lipstick, intimidating crosses on their healthy chests, that Jones girls were what I wasn't used to: *nice*.

Except for Slugger, who was built like the ten-sport Olympic athlete Babe Didrickson; a solid chunk of female, except breastier and with two prominent gold teeth. Her lay-down-collar blouses showed a startling amount of cleavage; she even walked like a stripper, swinging her hips, free and easy, well oiled. Slugger's "steady" was my fellow Rocket, Legs Glasser, who'd dropped out of school to be a full-time bookie's runner at Putty Anixter's poolroom and to raise the cash to get married. They were spoken for, foreordained: to the best of my knowledge, they are still married to each other.

Slugger was intimidatingly sexual. When Legs came visiting they held hands and snogged in the hallways, yet no teacher dared confront Slugger, who exuded a faint air of physical threat, a Lawndale survival tool even for girls. Curiously, she was popular with the other Miss Prims at Jones because she was so open-hearted and easy about herself in ways they could only envy. Her rough husky laugh echoed through the whitewashed halls; it was like having Mae West enrolled at your school.

I hung about on the fringe of Slugger's clique, neither a full-fledged boy nor an honorary girl but an in-between, bristling with unvoiced, sexually indeterminate rage, I suppose because my "masculine identity" was under siege at Jones, an ultimate humiliation for a machismo boy. Over time in the old neighborhood, I had painstakingly sculpted a whole new persona for myself: not one-ball-down one-ball-up crybaby Fatty, but a sixteen-year-old faithful copy of my Dad, a suave ready-to-rumble man-about-town. But at Jones Commercial, in my newly bought second-hand business suit, garrot tie, neatly parted hair sans Wildroot, shined Florsheims, and filed fingernails inspected every morning by Mrs. Craig, the typing-and-stenography teacher, I was Señor No Balls, looking more like a department store floorwalker than a hoodlum movie star like George Raft. But with Montefiore reformatory hanging over my head and my every step under the scrutiny of a juvenile court judge, what choice did I have except to knuckle under?

❅ ❅ ❅

Being a boy in a girls' school is no fun except in theory. This was it, your life was on a path as straight as a Chicago street, you were going to *work* for a living forever plus a day. Ma and Dad had ironed starched collars, I would wear one for the rest of my life.

Every morning when I swung into Plymouth Court off Harrison Street it felt like walking the Last Mile to the gallows. Hardly anybody else seemed to mind as much as I did; the girls were happy to be in Jones because most came from Depression-damaged families and were drawn by Jones's promise of a marketable skill and a job, a future. Before marriage, of course; the role model was Ginger Rogers in *Kitty Foyle*, who married the boss's son. But where was the role model for the only boy in Jones's one hundred-year history to major in stenography?

Billy Rose, Fanny Brice's showman-songwriting husband ("Does the Spearmint Lose Its Flavor on the Bedpost Overnight?"), was held out to me as a possible inspiration. Famously, he had started out by winning a "world's fastest stenographer" contest at sixteen. Maternally buxom, florid-faced Mrs. Craig, my sharp-eyed typing and secretarial teacher, was encouraging. "Mister Rose is of your persuasion, isn't he, Clarence? His real name is Sam Rosenberg, but he didn't let that stop him . . ."

For four long semesters I drifted along in a kind of neutered haze in Jones's waxed-to-perfection halls. We were expected to be, and were, little business robots. Clarence B. Carey, the school principal, a former Hearst newspaper editor, liked to call us "Jones Incorporated." His pledge to students, always honored, was to find every graduate a paid job as a clerical employee for a major company like Pullman, R. R. Donnelly,

Armour, Swift, McCormack, the Board of Trade and other pillars of Chicago's war-flush businesses — all of them patriarchal, hierarchical, and bitterly antilabor. Ironically, our school was located close by Haymarket Square, site of the 1886 riot where eight policemen and four bystanders were blown up by a bomb hurled by nobody knows whom during an anarchist meeting. The four German immigrants framed and hanged for the crime — Albert Parsons, August Spies, George Engle, Adolph Fischer — were honored names in our home. My mother was a friend of Albert Parson's widow, Lucy, who had died only last year in a house fire.

How could Jennie have flung me into this training ground for scabs?

※ ※ ※

Tap tap, tap TAP TAP, slap a crashing right hook to the Underwood typewriter carriage return, stare straight ahead at the blackboard, both eyes up, head erect, shoulders back. *Tap tap, tap TAP TAP*. The mesmeric clatter of machines launched me into an out-of-body experience, floating me like a hundred-eyed spider up to the ceiling to swoop back down on the typing class of Jones girls, with their neatly combed tied-at-the-nape spinster-style buns, this divine hell of cascading hips, breasts, naked legs, hair, eyes, necks, ears, more breasts, a Busby Berkeley chorus line of erupting nubility, a regiment of bras under skintight sweaters near to bursting at the nipple, my maddening eye searches under the warp of faux-angora for the ski-jump silhouette, avalanches of flat, full, and fuller chests. Exhale, inhale. O God. I'm going to faint.

My fuse overloaded, I got into the habit of excusing myself

in class to go into the boys' bathroom and, locking myself in a cubicle, whack off to a mental harem of Jones girls, as many of them as I could cram into my overcrowded fantasies. Two, three, four times a day, whence I emerged from the bathroom pale, drained, and exhausted. I could hardly lift the basketball in the tiny gym where the Jones boys, all five of us, met for phys ed under the mistrustful eye of Miss Sibley, who had short hair and Bronko Nagurski calves. I'd come from Marshall High, the All-City hoop champs, and I wanted to show Lawrence, Leo, and Donald some tricky west side moves. But, weakened by what Father Lenihan ticketed as the sin of self-abuse, I stumbled around the court like a zombie.

Then one day while everyone else was in class, I emerged from the bathroom in a half-daze only to encounter Slugger stubbing out a furtive cigarette and staring at me from across the hall. Smiling broadly, she strolled over and hooked her arm in mine. "I know how to stop Legs doing that. Need some help?" I gave her a punch, she pushed me back, and our buddyship was sealed.

❉ ❉ ❉

And then the movie star Errol Flynn got me into the worst trouble of my life.

"OH-H-H, ERROL! HEY, LOVER MAN! WOO-WOO!"

Rockets, on their way to after-school jobs in the Loop, were in the habit of stopping by Jones Commercial and, with all the might of their sixteen-year-old lungs, hurling insults and obscenities they hoped would rub it in that I was no longer in Marshall High with them. By sheer luck, one of their shouts hit the mark too well.

"'Bye, Errol. See you in jail!"

Instantly, the contagion spread from the snow-covered sidewalk outside Jones into its classrooms and hallways.

A few of the girls, leaning on the frosty windowsills whenever the Rockets paraded by, picked up on it. "Hel-lo, Errol," they'd warble, "how's Peggy?" or "Oh-h-h-h, Errol, sweetheart . . ." or "Clarence, I mean Errol, you make my heart go pitter-patter. Ha ha ha!" Like a virus, the joke propagated all over the school, teasing, taunting, kidding, sickening me with its cruel mockery. Until last year I'd been an overweight, ungainly, waddling kid with an undescended testicle and women's breasts I was so ashamed of that I hid in an ROTC uniform rather than expose my naked body in swim class. Back then everyone seemed privy to the secret that I was faking it as a man. "What's up with our little girl?" Dad would say to Jennie. Some joke. Being in a young ladies' school affirmed my nullity: "Jones Incorporated" robbed me of the one thing I'd made of myself, a street guy with a smart mouth. It pushed me back to being, once again, a potential hermaphrodite, a canceled check.

The bitter irony was that it was my *uber*-hero Errol Flynn who was laying a stone on my grave. For years on the street I'd copied his *Robin Hood* derring-do, his crooked grin, the pugnacious set of his jaw so like my Dad's, his daring swordplay and defiant laughter in the face of overwhelming odds, my wool cap set exactly at his cocky angle. But in reality, Robin had been caught cheating on Maid Marian. Presently, Flynn was on trial in a Los Angeles federal court facing prison for the statutory rape on his yacht of two fifteen-year-old girls, one of them a stunning brunette sex dream named Peggy La Rue Satterlee. Jones Commercial girls spoke of little else outside the classroom.

And then the busy little bees of their darting tongues stung me.

"Errol, sweetheart . . ."

Teasing, pitiless, persistent, strident, up and down Jones's waxed-floor corridors, on the staircases, in the lunchroom, Errol this and Errol that, it got so I was afraid even to go to the bathroom to jerk off because I was so sure everyone's eyes were on me. (My basketball game improved markedly.) At first flattered, I realized what they were telling me: I was a monster not of sexuality but of comic ridicule, the very opposite of cute and dashing. It soon got worse, much worse. A sort of hysteria erupted and swiftly spread. Girls I didn't even know jeered right in my face. "Errol Errol . . ." Gargoyle-sneering, inflamed, goading. Nothing so bad had ever happened to me in the neighborhood; I would have fucking killed anyone who persecuted me like this. But who could I slug at Jones without bringing down on my neck the Damocles sword of a juvenile judge and the Jewish Social Service Bureau? It was all the fault of my stool pigeon mother.

As the Flynn trial went to jury in L.A. amidst banner headlines, the voices at Jones took on a screeching, openly hostile tone. These well-mannered bobby soxers were metastasizing into cawing crows, throwbacks to their village grandmothers hurling scorn at some strange man because they had no other outlet for their oppression. And then the name-calling turned *physical.*

Even the nicest girls joined in. Girls I hadn't even *looked* at. Joyce and Margly and Ardell and Betty Jane and Edith and Fern and a flying squadron of Marys poked me in the ribs, trod on my heels, elbowed me aside on the stairs, slammed sledgehammer blows on my back. "Oooooooo Errol, you send me . . . Darling, Errol, I'm not doing anything Saturday night. Ha ha ha ha."

What made it infinitely worse was that Beatrice Podolny, a

gentle and lovely girl, the only classmate I dared to be in love with, also turned on me, screaming with horrible laughter and yes, actually kicking me!

Then they began pulling my *hair*.

I dreaded leaving class because it was like walking into a flock of vampire bats. Everyone in school, including teachers, knew what was going on and nobody stopped it. Something had happened to transform these Miss Prims into the worst bullies I had ever faced in my life. Who could I complain to? I could stop this bullshit with a single punch—and end up behind Montefiore's high yellow walls.

"Hey, quit your kidding . . . okay I get it . . . enough already . . ." I pleaded, my whole personality collapsing in a final cringing and whining indignity. But begging the girls to stop only inflamed them more.

Half a dozen of them would surround me in the hallway and pick, pick, pick at my clothes, tear at my hair, or knee me from behind. One morning after accounting class, I felt a stinging sensation on my neck. A girl had raked her unlacquered nails like a dagger just below my ear. The pocket handkerchief I put there came away stained with blood.

I dropped my books to look after myself.

Still the girls kept at it, their hot little angry eyes devouring me with a kind of aimless joy.

"BACK OFF, YOU PIGS!"

Slugger Lebedeff stepped between the bullies and me swinging her books like a scythe to clear an enemyless space around us. Instantly the commotion died. She was magnificent, standing over me like a gladiator in a skirt. The girls, shocked, retreated. Slugger's big brown eyes flashed fury. Where had she been all this time?

"Back the fuck off!" She again lunged out with her books sending the girls scurrying. Fuck?! At Jones. One *never* used bad language at Jones Inc.

The hallway emptied in an eyelash as the bell rang for eleven o'clock classes. Slugger used a handkerchief to dab at my neck. "The fucking asshole bitches." She breathed fire and for a minute I thought she was going to hit *me*. Then she flashed her tremendous toothy smile. "Rockets forever."

"You won't tell the guys, will you?" I beseeched her.

"Tell what?" she shrugged.

Relief oozed out of me. Slugger was the one person in the world I knew I could count on.

All that last semester we were inseparable. Wherever I walked at Jones in class or hallway, Slugger was a comforting —and menacing—presence. We began riding the same Roosevelt Road streetcar downtown so she could take me to school. My bodyguard.

On graduation night, with her fiance Legs Glasser and my mother Jennie in the audience, Slugger and I strode onto the stage, together, clasping hands, my champion. Rockets forever.

❊ ❊ ❊

True to its word, Jones found me work as a junior mail clerk with the firm that had the longest antiunion record in America, the Pullman Company at 221 South State Street. In late '44, coinciding with the Battle of the Bulge, I was drafted. Actually, I volunteered for induction because all the Rockets were gone to the military and I hated being left behind. On my first furlough home, I returned to Jones slim, trim, proud, hard and healthy, and confident in my dress uniform, a sharply tailored

"Ike" jacket, paratrooper bloused trousers, dubbined combat boots, my overseas cap with its distinctive blue piping set at a bombastic angle and — chickenshit, this — wearing my Marksman's medal. I was due to join the Fourth Infantry Division on its way to the Pacific fighting.

I felt terrific, but also had a moment's uneasiness as I pushed open the big bronze doors of Jones Commercial, arriving in time for change of class when the hallways were full of chattering girls. Everyone I'd graduated with was gone but these others would do; they *looked* like my former tormentors, even if they gave the visiting soldier admiring glances. (*I knew what evil they were capable of.*) The hallways emptied on the bell as I slipped into the main office to flip through the faculty mail. The system was, the mail carrier dumped incoming correspondence into a shallow open wooden box so that teachers had to sort through their colleagues' letters to find their own. Senders' return addresses were open to inspection and to my delight the most conservative Republican teachers were *still* getting mail from Communist front organizations on whose lists I'd placed them. Mrs. Craig, so dubious about Jewish boys, even had a fund-drive letter from *Freiheit*, the Communist Jewish newspaper. Hot dog!

I wandered up and down the stairs, in and out of the corridors, peeking through the glass-paneled doors. Up on the second floor there they were, still at it, Mrs. Hawkins, Mr. Wilkinson, Miss Thorning, Misses Jex, Lynch , Noelle, and — of course — Mrs. Craig, who taught me the only useful trade I've ever known, typing. Then it was time to go. But I badly wanted to leave *something* behind. So, in the dead center of the hall on the superhumanly polished floor that hardly showed scuff marks of generations of girls, I did a little jig in my hobnailed combat boots, stomping down hard, hard, *hard*, again and *again*. My boots set up a fabulous racket. Whomp! Whomp! Whomp! Doors swung open, teachers' heads popped out, Miss Birmingham, Mr. Deal, Miss Bittle. I gave the floor one or two final LOUD licks with my boots, then leaped as high as I could into the air and came down so hard that I left serious gashes.

Thrilled, redeemed, I ran downstairs to the ground floor and I did an impromptu dance outside the principal's office, where it made a glorious noise. When more doors flew open and plump Mr. Carey emerged pop-eyed from his inner cubicle followed by his clerks and I was sure to have everyone's attention, I raised my arms and flexed my muscles like Tarzan and let out a tremendous jungle yell:

"ERROL FLYNN! ERROL FLYNN! ERROL FLYNN!"

Clancy's graduation photo from Jones Commercial.
Age seventeen. Trying hard to be respectable.

12

To Name Is to Empower

1943–44:—*London V-2 "flying bomb" attacks. PT 109's skipper Lt. John F. Kennedy saves a crewman's life in Pacific. U.S. Marines slaughtered when Tarawa atoll assaulted. Janis Joplin born. "Don't Fence Me In" a hit song.*

The Pearl Harbor catastrophe was anything but catastrophic for us. The war brought prosperity, or at least a living, to many west side Chicago homes. It also served as an escape valve for all the family pressures that had been building up during ten years of privation. Parents were now at work all day, and kids— prototeenagers—started earning money and the right to live as they pleased. Between Jennie and me, a divorce was pending courtesy of the U.S. army, yet neither of us wanted to let go of the other until the last possible moment. I was the last Rocket standing, all the others having gone into uniform, and each time I tried to enlist in a different branch Ma and I went through a silent little tearless drama of splitting up, packing a shaving kit, strapping a money belt to my naked waist, but there was always an anticlimax when the Navy, Army Air Corps, Marines, and even the Coast Guard rejected me for one small reason or another (bad lungs, flat feet, that tricky testicle, etc.). However, as the war abruptly turned bad in the summer of '44 when I was seventeen, climaxing in the butchery at the Battle of the Bulge, even the blind, lame, and halt were selected. So my turn had to come next.

Eight of nine Rockets had gone into the infantry (Mendy already had a Bronze Star), and I assumed this was my fate. Dying in battle would be a cinch compared to my unwholesome fear of being buried under a Star of David headstone inscribed "Clarence." No sir, no way. All that D-Day summer, I experimented first with this, then that new name that I wanted to look just right in a warrior's cemetery. I'd wander off into new neighborhoods, never Angie Lombardo's, and introduce myself as Alex, Pat, Jack, Reggie (after one of my favorite radio sleuths), whatever occurred to me at the time. Nothing quite fit.

Then a cleft palate and a speech defect transformed me overnight from a nice little semi-suicidal Jewish boy with absolutely no future into a full-blooded American ready to take my place on the stage of history.

Waiting for my draft papers, I had a part-time stock-boy job at a Loop department store, Goldblatt's, the pearl of its seven-store chain. The job was fine because mostly I chatted up the sales girls or rode the escalators listening to the Mills Brothers—"You Always Hurt the One You Love"—piped in through the public-address system. Goldblatt's, with its Corinthian plaster columns, heavy scent from the cheap perfume counters, and constant whoosh of the circulating system of pneumatic tubes delivering customers' cash and receipts, intoxicated me. It was impossible for even the laziest worker (me) to get fired because wartime businesses were so man-starved. Even when Louis, one of the Goldblatt proprietorial brothers, a small dark man with eyes in the back of his head, erupted in rage at my idleness and chased me onto an escalator, my arms heaped with fake-fur winter coats, and tried to strangle me in a fury at how I was wasting his money, it never occurred to Mr. Goldblatt to fire me. Kids ruled.

Chester, my supervisor in a subbasement department titled "Will Call," was a partially disabled fellow with a gimpy leg and a malfunctioning palate that gave him a speech disorder. His life wasn't easy, and I didn't make it easier by dodging work assignments, which kept him constantly on the public address wailing, shouting, and pleading my name except that the best he could manage with "Clarence" was a strangled thick-tongued "Ku-la-n-see." *"Cla—ence! Ku—lans! Kulansee!"* eternally ricocheted through the store because I was usually asleep curled up inside a hollowed-out counter.

Kulansee!!!! A music department salesgirl giggled when she heard it and told her best friend in Notions who shouted it across the aisle to a passing inventory clerk who mentioned it to a spring frock buyer who told a freight elevator operator and in no time I was . . .

CLANCY!

Chester had touched me with fairy dust and made me into . . . well, what *was* a Clancy?

Not knowing made me feel powerful. This new Clancy was my unmapped future.

Now anything was possible.

In Old Celtic Clancy means "offspring of a redheaded soldier" and if that doesn't describe Jennie and me, what does?

Jennie in the Snow

A hard sleety snow buffeted the four of us as we trudged up a slushy sidewalk in the Detroit suburb of Royal Oak, Michigan. We—that is, Jennie, my fellow Rocket Nate Manoff in a Sad Sackish 85th Division private's uniform, his girlfriend Louise, and me in my George Raft velvet collar topcoat—(I was waiting for my draft papers)—approached the only house on the block without Yule trimmings, a plain wood two-story with a snowed-in front porch. In a small nervous voice Louise whispered, "There's my dad. Oh, God help me."

Royal Oak was the home of America's most notorious anti-Semite, the radio priest, Father Coughlin, who'd been so wildly popular that the Pope himself had to slap a lock on his mouth. By some wretched coincidence Nate, on his last furlough before shipping overseas, had met Louise Whittacre, daughter of a Ford foreman and a Christian Fronter from Royal Oak, at a serviceman's canteen in Detroit. Nate, with his large nose, small stature, and hunched shoulders, looked unmistakably like some bigot's idea of a Jew, while Louise, with her uptilted prom-queen nose and long dark straight hair, was Miss Gentile America. Both sets of parents—Jewish and anti-Jewish—freaked out beyond reason upon learning of the liaison. The young unnerved couple had begged my mother to intervene and use her negotiating skills to save them from the wrath of their rampaging hormones.

Louise's father, Mr. Whittacre—it had to be him—stood on his porch in blue overalls holding a short-barrel 12-gauge shotgun on us. He levelled the gun and yelled, "Go back where you came from—and take that Jewish-loving whore with you!" He meant his only daughter Louise. Except for us, leaning into the driving snow, the street was deserted. I liked the formality of his "Jewish," not kike, sheenie, or Hebe.

How has it come to this? Nate is nineteen, she is seventeen. He has a three-day pass from nearby Camp Custer, she is serving doughnuts to GIs, and somehow in the jam-packed city they find a motel room for the night. Nate goes on to Chicago where his mother screams bloody murder when she finds in his pants pocket the motel bill for "Mr. & Mrs. Nathan Manoff." Nate makes the mistake of his life by confessing all to his mom which brings on a threat—not to be taken altogether lightly on the west side—of suicide; Mrs. Manoff, devoutly Orthodox, phones the Whittacres in Detroit, Mr. Whittacre locks Louise in her room, Louise escapes out a back window to plead with Nate to rescue her; Nate panics and calls in my mother, who grabs a train for Detroit in the middle of a wartime winter. Now watch:

With a sawed-off aimed squarely at us, Louise begins shaking uncontrollably, trying to wriggle free of Jennie's iron grip but held firmly on the sidewalk in front of her father's shotgun. Mr. Whittacre is a dead ringer for Walter Brennan as a very angry Judge Roy Bean in *The Westerner.* Nate places his arm around Louise, which Jennie smartly slaps away. Whittacre twitches with the effort not to pull the triggers. Now Nate, too, attempts unsuccessfully to escape my mother's grip but Jennie won't let go of him either. "Don't you two dare move," Jennie commands them in her strike-captain voice. Then she ventures one foot on the lower step of the porch, fishes a Pall Mall from her purse, and politely asks Dad Whittacre for a match. He stares down at her: "Don't smoke."

As we near freeze to death on the sidewalk, Jennie launches her pitch. Oh, I knew that tone, the soft soap. Tranquilized and tranquilizing, calming, steady, soothing, no hint of argument or provocation, burbling about the weather, how pretty Mr. Whittacre's street looks in the snow, just like a picture postcard, the hardship of wartime travel—all without a word from Whittacre or his wife peering at us through her front window curtains. I am pissing in my pants with cold. Jennie flashes her Little-Eva-on-the-ice-floe smile. "Sir, I am a little chilled down here. A hot cup of tea inside?"

I think she is crazy.

Whittacre looks uncertain what to do with his shotgun. Jennie, little step at a time, eases up next to him on the porch and implores, "Or even a small glass of water?" I like that "small." What an actress! How can he shoot a shivering Chicago Jewess over a little water?

I can't recall how, but moments later we are all tensely seated in their living room with Dad Whittacre, having parked the shotgun in a corner, proudly showing off Louise's baby photos. Jennie commiserates. "Tell me, tell me, what happens?" she laments. "Such darling children when they're little." She stares disapprovingly at Louise and Nate—and me. "Now look at them." She shakes her head. "Stubborn. Stubborn as mules. My son over there. I could tell you stories. What is he doing in Detroit in the dead of winter when he should be home with me?" Whittacre relaxes in a wicker chair. "Oh, I don't know," he allows, "Detroit isn't as bad as they say. Would be fine if not for the niggers and Jews, beggin' your pardon, missus." Jennie just sits there nodding agreeably. I suspect Mrs. Whittacre knows Ma's game but is too paralyzed by having a Jewess in her house—three Jews!—to call her on it.

All through the early evening, talking soothing conceding sympathizing—by some magical alchemy of the negotiating process, Jennie parleys a settlement of sorts with the Whittacres. Even though I am there in the room, I don't exactly know how she does it. In the end, Whittacre and his wife, step

by painstaking step, agree to (a) forgive Louise this one time
(b) keep her at home but not locked in her room (c) loan her
money to enroll for a freshman year at Wayne State College
and (d) let Louise reimburse him by working part-time ("The
wage I sweat for is not going to pay for her defiling the Lord
Jesus," Mr. W says affably.) In return Nate agrees to stay away
from Louise until the following summer, during which he may
phone but not visit. While she is grounded Louise must faith-
fully attend church, but she will not be compelled to appear in
front of the congregation to confess her sin as Mr. W at first
demanded. In six months there will be a second family conference to decide Louise's long-term future. "You see," my mother
sweetly concludes, "nobody gets anything their own way in this
life. We all give up something. Your daughter has stumbled, but
as good Christians you have your obligation to redeem, to lift
her up. In God's good time, that is. Don't you agree?"

Aghast, I stare at her. The Whittacres are mesmerized.
Buying it.

✿ ✿ ✿

Our skins intact, Jennie and Nate and I skedaddle, leaving
Louise behind in the house to her fate. As we slip and slosh
down the snow-banked street with white flurries floating down
in the lamplight Nate, almost fainting with relief, turns to my
mother. "Hey, Jennie, some performance!"

Jennie stops abruptly to face Nate. "You silly—" she
searches for the right American word. "—twerp!"

We shuffle on in the snow looking for a taxi on Christmas
Eve. I say, "Ma, maybe we should take Louise with us, they'll
kill her." Jennie shakes her head. "I know his type. He'll

---

scream from *mitvag* to *∂ornstag*. He's common. Very common. But you notice? I made him swear on the family Bible. I've worked down South where he's from. Usually they don't kill in cold blood."

"I like that 'Usually,'" Nate says.

"Shut up," Ma says. "Twerp."

Of course, Nate Manoff broke the pact by sneaking back to Detroit to see Louise Whittacre while her parents were away on a religious retreat and found Louise in bed with a sailor whom she later married but not before she brought the sailor to Chicago for my mother's blessing. Nate came back from the war, having landed at Omaha Beach on D-Day-plus-one, missing two of his clarinet fingers, then, like most Rockets, he married a local Lawndale girl. On his wedding day he rang up my mother and me, cohabiting again in our usual one-room flat, this time in Los Angeles. Nate said, "Thank God for Jennie. Louise's father was right. She *was* a whore. Your mother saved my life."

After hanging up I turned to Jennie. "Ma," I asked, "did you believe any of that stuff in Whittacre's house?" She lit another Pall Mall before replying.

"Whittacre wanted to make a deal," she said. "Any fool could see that. But there was nobody to make a deal with. He was helpless. I just made it easy for him."

She narrowed her eyes at me. "But," she said, "if it was you who wanted to jump into bed with that slut Louise I would have pulled the trigger on her myself."

13

Divorce, Chicago Style

1944:—D-Day landings in Normandy. Attempt to assassinate Hitler fails. President Roosevelt elected to unprecedented fourth term.

A strange peace settled on my mother and me as a wartime couple. Most of the outstanding issues between us seemed to have been settled or set aside for payment at a later date. We were like two punched-out boxers hanging onto each other in the last round. Because I'd soon follow the other Rockets into uniform, there was nothing left to fight about. Our divorce had already been negotiated, so we could let go and enjoy the west side's pervasive sense of relief that the worst was over, maybe not in the war itself but in our lives. Something good and greedy was happening to Jennie and me.

The blood cost was high. Gold Stars for a dead son, husband, or brother were showing up everywhere on Lawndale windows, but if it didn't happen to you personally, or somebody you were close to, you rode a wave of optimism that things were getting better and might even stay that way for a while. Somewhere somehow an idea had taken hold that the war was turning into a great social crusade that would slay the dragon of mass unemployment once and for all. Life was opening up.

One little problem for Jennie. I'd become her worst enemy, a Communist.

The Permanent Soldier

"Soldiers are the only real people."
—letter from Winston Churchill's wife, "Clemmie," to her husband in the trenches in 1916

Long before I joined an actual army I was a boy-soldier-in-my-head, in perpetual training for a final conflict between good and evil. A juvenile cult of the military ran deep in me despite everything I knew about the "merchants of death" and soldiers getting their faces blown off in the Flanders mud. My childish thinking was martial; my games were service-related; my playground vocabulary naturally fell to tactics and strategy. I put myself to sleep on dreams of battle glory. I was a Marine charging the Kaiser's spike-helmeted hordes with my bayonet at Belleau Wood; I served as one of Emperor Haile Selassie's barefoot Ethiopian warriors armed with a rhino hide shield against Mussolini's dive bombers; and of course I joined cousin Charlie on the Ebro with the Lincoln Battalion against the Spanish fascists.

Radical pacifism might be part of the family faith — *believed* — but to be *soldierly,* a variation on Jennie's iron self-control — stoical, overcoming fear, humping your pack without complaint—well, I couldn't imagine a better way to die for one's country, or at least serving "with distinction" whatever that meant. Fighting was in my blood, preferably in some sort of uniform.

Soldierness was a perfectly rational technique for organizing one's fears about the outside world's chronic war fever. If nothing else, war taught me geography, with all those nonstop crises in Manchuko, Addis Ababa, Barcelona, Danzig, Saarland, Warsaw, and Pearl Harbor. It also helped subdue my anxiety about things at home. No matter how badly Jennie and Leo and I treated each other, I was going to accept it like a man in brass-buttons-and-khaki, take up my sentry post on the tall domestic wall, do my duty, and refuse to go AWOL except in my imagination, which sheared away from domestic chaos into the ordered structure of a military dream life. Naturally, just as I chose what kind of Jew I was, I *chose* the type of soldier I wanted to be—certainly not a bloodthirsty bully like Major George Patton, or General Douglas MacArthur, who led the cavalry-and-bayonet charge against unarmed Bonus Army war veterans in the "battle of Anacostia Flats" in Washington, D.C.—but a special kind of warrior.

My models then, and in some ways continue to be, were three great unorthodox military men: General Joseph "Vinegar Joe" Stillwell, the testy, outspoken commander of Allied forces in the China-Burma-India theater of operations in the bitter 1942–43 retreat from the Japanese ("We took a helluva beating"), under whom I was to serve after the Washington brass-hats exiled him from combat; Colonel Evans Carlson, creator of the U.S. Marine Raiders, who borrowed Chinese Communist army tactics, including their war cry, "Gung ho!"; and General Orde Wingate, the strange, Bible-thumping,

Scottish-born Presbyterian strategist who created the Israeli Haganah and whose permanent legacy is "Yemin Orde Wingate Village," famous for rehabilitating hundreds of war-broken and abandoned children.

I was "Gung ho!"

So signing a Communist Party card at fifteen was a little like joining my army-of-the-mind if only because the Party's language was so militarized. All those "soldiers of the proletariat" forever "on the march" in the "battle against fascism." The Party's songs, rhetoric, and psychology emphasized fighting as the ultimate virtue; in fact, many Communist apparatchiks managed, despite intense FBI screening, to get themselves into World War II combat. National organizational secretary, Bob Thompson, won a Silver Star in the Pacific; John Gates, editor of the *Daily Worker*, served bravely; and Milt Wolff, a raving Red, was a combat aide to "Wild Bill" Donovan, head of the OSS, precursor to the CIA.

It took some mind shifting to get used to the idea that I was hooking up with card-carrying Reds my mother and father loathed to the max and whom I regarded as definitely uncool. They were all over the neighborhood and *very serious*. But if you had the war fever and believed in soldiery and liked the up-front activism of the west side Communists (coming in platoons to move evictees like us back into their apartments, calling rent strikes, etc.) and knew the Russians were fighting on our side and identified it all with my much-admired cousin, Charlie the Spanish Loyalist fighter, and looked forward to some really great arguments with Jennie, why, what choice was there?

✳ ✳ ✳

Jennie's to blame, naturally. For years we had honed our skills on each other by debating "the issues of the day" at the dinner table, hammering our personalities out on the anvil of the other's beliefs. When it became clear that a chapter was closing in our lives, courtesy of the draft and my eagerness to get in the war, I thought about what farewell gift I could give Ma guaranteed (a) to piss her off and at the same time (b) assert my own autonomy and (c) simultaneously show her that she had raised a *serious* son. By a process of elimination, signing up and dropping out of Lawndale's many youth groups—Young People's Socialist League, Young Fourth International, Young Slavic Workers, and the Zionist Habonim, Hashomir Hatzoir, Hashomir Hadati, and Betar (Irgun)—I deduced which would be the most repellent to her. Mere juvenile delinquency didn't cut it anymore. We were a *political* family, after all.

Though mostly tolerant of other people's beliefs, Jennie reserved a special place in hell for Communists because they betrayed the 1917 Russian revolution, murdered the mutinous Kronstadt sailors, split the American labor movement, and oh yes by the way a Communist goon had damn near fractured her skull in a New York alley brawl. What could be more logical than for me to become a Communist?

Hard to believe now, but it wasn't an unpopular thing to do then. Communism had become so conventional, not to say chic, that a wartime *New Yorker* cartoon showed two rich society ladies at Carnegie Hall, standing for the Soviet hymn, "The Internationale," the traditional call for workers to overthrow the upper class. One dowager whispers to the other, "If you don't know the words just move your lips."

Pro-Soviet fervor swept the nation because most Americans, including Jennie, felt grateful to the Russians for taking the brunt of the war casualties, twenty million at least. Hitler's invasion had taken the edge off her anticommunism because now it wasn't Josef Stalin but her beloved country of origin, Mother Russia, in peril. And her long-lost sister, Rose (Surkah), who refused to emigrate to America in order to marry a shoemaker, was trapped in the war zone at the mercy of SS *einsatzgruppen*, the extermination squads.

It took some mind changing of her own but, even though she abominated Joe Stalin, Jennie flung herself passionately into the war effort to sell U.S. War Bonds from a street corner, regularly donate blood, save the silver foil from her packs of Pall Malls, throw her old aluminum pots into a community bin, and even offer her services to Russian War Relief to roll bandages. She still spoke fluent Russian, which is why, when the official translator fell ill, Jennie was asked to interpret for the famed Soviet army woman sniper, Ludmilla Pavlichenko, on a morale-building tour of America that was passing through Chicago.

What do you do if you hate the Soviets but love the Russians? Jennie did much heart searching before agreeing to accompany Pavlichenko on her Midwest speaking engagements. "Hey, Ma," I slapped her on the back, "I'll make a Communist of you yet." She eyed me coldly. "The day you raise Ehrlich and Alter back from the grave, I'll join." Henrich Ehrlich and Victor Alter were Polish socialists murdered by Stalin.

Jennie dressed to the nines for her stage appearances with Pavlichenko, who spoke to huge Chicago rallies. (Jennie got into some of her newsreels). One night I came in from a street-corner meeting to find Jennie and Ludmilla, in full splendid Red Army uniform dripping with medals, exchanging photos of me as a baby and the sniper's family back in Russia. Ludmilla was young, beautiful, and "raven tressed," a sort of brunette Judy Holiday, my kind of gal. The killer of 309 Nazis in my apartment! I was speechless, but not for long.

I plopped myself down on the couch next to her and in pidgin Russki reeled off the only Russian phrase I knew, "Arise, workers of the world!" (Phonetically, *vistavi padamonsi raboche narod!*) Ludmilla gave me a strange look and moved away uneasily. Jennie spoke in Russian to her and they both smiled indulgently and went back to their photographs. The remains of a matzoh brie-and-brisket dinner were on the table. I kept interrupting them, prodding Jennie to ask Ludmilla questions for me—had she ever been wounded? did her rifle have a scope?— which the Soviet soldier blithely ignored. Ludmilla and Jennie were chattering away like old friends and at one point began to cry and lament together. I hated being ignored by these women. My Russian wasn't working, so I tried the west side method of subtle flirting by putting my leg alongside Ludmilla's. Jennie stared at me with subzero eyes. Ludmilla, on the couch with nowhere else to move, slowly turned a sultry gaze on me and said something in Russian that caused Jennie to almost fall off the couch, in merriment. The two of them threw their arms around each other, swaying back and forth laughing. I shifted to the far end of the settee and sulked. All this time, Ludmilla and Jennie were holding hands like sisters.

The hall buzzer sounded, Ludmilla's U.S. army chauffeur. Jennie's eyes urged me off my duff to bid a gracious good-bye to our visitor and this time I didn't try anything, but Ludmilla did. She grabbed me with one of those colossal Soviet kisses on both cheeks, held me at arm's length, and said something in Russian ending in "tovarich." Then she and Jennie embraced, flowing over in Russian to each other. Jennie's eyes were wet as she watched Ludmilla and her driver march down the carpeted hallway.

I leaned against the door jamb. "Ma," I sighed, "she called me comrade." Jennie pulled out a Pall Mall, lit it, blew out an iridescent circle of blue smoke, and said, "Too bad you don't understand Russian. That's not all she called you."

Jennie on the Dating Scene

Jennie and I honored Sundays as our "date" day, truce time, an armistice in the war of love and hate between us. Our custom on late Sunday mornings was to promenade arm in arm along busy Roosevelt Road, dressed up, mother and son, young Henry Fonda to Jane Darwell, saying howdy to the folks. Jennie was intensely proud of these strolls climaxed by lunch at Silverstein's restaurant and an early matinee where we watched the latest Paramount release at the Central Park Theatre, part of the Balaban & Katz chain of ornate movie palaces that made life in Chicago bearable. She adored Mae West and Myrna Loy and loved going to the show with me. Occasionally we even held hands in the darkness. Of course, she wore gloves but still it felt fine entwining my fingers around her kid leather hand as long as it stayed dark and she didn't draw attention by laughing too boisterously at how Mae twirled men around her chubby little finger.

Afterwards, we'd stroll in Douglas Park and chew over the plots. Jennie: "William Powell, now there's a gentleman." Clancy: "Ma, that mustache?" Jennie: "Suits him." Clancy: "Sol Schechter has a mustache. What's it like to kiss him?" She froze up. Ah, I thought, so it was Sol Schechter, was it? I was always on the prowl for Ma's other men, real or imagined.

Jennie never looked at another guy as long as there was even a sliver of hope Leo Sigal might walk in out of the night. But when it became obvious that he was phfft for good, the TLJs—tough little Jews, Meyer, Sam or Abe, squat compact Ukrainian-Byelo-Russkis, often Dad's friends, usually married, rarely over five foot three or four and scenting Ma's loneliness —came casually calling, often around dinner time. She used me, her teenage son and accomplice, as a screener to pass judgment, size them up, and dust them off if unacceptable, which they always were in my eyes. *"Shalom Yenni! Vie bist du? Vos machs du? Und dien zun, vie geitz mit der?"* And if they dared sit down at our dinner table I'd shove my face close to theirs and give them my Boris Karloff smile. "And what do we have here, little man? Embalmer's night off." The point was to keep the animals off Jennie, which usually worked not always to her displeasure. Her mouth might turn down reproachfully, but her eyes sparkled at my effrontery, which reminded her so much of Leo Sigal's boldness. "You're so awful to my guests," she'd try to frown and would end up grinning.

Then trouble. A guy over six feet showed up.

Sol Schechter was that rare animal, a prosperous businessman and a fatally available widower. He was one *big* Jew. Handsome, hawk-nosed, wide sloping shoulders like a Chicago Bears lineman, and a deep authoritative basso profundo voice, he starred in amateur Shakespearean productions at the Labor Lyceum's Yiddish Theater and was a well known "social figure" in his crème suits and quick smile. When Jennie told me me that his King Lear made her cry I got really worried.

By reputation Schechter was decent, honorable, respectful, friendly, and warm, hence a dire threat to me when Ma invited him one night to dinner at our place .

At her strict instruction I wore my Jones Commercial double-breasted suit and my school manners, hands folded at table as if in prayer, sitting so modestly silent that it rattled Jennie, who leaned over to whisper, "You sick or something?" Around dessert of Dole's canned fruit cocktail with a maraschino cherry, I artlessly interrupted their small talk: "Mr. Schechter, sir, what kind of business are you in?" Ma shushed me but Schechter smiled tolerantly, "That's all right, Jennie," he said, putting his hand on her arm possessively. I visualized wielding a small axe and chopping off his hand at the wrist.

Schechter declared that he owned a wet wash company, a commercial laundry, over by the north side. Wet washes were steamy factories full of heavy machinery — extractors, mechanical pressers, huge vats full of boiling water, mangles — used to process mountains of dirty laundry. Workers, the majority women, sweated twelve-hour days in intolerable heat for low pay. These factory laundries hired truck "commission" drivers who belonged to the crooked Teamsters' union. At one point, Dad had been chased out of town by a Teamster thug, Klondike O'Donnell, who was in the pay of Ralph Capone, Al's brother. Chicago's entire laundry industry was overrun by union criminals like the Capones, and "Red" Barker and his mob henchman, Murray "The Camel" Humpreys. (Even by Chicago standards Barker's assassination was remarkable: he was shot thirty-six times by a rapid-fire, water-coooled machine gun mounted on a tripod.)

In my best Mickey Rooney voice I sprung my trap.

"Say, Mr. Schecter, that's swell. Imagine, all those workers working for you." Beat. "What union did you say you're signed with?"

Jennie glared at me.

Schechter's body language conveyed an urgent desire to change the subject.

"My employees are of two minds about unions," he replied carefully.

"Run a nonunion place, do you?" I wondered.

He chose his words. "I am one hundred percent union. I do my part," echoing the now-defunct FDR Blue Eagle pledge. "In fact, two hundred percent union." His people were signed up in separate unions, the inside laundry workers in one local and the laundry-wagon drivers in another. "So they are well protected." For a man easy with himself, he looked a little under strain.

Sweetly, I said, "These two locals, would they be the Teamsters?"

Schechter nodded.

Clear as glass. Schechter the boss, a truly nice man, had signed a sweetheart agreement with the corrupt International Brotherhood of Teamsters to bribe the local officers in exchange for labor peace, and screw the workers. It was done all the time. God forbid an employee should ask for a free, fair, or honest ballot.

Schechter, sensing he was being jammed, looked imploringly to Jennie, who sat sphinx like behind a curtain of cigarette smoke.

Somehow, the inglorious evening ended. At our apartment door Schechter formally shook Jennie's hand for the benefit of the kid who was wondering what they got up to when he wasn't around. He gave me a look, hesitated, started to say something, thought better of it, shut the door quietly after himself.

Jennie and I cleaned up the dishes after he left. For the longest time the only sound was the tap water running and me cheerily whistling "Begin the Beguine." After a while of passing dishes to each other we started bumping hips boompsadaisy at the kitchen sink, a game we hadn't played in a while, whereupon she threw a vicious bodycheck that sent me crashing against the wall, where I almost dropped a plate. She leaned her hands on the sink and made a sound that wasn't laughing, wasn't weeping.

And drew a slow big breath. "Well, that's that."

Sayonara, Sol Schechter, we hardly knew ya. Score one for the Last of the Rockets.

※ ※ ※

That night, as we were preparing for bed, I called across to her in the darkness. "Ma, did you at least sleep with him?" Me, Mister Sophisticated.

Silence, because I'd stepped over the unmentionable line. Then she gave an answer that would stand the test of time for years to come.

"And what," she softly asked, *"will I talk to him about afterwards?"*

Called my bluff. All the horsing around and flirting and boompsadaisy came down to this; *"What will I talk to him about afterwards?"* It was Jennie's only acknowledgment to me in sixteen years that she was accomplished in a world of forceful raw sex that I was yet to be initiated into; she had *done* it and, given a choice, would *do* it again. My head ached. I jumped off the couch-bed and, pretending to need something, snapped on the light and looked at my mother, really *looked*. The night was warm and she was lying in her rose-and-shell-embroidered cotton shift. She had large streaks of gray in her red hair and wrinkles around her eyes and sagging underarm flesh and fading freckles and her stocky legs were crisscrossed by intricate traceries of varicose veins. Where had my Jewish Carole Lombard gone?

I turned off the light and climbed back onto my couch. I felt so tired. That last word hung in the air: *afterwards*? It was out in the open. Leo Sigal would forever and always be her "afterwards." Nobody else would ever take his place in her life. Not even me.

Venus (Assisted by Cupid) at Her Dressing Table

Friday, a warm spring night in wartime Chicago. Hip to hip, Jennie and I are crammed into her "beauty alcove" improvised around a half-length mirror screwed to the bottom of the retracted Murphy bed in our one-room-plus-kitchenette apartment at Douglas Boulevard. We're in the money, jobs are plentiful, and so are paychecks. A low-key madness enters our souls: people are dying overseas; in Chicago they're *living* for the first time. Separately, Ma and I are preparing to go out for the night. She claims to a meeting of the Riga-Baltic Progressive Ladies Society; I to the movies. We are both lying.

Even after we moved into our very own place we continued to dress and undress in front of each other. But now when I lean in to study Jennie she stiffens uncomfortably under my stare, even turns her back when putting on her Van Raalte chantilly lace slip and waits for me to turn away before she tries on her panties, girdle, and almost-impossible-to-obtain, full-fashioned stockings. Vaguely, I feel cheated.

I weave and bob in front of the mirror to get its full attention, and Jennie's. She carefully assembles herself for the evening. Not bad. Open-throat rayon blouse showing more bosom than usual, elbow-length Belgian velvet gloves, red-banded straw hat set at a flirty angle, pleated skirt with medium-high hemline, a dab of Jergens Lotion for a set of the front bob in her "casually yours" hair style. She's on her way to the Riga-Baltic Ladies, oh yeah I'll bet. Automatically she turns for my approval, catches herself, realizes it isn't appropriate anymore. But I give her my Robert Mitchum slit-eyed sultry look. Jennie doesn't like where this is going so she narrows her blue-shadowed eyes on me, but she's blushing.

It's my turn.

Now check me out. I mean, *cool*. Pork pie extra-wide brim fedora with a rainbow-colored feather stuck in the hat band, orange fluorescent fake-satin shirt with wide lay-down collar, double-knotted fifty-two-inch shiny burgundy wool-cable tie with cream and navy abstract pattern and tied in a Windsor knot, one-inch-wide green corduroy suspenders holding up "reet" cuffless chest-high trousers with baggy thighs and strangled ankles, a Texas cowboy-style belt with a silver-plated buckle engraved CS, pale mauve imitation angora single-breasted cardigan-type blazer jacket, checkerboard-crocheted argyle socks and oxblood high-shine shoes with metal taps heel and toe so they can hear me coming a mile away on Roosevelt Road, and, of course, a double spiral "gold-plated" key chain clipped to my belt and plummeting to the sidewalk and halfway back up, a small-arms weapon as well as an ornament.

Venus, the observed, observes with sinking heart. We stare at each other in the mirror.

Her look says, where did I go wrong?

✳ ✳ ✳

Joe Franklin, ten as of this writing, has begun spreading smelly guck on his hair to make it look spikey. He spends incredible amounts of time in front of the bathroom mirror microscopically examining his blonde mane while snapping his fingers and wiggling to gangsta rap lyrics,

I'm a little boy but live a big man's life/
I got grown women wanna be in my life . . ."
Exhales. *Blah Blah Blah . . . gotta split heads tonight . . .*

Where did I go wrong?

14

Reds

Maybe in Topeka or Laramie you don't find many "ists," but they were everywhere in Chicago, agitating on street corners and in taverns, helping to drag furniture back for evicted tenants, turning out at dawn at factory gates to hand out leaflets exactly like Barbra Streisand's Katie Morowsky in *The Way We Were*. They were your neighbors. Signing up was as easy as shouting across a clothesline.

If I wanted to get Jennie's goat, why didn't I go all the way and become a Republican? Quite simply, I never met any Republicans in Lawndale because they were an endangered species. Our local Twenty-fourth ward habitually turned in 95 percent Democratic votes, and, in one election, more than 100 percent (Chicago mantra: "Vote early, vote often"). The president, FDR himself, hailed the Twenty-fourth as the most Democratic district in the nation. I've met South Wales miners who have gone through life without ever meeting a Tory; they would have felt at home on Kedzie Avenue.

It starts this way. "Some performance you put on there." This tall, awkward, intense kid put his hand on my arm outside Miss Saunders's class at Marshall High. Max Weinstock said, "If you're interested, I can show you some *real* Communists." I said, "My old lady had her ass kicked by you Communists. Screw off." But since I'd tried every other group, grouplet, faction, and Young-This-Or-That on the west side, I figured *What do I have to lose?* And went along for kicks.

The Young Communist League meeting in somebody's front room was not exactly a hoot. There were dusty pictures of Karl Marx, Lenin, and Joe Stalin on the wall, and the YCL girls looked as if they all got all As in class and not a neighborhood slut among them. An older woman with a pronounced lurch-limp paced up and down expounding on "wage, labor, and capital" and recommended a pamphlet from the Little Lenin Library; my head fell on my chest with boredom and I soon slipped away. Max followed me out into the street, where I told him, "Next time, warn me so I can blow my brains out first. See you around," and went off into the night.

Six months later I saw Max Weinstock again when he was standing on a wooden orange crate punching his fist up to the sky on the corner of Roosevelt and Turner calling for "Guns for Russia!" A fight started, he was grabbed off his soap box, and a couple of other guys, I assumed Young Communists, hurtled to his rescue, fists flying. Ah, unlike "wage, labor, and capital," this was a language any Rocket could speak.

On his way out of the crowd with a bleeding lip, Max spotted me. "Still on the sidelines, Sigal? We'll never win the war that way."

Something about the brawl intrigued me. The inefficient way Max fought back, all awkward arms and flailing legs and no rabbit punch, and how those two other kids dived in to save him. Curiosity pulled me in.

What a difference six months makes. This time, the YCL met under a new "front" name, American Youth for Democracy, in a big room at a local People's Institute, where pinned on the wall was a large American flag and portraits of George Washington and Abraham Lincoln, not Lenin and Marx. Same girls, same boys, same older limping woman, different lecture, "Communism is Twentieth-century Americanism." It was like attending an American Legion convention.

My big mistake was dragging some of the Rockets along— Deaf Augie, Stash, Albie, and Ike, all army bound—to the AYD meeting, which ended badly when they made boors of themselves by yawning like hippos and pawing the "broads," and I was asked—no, told—never to bring them around again. But I still *dressed* like a Rocket, so this, too, became an issue. Or, as the limping woman, my section leader, a veteran Communist organizer, warned, "Bohemian is so bourgeois. The norms of comradeship require an appropriate response to the culture without surrendering to it." I had no idea what she was talking about except that it sounded like a Jones Commercial sermon.

A culture clash was inevitable. While I was keen on necking, petting, cussing, and chasing girls, AYD was dedicated to clean living, healthy exercise, and fresh air, like the Boy Scouts except without the hi-top boots. Whoever circulated the rumor that Bolsheviks were into free love was a liar or way out of date. I'd conned myself into the west side's most conservative organization outside the synagogues.

Again I tiptoed out of the meeting, meaning never to return, when from an adjoining room came the squalling sound of a guitar followed by young voices belting out a Sigmund

Romberg showstopper with weird new lyrics. I paused in the hallway to listen.

The sky was blue and high above
The moon was new, so was love
This eager heart of mine was singing
Krupskaya, * where can you be?*

Aha, finally somebody with half a sense of humor. I opened the door into a whole new life.

The voices belonged to Max Weinstock and two of the guys who had hustled him away from the street corner scuffle. Max and his friends, Arthur and Ginger, called themselves the "Corpuscle Trio" for no known reason except that they liked to get together in close part harmony, a sort of curbstone doowop version of the Mills Brothers adapted to Woody Guthrie lyrics with send-ups of Tin Pan Alley standards. Cool. When I asked to sit in, the Trio put it to a vote—everything was voted on—and that afternoon the group became the "Corpuscle Quartet." For the rest of the war and beyond, until Senator Joe McCarthy and amnesia set in, that's the way it would be, the four of us, just like the MGM film *Three Comrades,* plus one.

Intensely competetive, dying of hormonal glut, fighters more than rebels, noisy and bad mannered, the Corpusclers were not anything like the lovable sleazeballs I was used to. Max and his friends had their eyes set on something we Rockets simply never thought about, the future. The future—hope—promise—a better day—singing tomorrows were written into the Communist songs and pamphlets and their perspective on life.

* Lenin's notoriously dowdy wife

If I had gone into a conventional Red branch I would have marched out again in ten seconds. I called it the "comrade kids" syndrome, patronizing and cynical at the same time. But the Corpusclers occupied a fringe of their own: quick to shoot down authority, they liked "doing the dozens" and making fun of their own party leadership, Marxist dogma and "marching into the dawn" type songs. Although loyal Communists—as I would become—they gave themselves plenty of room for satire and put-downs, erupting in their—our—versions of the Old Anthems (*"I dreamed I saw Joe Hill last night / In bed with Emma G / Says I to Joe you're ten years dead / It never died says he"*) or scatalogical jokes or defying the ever-changing party line with gags. Call it style. It angered the ancient members and the bureaucrats, who tried to shout us down, split us up, promote us, educate us out of our "absence of proletarian discipline," a phrase we loved to roll about our tongues to see what new puns we could make of it. (Not very good ones, admittedly: "Absinthe makes the proles grow fonder." Ugh.) Premature punks, we rampaged through the Chicago progressive movement drawing large audiences of wildly appreciative young fans and disapproving frowns from the party mandarins and Old Believers. Of course, it never occurred to me to bring Art, Max, and Ginger to my Flukey's hangout joint. Innocenza Dominici would eat them up alive.

❊ ❊ ❊

Because the Corpusclers were smart and lively, the "downtown leadership" (party hacks) chose to honor, and cage, us with scholarships to a sort of West Point called the Abraham Lincoln School for budding "cadre," or potential leaders. Our most charismatic teacher, Socrates to us disciples, was a musician and artist named Arthur Stern, a singer with Woody Guthrie and Pete Seeger in the Almanacs, radical folkies who were the spiritual godfathers of Bob Dylan and Springsteen. Arthur Stern was pugnacious, irreverent, brilliant, analytical, scathing, generous, dogmatic, and loved young men. He put his stamp on us for years to come, tugging us out of childhood into a world of massive abstractions against which our main shield was sheer adolescent fuck-you. In time, each of us in turn was sent to the Lincoln School principal, an African-American super-Stalinist, for correctional lectures which only furnished more material for our improvised satires. We were not about to let ossified minds throttle back our idealism or our instinctive faith that by ourselves alone as Corpusclers we could remake the world, even if we had to do it as Communists.

An American Comedy

Normally, being radical is a good way to stay poor. That was certainly true of my mother and father. But, as I was to learn, if your timing and connections are right it can boost you right up the status ladder.

Aside from teachers and probation officers, I had no personal contact with the middle class, the so-called "bourgeoisie." Even at sixteen I had no higher ambition than to connect with the neighborhood lawyer Mr. Freyer and his daughter Annette, who clearly found me a social disaster. Without resentment, I had accepted their judgment; indeed, their silent censure released me from any obligation to aim above my station.

But then one night the Corpuscle Quartet was asked to perform at a benefit at a south side Hyde Park venue, one of many we accepted because it was fun to sing our hearts out for

an audience. But this was different from the workingclass pic-
nics and halls we normally appeared at. The home belonged to
a Chicago businessman whose daughter, let's call her Antonia,
was a young radical.

I'd never in my life been in such a palatial palace, a three-
storey Frank Lloyd Wright-style house with porches and eaves
and low-slung wooden beams and a fabulous dance-hall-size
living room with *two* grand pianos, a kitchen as big as our whole
living quarters at the back of the Family Hand Laundry . . . and
a separate bedroom for the parents, a walk-in closet and a
whole room to herself for fifteen-year-old Antonia.

I was impressed . . . and how! And so were Max and the
homeless Ginger though Art, whose father was in work and
therefore socially a micromilletre above us, affected a gentle
superiority to his surroundings. But not me. "Shut your
mouth—you're gawping like an ape waiting for his banana,"
Max said.

After we performed successfully to a room packed with
middle class sympathizers, we sat crosslegged among them to
listen to the next act, Big Joe Turner belting out the blues
accompanied by the boogie-woogie Kansas stride artists Al
Ammons and Pete Johnson. Two things immediately struck me
staring up at them in astonishment. I had never before heard
anything like this—Turner snapping his fingers and shouting
"Roll 'em Pete" while Ammons and Johnson ran their fingers up
and down the piano keys in a thundering locomotive of sound—
until then my idea of music was Kay Kyser's Kollege of Musical
Knowledge's "Three Little Fishies"—hit me like a religious
thunderbolt, and my life changed on the spot. And, gazing
around at the guests, my eyes picked out the women all of whom
seemed elegant beyond compare. They dressed and even stood

still differently. Had I seen them in Lawndale I might not have given them a second glance. But they were *here* amidst all this glamor . . . and money. (Over a thousand dollars was raised: Orphan Annie's Daddy Warbucks was here in spirit.)

They may not have been wearing perfume but I *smelled* the difference.

F. Scott Fitzgerald, in the persona of his fictional hero Amory in "This Side of Paradise," famously envied the inherited arrogance of his Princeton classmates and their wealthy friends. But I did not want what these people had. For one thing, it was unimaginable. But, (almost) virgin as I was, I wanted every single woman there, to possess them. For me to rise into their comfortable middle class—those silk cut-on-the-bias dresses, that streamline moderne furniture!—was clearly an impossibility, and a betrayal of my convictions. But taking "their" women . . . *that* I could imagine.

Thus, rock 'n roll—for that's what Ammons, Johnson and Turner played—and a determination to have what the men in this room had—their women—entered my life at the same time.

Even then I had read Dreiser's *An American Tragedy* and identified strongly with its pathetic hero Clyde Griffiths, son of wandering preachers. He, too, had tried "getting up" through sex and ended up in the electric chair. Poor fool, he'd never heard of condoms.

Jennie had taken care of that.

❊ ❊ ❊

Jennie now faced a Hobson's choice. Her son—forget getting kicked out of high school, the neighbors' gossip about his behavior, or the next-door rabbi's outrage at atheistic slogans in Crayola crayon on his temple's front steps — had strayed into her personal Land of Horrors by linking up with the despised Reds. She could expel me from her bosom as Leo Sigal had — or deal with me as she treated hecklers in the hall, kill them with kindness.

Guess which.

She kept her composure and armed herself accordingly. Whatever it took, she was determined to keep me as her son.

Hospitality was her weapon of choice. Somehow she maneuvered me into inviting the Quartet up to our place for cookies and milk. ("What, I can't handle young criminals? May I remind you, sir comrade, that when you were little we once had Homer Van Meter to breakfast." Hey, yes. Van Meter, John Dillinger's right hand man, blazed it out with cops in St. Paul and fell dead with a smoking .45 still in his hand. He'd been a distant pal of Dad's.)

I dreaded a confrontation between the Corpuscle Quartet and my Communist-hating mother. Grudgingly and ill-temperedly the Corpusclers swaggered up to the house on their worst behavior. Ginger, thin and wiry and salty-tongued, sauntered in as if he owned the place, kicked off his sneakers, and stretched out his smelly bare feet on the kitchen table and left them there as an insult to Jennie despite her unblinking stare at his filthy toes. Art loudly noted the absence of bookshelves. "Your mother doesn't read? How interesting." And Max, practically before he was across the threshold, baited and taunted Jennie as a "social fascist" while I kept a miserable cowardly silence.

All the while, Jennie just kept smiling her all-American Mom smile in the face of their really mean blistering attacks, offering "More cookies?" instead of venom, slowly grinding them down with her civility. It drove the Corpusclers crazy.

"What's wrong with your mother?" Ginger demanded in her hearing. "Isn't she a serious person?"

She was infinitely more devious than anything they had ever met before.

Soon the Corpusclers got into the habit of dropping by Jennie's place any old time, to see, and provoke, and be comforted by her. She always kept fresh *cholla* and jam or Nabisco wafers and milk on hand for them, and I hung around just to watch Ma do her magic act, except that her hand was quicker than my eye and I never did catch her at it. Some kind of internal guidance system, a talent for enchantment, told her to use a different approach, even a different tone of voice, for each of the Corpusclers, around whom she slowly and protectively wove a net of maternal charm. Counterintuitively, she freely laid her hands on tall gawky Max, the group's unofficial commissar, who hated being physically touched; gave a duplicate of our apartment key to Ginger, who was basically a homeless street orphan sometimes beaten by his half-insane stepmother; and sat with Art for hours teaching him Russian folk songs until he got the chords and intonation right. Ma's intuition told her what each of them needed emotionally, what they lacked at home or, in Ginger's case, no-home, and she gave of herself warmly, generously.

Neither Jennie nor I had reckoned on a wild card, the jealousy devil biting my ass. The Corpuscles were taking my mother away from me, I felt, and in a sulk I distanced myself from them and slithered back to the streets to try to regain what I'd lost, my Rocket soul. But all the others were in the military (and Stash in jail) and our basement clubhouse had been taken over by a bunch of younger kids, sixth graders, who called themselves the Daring Dragons and stared at me as if I was the Old Man of the Mountain until, flustered, I backed out in confusion. Upstart little pishers.

My own choices were to resume my post on the street corner in full zoot suit regalia to hang out with the pishers and

4-Fs or to take up again with the Corpusclers and their new den mother Jennie. But I needed my mama.

In moments alone I needled her, "You going Communist on me, Ma?" Out came the usual ciggie, the lit match, the lazy smoke ring, looking me in the eye as she suddenly belted out her version of the Communist anthem, the "Internationale."

> *"Arise, ye prisoners of starvation*
> *Arise, ye* RED SHIT *of the earth . . ."*

And howled with laughter at her joke on me.

P.S. The Corpuscle Quartet lives on in two-and-a-half of its members. After the war, Max Weinstock went to work as a laborer in a steel mill to "colonize" for the party and then became a probation officer in California and had second thoughts about his youthful radicalism, which he said was out of touch with the real human natures of the hardened criminals, rapists, and

Nineteen-year-old Clancy (right) with one of Corpuscle Quartet.

(Courtesy of Robert Berkovitz)

murderers he dealt with daily. He lost his mind, probably because of an undiagnosed brain tumor, and reverted to exquisite recall of ancient ideological disputes; he couldn't let them go. In our last dinner together, at Alice Waters's restaurant, Chez Panisse, in Berkeley, he giggled a lot, slapped his knee, shouted old-time slogans, called the nearby customers "comrade," and dredged up from his relapsed memory, sneeringly or straight I couldn't tell, the words of the Russian writer Ostrovsky that were printed in Communist membership booklets,

Man's dearest possession is life, and it is given him to live but once. He should so live that dying he can say, "All my strength and all my life have been given to the finest cause in all the world: the struggle for the liberation of mankind. . . .

Over their coq au vin and apple martinis the Chez Panisse patrons looked extremely uncomfortable at Max's outbursts and several chose to move to distant tables. I got angry at them and began shouting, too. "What are you scared of? Somebody raised his voice. Big deal. So NPR won't hire him. Enjoy your meal!" When I said goodbye to Max, he held my hand on his porch and just couldn't stop laughing at a joke he saw and, at the time, I didn't. He's gone now, the boy who believed he could box the circle and resolve every human contradiction through sheer brain power and the force of the Hegelian dialectic. He couldn't play baseball, football, or buck-buck, but he was Casey at the Bat when it came to having the courage of his convictions.

Ginger, despite his small frame, also "went into steel" for the Party, sweeping floors and shoveling coal, and survived the McCarthy period when factory workers were flinging lefties like him from top floor windows. Eventually he went on to grad school, took his degree in psychology and became warden of a shelter for homeless boys precisely as he once had been. At our last meeting Ginger professed blank ignorance of our shared past and had to be prompted by his wife to whom he apparently told everything before self-obliterating his political memory, a common condition among "ex-es."

Art, the singing satiric troubadour, Lenny Bruce *avant le mot*, now a scientist on the East Coast, and I are in almost daily contact. Recently he wrote me about his feelings as a young Communist. "It was as raw as naked sex standing up. I never had felt a part of the life around me before I attended [an AYD meeting] . . . What I felt was an apparently spontaneous and sincere outpouring of warmth and friendship directed at me, personally . . . I just bathed in it. Joining the party was like getting a medal for service and bravery . . . If there was a secret handshake, I never learned it. If the feeling of exaltation, of being a comrade among comrades, would not last forever, I could not imagine that it would dissolve. Hey, we were the Corpuscle Quartet and wouldn't ever break up."

But we did.

※ ※ ※

D-DAY—WE INVADE HITLER'S EUROPE! the headlines screamed, and it was happening without me.

The Rockets had gone, and now the Corpusclers, Max (tanks), Art (Merchant Marine and Navy), and Ginger (infantry). Jennie knew she was going to lose me, and at odd moments I'd catch her looking at me as if she was saying goodbye to a seventeen-year-old person neither of us knew very well anymore.

At Christmas, during the Battle of the Bulge, I was drafted into the infantry. Jennie helped me pack a small bag and gave me a double-thick baloney sandwich laced with Hellman's mayo and French's mustard for the troop train that would take me to Fort Sheridan. Awkwardly, we embraced, not knowing where to put our arms and lips. Her self-control was unshakable. We had agreed she'd stay in the apartment and not walk me down to the corner bus. " 'Bye, Jennie," I waved in the hallway. She just stood there mutely and as I went down the stairs I prayed she'd keep her cool.

Outside a cold snowless day. The Douglas Boulevard bus came and I boarded it. When it began to move I turned in my back-row seat and my heart squeezed hard. Jennie had come out of the building in her housecoat and was running after the bus to keep up with it. Then the driver shifted into drive and rumbled away, leaving her on the sidewalk still running and stumbling, a dwindling figure in the west side landscape. Finally the little person stopped and put her apron up to her eyes.

※ ※ ※

At Fort Sheridan I got into the chow line served by fantastic-looking Afrika Korps POWs tanned and hard from the desert war. These were the Nazi giants I wanted to fight? Immediately, I shriveled down to midget size, but as always the wise guy in me came to the rescue. On the off chance there was a secret Red among them I began whistling what I'd always been led to believe was an antifascist tune, "Hans Beimmler." (*"Eine kugel kam geflogen/Aus der "Heimat fur in her . . ."*) The largest POW, an immense guy, sidled up to me inquiring in thickly accented English, "You are Jair-man?" I almost dropped my

food tray and stuttered, "J-jew." He went back to the line of
POW servers and whispered to them and they grinned at me,
nodding agreeably. Then they all began humming "Hans
Beimmler," in unison, only it sounded like the Nazi anthem
"Horst Wessel," fiery and threatening. (Later, I learned it was
an old German folk tune.) My skin crawled. I had to make a
gesture, anything. I'd prepared for this moment for years. I had
the power. I was an American soldier, they were my prisoner.
So why did I feel like theirs?

I wanted Hitler to know I was from Lawndale, where we
took no shit. I went back to the chow line for seconds and as I
moved down the serving line I blasted out into the faces of the
German POWs the Rockets' marching song, our nonsensical
defiance of everything in life that wanted to kill us:

> *We're the Knutes of Rocket High school*
> *Colors black and blue, bumdebumdebum*
> *We always Knute our blair boys*
> *And our fitzes too, bumdebumdebumdebum . . .*
> *Don't Knute your blair too often*
> *Or you will not be, be, be, be*
> *A Knute of good old Rocket High School*
> *K-N-O-O-T!!*

War Is the Health of the State

We were soldiers long before the draft notices came. In the lim-
ited anarchy of the streets, we kids ruled ourselves, but our
moms, dads, and surrounding culture drilled home a contrary
lesson, the discipline of keeping pain to ourselves. From Jennie
and her generation we learned, despite all our wild games, to
shut up and keep marching or die. And then the U.S. Army

made official what we'd always known as children, taking shit (orders) was the key to life.

Rewards for military obedience were real. I had never been better fed, clothed, and looked after than in the service. I made Staff Sergeant and temporarily commanded a regiment (in the absence of a drunken colonel) as Sergeant Major until one of "my" men put an M-1 rifle up against my chin and swore he'd blow my Jew-face off if I made the troops do anymore morning phys ed. Yet I almost re-upped because I'd found a home in the army. When two of my buddies saw me with reenlistment papers at the separation center at Camp Roberts, California, they wrestled the forms away from me and flushed them down the toilet. One of them sneered, "You're a chickenshit with stripes. I just saved your life, you jerk," which woke me up to my new civilian reality: the Hitler war was over, the Cold War was starting, and, this time, whoever it was had his sights set squarely on me.

15

Venus, Released

After I left for the service, Jennie embarked on a secret mis-
sion to track down Leo Sigal in New York under cover of visiting her sister Pauline. My Aunt Fannie testified, "Jennie was
crazy about that no-good man. She never even bothered to see
Paulie. One thing only on Jennie's mind, that animal Sigal."
I don't know if Jennie found my dad or what happened if she
did, but when she returned to Chicago she packed up and put
3,000 miles between her and Manhattan, emigrating to postwar
Los Angeles to find work in the prospering summer garment
industry. In L.A., she settled down as an hourly machine operator at Catalina Swimwear, joined the union, paid her dues,
struck when called out, but no longer leaped on tables to stir up
the workers or lead wildcat strikes. "The Spanish are coming in
with their own language, their own ways," she observed of the
wave of immigrant Latina women supplanting the older generation of Jewish needle trades workers. "Let them organize

themselves." *Let them organize themselves*? I'd never heard such words from Jennie before. She was getting tired.

Physically, she was running down—she had put in a five- or six-day week, eight or more hours a day for forty years without letup—and confessed that sometimes while running the machine her mind got caught up in its implacable puk-puk-puk-puk rhythm, taking her back as in a dream to the past and her childhood. She feared going insane. "How would you deal with a crazy mom, Kalman?" She'd shake her head as if to throw off the weight of memory. "But you," she commanded, "you stay sane, hear? For me." I was her last great hope.

❉ ❉ ❉

As Jennie aged, she became more disappointed in herself for what she felt she had not accomplished compared to her heroines, the President's wife, Mrs. Eleanor Roosevelt, and Dorothy Thompson, a glamorous and popular newspaper columnist. "Ma," I'd say, "be realistic." Meaning, you're an immigrant girl who left school at twelve, led her first sweatshop strike at thirteen ("The boss hated us going to night school so he kept turning the time clock back, the schnorrer") and carried a bastard child from a fugitive lover. "Be realistic," I'd repeat.

Ma would scan me through her veil of Pall Mall cigarette smoke, "I *was* realistic—and look where it got me. Dreams are the only real thing. They matter. Hold on to them even when they drive you crazy. You're old enough now to listen to yourself."

Jennie never lost her pride, laced with disenchantment, at what unions had accomplished for their members, even if it hurt her that the younger workers had no idea of the sacrifices of her generation that built the labor movement. "We gave them more money and a better life but where was their education?" It was hard for her to accept that a buck fifty more hourly wage wasn't accompanied by a huge explosion of interest in Dostoevsky and Verdi. She'd point to the tiny sixteen-inch TV I'd bought her for Christmas. "That's an education?"

When I'd lugged the second-hand TV up to her apartment she at first locked it in a closet and regarded it as a personal enemy, although I did once catch her watching *I Love Lucy*. "I personally knew Lucy when she was a socialist," Jennie said and I thought, Ma's losing it for sure. Later it came out in a House UnAmerican Activities session that Lucille Ball had indeed once registered to vote Communist. O Lucy! What would Ricky say? So, even if Jennie's knees and fingers were stiffening, her mind shone in the old way.

After the war I moved in with her as a college boy, which crimped both our styles. She badly wanted a grandchild but I was already mentally zipping my bags to get out of the country before somebody nailed me for something. The FBI, two agents with the usual Marine buzz-cut I named "Mutt" and "Jeff" after old-time cartoon characters, regularly dropped by Jennie's apartment house in L.A.'s Pico-Vermont district to grill her about me, and of course she was unnervingly polite, served them coffee and cake, and sent them away, their ears burning with, "Do your mothers know what you do for a living?" Jennie couldn't do much about the FBI chief, J. Edgar Hoover, but when I told her that the L.A. police department Red Squad was also snooping around and taking photographs of me, she called in one of her markers from the mother of L.A. Chief of Police William Parker, a notorious conservative. Mrs. Parker lived in our building and she and Jennie had struck up an unlikely friendship based on Ma knowing how to locate home fabrics wholesale. Now Ma went downstairs to have a private chat with the chief's mother and a day later I lost the Red Squad tail. "What did you tell her, Ma?" I was curious. Jennie replied, "I said, "What if the damn Communists took over and made life miserable for *her* son? How would *she* feel?' She got it right away."

Anything else?

"Oh sure," Jennie added. "I cried and said I was so upset I couldn't go bargain hunting with her anymore. That's what did it. She's got a heart like a stone rock."

Smile!

When a Hollywood studio blacklisted me, and I embarked on a series of "nothing" jobs (as Jennie called them)—taxi driver, banana boat dock worker, saw mill operator—she moved swiftly to repair the damage by quitting Catalina Swimwear to hire me as her short order cook in a hamburger stand she rented in a supermarket at a southwest corner of Los Angeles. "This is our big chance to break out," she vowed. Oh, yeah. Even if the market hadn't been collapsing into bankruptcy, myself as chatty chef Emeril of the flat-patty sizzler and Jennie as welcoming waitress, it reeked of the Grenshaw Home for the Aged as a money loser.

To attract male customers because aircraft plants were located nearby, Jennie bought a stack of fashion magazines and then came to work with her thick gray/auburn hair tied back in a ponytail like teenage Gidget, wearing Hazel Bishop indelible lipstick, June Cleaver twinset "pearls" and noisy bracelets. Anything to bring in customers.

Unfortunately, my slapdash cooking lost us business in a rush to the exits which were usually clear of clientele anyway because the mark of Cain was on the defunct store. Every hour on the hour like a cuckoo clock the desperate manager popped out of his second floor office to prowl the balcony cheerleading into his p.a. system, "Smile . . . everybody, smile! Happy faces! Remember—a smile is a frown upside down!!" Ma and I would look at each other and say, "Go ahead, you smile first." "No, you first." And crack up.

Then one day she said, "Make me a hamburger so I can have a taste." She had never before eaten one of my dishes, preferring to brownbag it. I cooked her a Super Clancy Special with all the trimmings and set it down in front of her. She studied it, took a bite, a second bite, put the hamburger down, and inquired, "That's what you've been giving our customers?" "Sure thing, Ma."

She started to laugh, took off her greasy apron, tossed it behind the coffee maker and said, "Let's get out of this funeral home before they arrest you as a mass murderer."

I tossed away my apron too, and rather jubilantly we strolled out of the cavernous, ruined market, leaving behind our very last chance to break out, whatever that meant.

* * *

In Los Angeles, wherever and whoever her body lay with, Jennie's emotional life was again centered almost entirely on women, two in particular: Charlotte, the teenager, abandoned by the Navy Pier sailor in Chicago, who had followed Ma to the West Coast, got her a new life and job as a waitress; and Dinah Farrar, a very soigné fashion designer at Catalina Swimwear who also came West from Regal Frocks in Chicago. Dinah, Charlotte, and Jennie became a threesome on dates together to Vegas and Tijuana clubs. Charlotte told me, "Your mother loved dancing. She'd put that wild red henna in her hair, get her nails painted blood crimson and off we'd go. Check into a hotel, put on fancy dresses, order room service and kick back. Guys half her age would see her coming and fall over their own feet to get Jennie to dance with them—her more than me, and I'm eighteen years younger. Jennie liked men and they liked her. A guy didn't need to be political for her to go stark raving mad over him."

Dinah, with her slightly aristocratic manner, didn't trouble to conceal her dislike of me as an unmannerly klutz. Her aquiline nose seemed to quiver in my presence, as if scenting a bad odor, and we bristled around each other. She was extremely close to, and protective of, Jennie, two women of a certain age on the loose while sharing a subtly scornful attitude to men in general, based, no doubt, on experience. At the same time, Jennie was clearly the leader in their Vegas/Tijuana forays on the wild side. I was a little afraid of Dinah's high style and intimacy with Jennie. Later, when I read an "explicit" biography of the woman Jennie most admired, Eleanor Roosevelt, whom Jennie had once met and (to her immense pride) debated with on one of Mrs. Roosevelt's charity tours of the Lower East Side, I began to get it that both Dinah and my mother came from a Victorian-values generation where it was possible to be fond of, deeply close to, another woman without necessarily fucking each other. But sexualizing my mother was a habit hard to break. When I asked young Charlotte if Jennie and Dinah Farrar were "something more" she stared at me coldly. "You know Clancy, I've never told you this. But you really are stupid and age hasn't improved you. *Your mother found it impossible not to love.*"

Venus, at Rest

Jennie died alone, and I let strangers bury her. "She's gone!" crackled Charlotte on the phone from Los Angeles. "Yes, a heart attack. Coming back from, where else, the beauty parlor. It's taken days to track you down. Where are you, lost in Camelot? It doesn't matter. We took care of it. We buried her — Dinah and me and a few friends from the shop. Where is she? In the ground at Workmen's Circle, of course, among her friends. God, you piss me off sometimes." She hung up.

A minute later the phone rang again. Charlotte. "Borrow some money and start therapy. You'll need it." And hung up again.

I hadn't seen Jennie in the three years since I'd been away from America.

For a while I tossed the phone from one hand to the other, then put it down in the stone-cold living room of the old slate house in Halifax, Yorkshire, and turned to the other people staring mutely at me. They included some of the best friends I'd made in England. Until interrupted by the phone call, we'd been having one of those intense political meetings charting the future of the known universe.

I said, "My ma just died."

No one got up to put an arm around me or say how sorry they were. Most of them looked acutely embarrassed, as if I'd farted in public or mistranslated Sartre's *Being and Nothingness*. Somebody cleared his throat impatiently. I didn't expect or receive sympathy; we had a vision more important than feelings, so I walked upstairs to my room and sat on the narrow bed and stared out at the frosty Yorkshire moors, beautiful and austere in the moonlight.

I missed my mom. We couldn't live together and we couldn't not be together and her apron strings stretched all the way across the Atlantic and I had a startling lightness of heart. How could this monstrous reaction be? The thing I'd most dreaded had happened. It was all over, the decades-long worry over when and how and if. I wouldn't ever again have to fret about her dying; it was done, over. At first, I felt no grief, shed no tears. Iced up. I was like those English people downstairs, armored against emotion and fixed on the life of the pamphlet. More than anything, I wanted my father to be with me now, take my hand, *do something*. Was he even alive?

Charlotte had it nailed. I *was* lost in Camelot. For two years, as an illegal alien on a canceled U.S. passport, I'd been living in half shadows in England, moving from place to place, humping my old canvas GI duffle bag stencilled "Sgt C Sigal 36929935" and a twenty-year-old Corona portable typewriter, all my equity in the world. Before the British police acquired computers and CCTV cameras on every street corner, it was a snap to hide in England if you kept on the hop, the habit Jennie had taught me. Like Dad, I seemed to have been bred for a life on the run, fading into the general population, scuffling and skiffling and collecting raw experience—except that I *still* couldn't write. To fill up time and pay for a Rowton House (workingmen's hostel) room, I took off-the-book jobs here and there, digging clay trenches for McAlpine on South Bank, messengering merchant bank transactions on a Vespa along Threadneedle Street, washing dishes at Nick the Greek's in Soho. Some nights, I slept under Charing Cross Bridge; days I kept on the move, shaving in public toilets. I lived in alleys or on the hospitality of kind women. Clippies on the big red "doubledekka" Routemaster buses liked chatting me up and taking me home and I waited to be arrested and deported or for literary lightning to strike, whichever came first. I was strung out on the adrenalin of gambling on myself and, so far, it was not paying off.

Living like a bum was an insult to Jennie. For this she had worked at a machine her whole life? I could almost see her shaking her head as she often did, "What will it take you to learn?" I was so glad she couldn't see me now.

Up in Halifax, I don't know how long I sat on the cot in the narrow freezing-cold room, minutes or hours. I was sure only of one thing. My life as a boy was over.

A voice from downstairs. Oliver Rossiter, the sturdy little ex-commando veteran of the Dieppe and Norway landings, was one of the few London lefties who actually liked Americans. "We're going out cavassing in the North End ward. Feel like coming along?"

Later, when they came back, Oliver sat on the bed next to me. "Don't be too hard on us," he said. "The war. The English. Somehow a feeling you expect more of us than we can give."

I turned to Oliver. "I'm not going to cry," I said.

He got up to go. "More's the pity," he said.

Oliver's father was a world-famous psychoanalyst and a close collaborator of Freud. I'd never gone to a shrink, but Charlotte had suggested now was as good a time as any. I asked Oliver, "You ever been in, um, therapy?"

He smiled. "No, it would be like going into the family business. I skipped that stage and went straight on to the loony bin."

One of the things I most liked about England was that half the people I knew had broken down and they treated it like any other domestic chore, without drama or self pity, just something that happens.

Back down in rain-whipped London, I locked myself in my Swiss Cottage basement bedsit (rented under an assumed name—here we go again!), and sat cross-legged in the middle of the frayed carpet, trying to feel what I was supposed to feel but feeling only numb and addle-headed and an emotion that at first I couldn't pinpoint: who *was* this woman who had just left me? It didn't *feel* as if she were dead, never would; she just wasn't here anymore, that's all, and it was hard to breathe. There was nobody I could ask or appeal to, no family or rabbi or priest. My father, for all I knew, lay dead in a pauper's grave or in a block of cement at the bottom of the Hudson River.

Without checking in the mirror nailed to the wall over the Valor paraffin heater, I carefully, blindly shaved my head with an old-fashioned straight razor—the kind Dad used—that I'd bought at the local Boots. Then I turned the mirror and my posters to the wall and sat perfectly still, as empty-minded as I'd ever been. Something unfamiliar took possession of me. My shaved head kept bobbing up down up down, the way I'd seen the old-timers in Lawndale *schuls* pray, and to my astonishment, but not surprise, words from somewhere bubbled up, *"Baruch Elokeinu melech haolam, dayan ha'emet . . ."* I felt porous, transparent, stranded in my heart.

Several days later—not sure how long, no eating—as if awakened by a pistol shot, I straightened up, dry-eyed, got dressed, and went to my typewriter on a table in the corner. Fasting, or Jennie's ghost, had unjammed the memory machine and my fingers flew over the keys. (God bless Mrs. Craig of Jones Commercial!) The piece that rattled off the roll of yellow copy paper, a trick I picked up from Jack Kerouac, had nothing to do with Jennie but came easily and fast, a short story out of nowhere. I copyedited it and slipped it into an envelope, walked down to the corner red pillar box, and mailed it to the magazine *New Statesman and Nation*. A day later, such was the efficiency of the British postal system then, the editor rang with an acceptance. Did I want my cheque in pounds or guineas? "What's a guinea?" "A pound plus a shilling," he replied. A guinea, of course, I said.

And I was on my way.

❊ ❊ ❊

Jennie's death, which even today I have a hard time believing in, took a weight off me that I hadn't even known was there and gave me a sense that I was now and forevermore alone in the world and therefore had to make something of myself. I owed her that. Other writers have told me that they, too, feel they "bought" their talent upon the death of someone close to them, including J.K. Rowling, Harry Potter's creator, who kick-started her first book when her mother died.

Not even for a moment have I doubted that Jennie is alive within me, watching me work out my life, including this story. It was my first literary lesson, that sometimes there's a body buried in any writer's skull, a sacrifice as primitive as any Aztec's. Jennie's death, the sum of her life, was giving me the push to go where I had no faith in myself to go, but where with all my heart—the heart that belonged to her—I knew I had to.

Jennie neither discouraged nor inspired me to write, except that her silent guidance system—the arched eyebrow, the invisible nudge, a tone of voice—unmistakably conveyed her acknowledgement that writers and poets were valuable. She read widely and joyously, everything from Gorki to Sholem Asch to P. G. Wodehouse to Mrs. Roosevelt's "My Day" columns; she devoured the literary pages as well as the "Bintle Brief" advice column letters in the Jewish *Daily For-ward*, which was her version of going to the public library. Names like Zola, Sinclair Lewis, and Tolstoy—whether she had read them or not—were her common coin. Despite my "low normal" IQ, she never lost faith in me, and even when she disapproved she signaled that it was okay to go beyond myself and to strive for that which had been denied her, a chance to fly as high as dreams could take us. I could not let her down.

The moment my fingers touched the Corona portable keys to commence serious work it's fair to say I experienced Ma's rage as well as her beneficence. Her strength had a dark side that fed into, but also propped up, my weakness. For all her life she had maintained, at great cost, her steely self-control. Now, it seemed as if all that anger, resentment, and pent up fury she could never articulate, for fear of being consumed by it, shot straight into my veins. I don't believe in the transmigration of souls, but this sure came close. Insofar as I have a "personality" as a writer it is, at least partly, something I borrowed from her. All this time she was teaching me how to be a writer.

At no point while she was alive did it look as if we'd even come close. Her most conscious worry, voiced time and again, was that her little prince would end up in Cook County jail or even like her acquaintance, Homer van Meter, gored by police bullets in a snowy alley, or just an ordinary tramp with his hand out. Yet, at my worst she never gave up on the "something" in me that neither of us could exactly define. She *let me be*, and if I wanted to go to hell she would have to let me, except with this proviso communicated by a toss of her brilliant red hair: *I am really afraid for you but don't you dare be afraid for yourself*. Do what I and your dad have not been able to do. *Be better* than us.

I chose my mother wisely. Her hands are on these keys.

No guilt, no shame, just a job to do.

"I'll Be Seeing You in All the Old . . ."

Shortly after Jennie "passed on"—a phrase I used to laugh at but don't anymore—I began seeing her in all the old familiar places, and some unfamiliar ones, too. Her death not only liberated me to write but had the strange side effect of triggering hallucinations, visions, mirages, and delusions, where I could swear that she slept side by side with me in my Swiss Cottage bedsit, strolled *a deux* along a Regent's Park canal path, and jiggled my elbow at the Prince of Wales pub. At such moments, she appeared so lifelike, so real, so human and spontaneous that I reached out to touch her. That's when my public behavior began crossing the line. My magazine editor or BBC producer would eye me warily when I mumbled to myself and gesticulated with strange body language (actually, like Dad, pounding my fist into my hand to make an angry point) when all I was doing, really, was arguing with Ma, who was *there*. Occasionally, from the top of a crowded Big Red bus, I'd audibly point out the sights to her, the Houses of Parliament, Soho's Gay Hussar café—formerly Karl Marx's home—Whitechapel Road, where one of her favorite authors, Jack London, wandered in the fog with gold sovereigns sewed into the lining of his shabby pea jacket, anything that might interest her.

Instead of going gently into her grave Jennie began to loom larger in my life in some way more real than ever before; now, when I spoke to her, she *answered back*, the start of a process of my withdrawing from social reality into a private world of my own. A great benefit of this "craziness" was that I'd never felt so close to Jennie or felt her so near at hand. We achieved an intimacy that was impossible when she was alive. Ma, though intensely maternal, had never been a great toucher. So, even in her death, we maintained a respectful physical distance which stays with me to this day. Proprieties must be observed on either side of the shade.

My son Joe, who knows almost everything I know about Jennie, is also in the habit of "seeing" her, as I do. He'll step out of the shower and wrap himself in a towel and look over my shoulder and say quite conversationally, "Hi Grandma, want to see my spitball?!"

❁ ❁ ❁

I want to get into Jennie's head, to think what she thinks, to keep her with me, but even in death she resists. The closest I can come to it is my own attitude to Joe when I look at him as she used to look at me, with a mix of love, admiration, amazement, disapproval, anxiety, and an only half-successful effort to keep his strong-willed personality separate from mine. In Chicago's Lawndale there weren't many "nice" kids Jennie could unfavorably compare me to since we Rockets bonded at the lowest level we could sink to as a matter of pleasure and pride. But today, like Custer at Little Big Horn, I'm besieged by bright, chirpy, homework-focused, get-the-class-project-done-on-time, "creative" children sometimes enjoying private tutors or sent to expensive schools who are clearly headed to a Nobel Prize, or at least a law firm partnership. By contrast, my Joe is working hard on his Mariano Rivera sinker-slider and loves hip-hop. Secretly, I long to put up a bumper sticker, "My Child is Scholar of the Month at Snootyville Elementary." What hypocrisy. I don't know how Jennie or Joe put up with me.

It comes full circle. I am the mother I spent my life escaping from.

16

Percy Comes Home

1963:—President Kennedy murdered in Dallas. Chicago Cubs come in seventh in National League. Martin Luther King's "I have a dream" civil rights march on Washington, D.C.

A London therapist raised her skeptical eyebrow just as Jennie used to. "You start out talking about your mother but keep coming back to your father, so why don't you find out if he really is at the bottom of the Thames with a fish in his mouth?" One reason I'd gone to the shrink was that I'd become obsessed with stalking dossers, homeless tramps, all over London, thinking they might be my Dad, grabbing them by the scruff, staring into their sunken alcoholic eyes. In the end, I simply looked up Dad in the telephone directory of his last known city, New York. American phone books were kept in the library of the U.S. embassy in Grosvenor Square, which I had not dared enter until a Supreme Court decision freed up passports for "subversive" Americans.

I found Dad's name in the Bronx directory and, after procrastinating for days, called him but panicked when someone at the other end picked up.

I shouted, "Is this Leo Sigal? This is, um—" Which name did he know me as?—Clancy, Clarence, Kalman? At the the New York end the voice growls, "I've seen reviews. You're the writer. So write me a letter." And hung up.

He was alive.

And he knew who I was.

All through that Cuba missiles autumn, Dad and I exchanged letters to arrange a high-level summit in New York. He kept postponing firm dates for us to meet, on this or that pretext, the last being that he had to clear it with a certain "Judge Goldfarb," his *consigliere*. He added, "And I have to prepare certain other people." What other people?

❊ ❊ ❊

"Percy, you're not wearing shoe lifts, are you?" were his first words to me in twenty-three years.

Percy who?

This little old guy in his immaculately laundered shirtsleeves blocked the doorway and peered up at me towering over him. For just a second I thought he was going to wallop me with one of his rabbit punches. *Cut it out, Clancy, you outweigh him by forty pounds.*

He had that same tight combative grin, compact fighter's body, thick swept-back black hair almost hardly any gray, narrowed eyelids—the resemblance to the Chicago mobster, Sam Giancana, was amazing. Dad probably would not have objected to the comparison.

A woman's voice from inside: "You're in his way, Leo."

He stepped aside.

In his small cluttered comfortable Bronx apartment, he gestured me to a wooden straight-back chair opposite the soft chair he took. We hadn't known whether to shake hands or hug, so we left it.

A sturdy, pleasant-looking woman Dad's age came in bearing a tray of cakes.

"Sarah, my wife," Dad said quickly.

She smiled a shy welcome. "You take tea?" I thanked her, and she disappeared behind a curtain into the kitchen, hardly to reappear that afternoon.

"My second wife," Dad added.

"Counting Jennie?" I asked.

"Listen, Percy—" he jerked his head toward the kitchen. "It hasn't been easy putting all this together—"

"Dad, I'm Clancy. Or Clarence. Or Kalman."

"Okay, Percy, have it your way."

"Clancy. It's Clancy. Clancy Sigal."

"Don't patronize me, Percy. I read about you in the *New York Times*. Your picture in the paper. I didn't recognize you, but Percy did."

"You didn't know it was me?"

"Of course, Percy."

I gave up.

Dodging and weaving, a Jack Dempsey of evasion, Dad fended off all my personal questions by constantly changing the subject to the British cultural scene—he was remarkably up on then-current British writing—just to let me know he wasn't to be trifled with. His eyes sparkled with curiosity and malice. "That South African dame, the one who put you in her book, she really hooked it to you, didn't she?" He bared his tobacco-stained teeth in an innocent smile. "How did you let yourself get sucker punched like that, Percy?"

I slipped his jab.

"Who," I pressed, "is Percy?"

Most of the afternoon was like that, an interview with a dodgy source more than the reconciliation I'd dreamed of. Stiffly, we chatted, sitting opposite each other, Kennedy and Khruschev, while Sarah uneasily tiptoed around the cluttered flat on Nelson Avenue trying to stay out of the way. This thing was going wrong and I wanted to retrace my steps to start afresh.

He leaned forward and tapped my knee. "Hey, put your notebook away. I don't want to sue you for slander. I should have taken you to court what you said about me in your book. Your old man is no drunk in the gutter. What happened, you run out of inspiration?"

He'd read it!

I said I'd made up that part about him out of literary license and my worst fears about his fate. He said, "You better get that license renewed. I'm doing pretty well on Social Security."

All the time I was there, Dad examined me closely as if not quite believing I existed. He was making up his mind about something and waiting for Sarah to disappear again.

Then: "Confidentially," leaning in to speak out of the side of his mouth, getting right down to it, "your mother and I were crazy for each other. Couldn't keep our hands off. But it was hell when we were together. She had a mouth on her like a river of fire." He sat back with folded arms. Before I could react, he threw in, "Children bore me. But I'm a *great*-grandfather. Ask Percy."

He paused, looked to the ceiling, clasped and unclasped his

fingers, stared me into the carpet, set his jaw, and decided with a long sigh. "Okay kid, it's time."

And came clean about the whole thing.

"Her name was Lena," he said.

Lena was his first wife, Dad revealed, by whom he had a son and a daughter, whom he abandoned for Jennie and to whom, "after some adventures we don't want to get into right now," he had returned after leaving Jennie and me. Boom, that was it.

So I had a new half brother and half sister out there somewhere. Dad had kept putting off our meeting to give himself time to prepare his "real children" (his phrase) for the shock of a surprise brother. "Your sister is all right with it, she can't wait to see you, but your brother, he's having a problem."

I waited. More, surely. Just this?

With many detours the rest of the story came out.

They—Jennie and Leo—had met in New York in 1919 on the crest of a national general strike wave and had fallen hard for each other. Leo believed he saw in Jennie the sexier, laughing, militant, experience-hungry rebel girl that his legal wife may once have been but wasn't anymore. And Jennie saw in him exactly what? Dad flashed a grin. "You kidding? I was an eagle, flying, up way up, nobody could touch me, she thought I'd snatch her with my claws and swoop her to the top of the mountain. That was the plan. God thought otherwise."

He'd been a married man with two young children, my mother a twenty-four-year-old bohemian virgin with four pissed-off brothers who had sworn a virtual blood oath on Leo Sigal after the sudden collapse in anguish of their widowed mother on hearing my father spring his brazen proposal—"a negotiating point," he called it to me—to split his domestic life equally between his legitimate family in the Bronx and Jennie at the Persily house on Manhattan's Twelfth Street. Uproar, bellows of outrage, threats, shouts. Pursued by the Persily wrath and the puritan furies of the socialist movement, Jennie and Leo fled west into the American industrial heartland to make a new life. "Your mother's family made it tough for us to earn a living in New York so we kept moving around, pulling up stakes, even after you came along. We'd make out somehow. We had each other, the movement and, what the hell, we were young."

"That," concluded Dad, "was when my bad luck started."

"When was that?"

"The day you were born."

It stung like he had torn open my eyelid.

Until now, I'd kept my feelings in check. Why is he speaking to me like this? I couldn't reach down deep enough to find my rage and sadness. It may have showed on my face.

"You came here today for a reason, right? Don't be yellow. It's just you and me. Don't go soft on me."

I asked who Percy was.

"My son Phil. A pet name."

Except that Dad kept calling me Percy all afternoon.

I took out my notebook again.

By now, the living ghost of Jennie had taken her usual place at my right hand, invisible except to me. Her large open freckled face was rapt and profoundly unconvinced by Dad's tale. But I bought it.

Nothing would stop him now from telling it his way in a stream of consciousness, Jackson Pollack dripping on the canvas, carelessly rattling off like a memory machine gun.

"The General Strike . . . cigarette girls wanted a nickel an hour more . . . William Z. Foster . . . Red bastard . . . the

Amalgamated . . . Executive Board . . . per capita . . . Teamster goons . . . Ralph Capone that *momser* . . . the shooting in Gary— no wait, it was Whiting, Indiana—"

"The what where?" I asked.

"—Carmichael tossed you over the counter and you bumped your head and Jennie went crazy when we got home, your skull is fractured, you're going to die, the sky is falling . . . she always wanted you a sissy, succeeded, too, by the look."

Tell me about Gary or Whiting, Dad. It really happened?

But when he saw how curious I was about the shooting episode, he clammed up and then changed the subject. He was on a roll, conjuring up fairy tales about our "many" idyllic times together as father and son fishing in the lake.

What lake? What fish?

"Our luck held till she got pregnant, and I put my foot down and said one more is too much for me to handle, but she wanted you and I gave in, your mother was too strong for me, what could I do? Teamster hoodlums chased us out of Chicago that time. I wanted to buy another gun, like in Flint. Your mother said no more guns, said we had to protect you. *You, you,* always *you.* So we sold the store and ran." Spitting out the word ran. "You made me run. Always *you.*"

Dad looked over his shoulder to locate Sarah, still in the kitchen boiling and reboiling the same kettle. His knee touched mine. "Your mother," he spoke low, "a wonderful woman, wonderful mother. Her luck, too, changed for the worse when she met me, I'm sorry to say." Then leaned in to whisper.

"And just between you and me," he repeated, "when you came along, no offense, everything went . . ." his hand dived and fluttered to mimic an airplane spiralling out of control. "Get my meaning?"

He sat back to assess the damage. "Your mother and I, crazy for each other." Another look into the kitchen. *"Crazy."* He yawned. "Percy, what kind of name is Clarence? I begged her to nix it. Such a cross to bear. Clarence."

"Does Percy know about me, Dad?"

"Don't try to see him."

"If you say so," I said.

He sized me up again. "Not much of a scrapper, are you, kid? Living in England all this time make you a gentleman? You haven't changed. That time in Chicago. I made you fight them. You've forgotten. I thought writers had good memories."

Christ. He remembered how I'd fled from a bunch of boys and he'd shoved me back at them. He despised cowards, whom he called "yellowbellies."

I felt the same way. What kind of son runs away from fights, or when trapped screams like a girl and pulls hair and scratches with his nails and flinches away from a *kishke* jab? I carried Dad's genes but not his nerve.

Jennie leaned over from her perch on the arm of my chair and reminded me of something she'd said on one of those nights we'd lain together in the big four-poster in the back of the Family Hand Laundry waiting for Dad and his fury to come home. In the darkness, she'd given a little laugh. "He tries, your father. He didn't bargain for all this. He's a fighting man, not a married man."

I put my notebook away again and Dad nodded triumphantly at my gesture of resignation. His look was almost tender. "Percy," he said softly, "we did not intend a rough deal for you. I read your book. You are a troubled person. Don't be a sorehead. It won't get you anywhere. Be a man. What choice do you have?"

He stood up and said, "Sarah! Clarence is going!"

Clarence. That was something.

Sarah parted the fringed curtain that separated kitchen from living room, nervously wiping her hands on her apron. I embraced her and she hugged me back, tears in her eyes. Dad stuck his skinny paw out a mile to block me from wrapping him in my arms, and I brushed it aside to try to crush him to death, inhaling that familiar aroma of cigars and shirt starch. He almost fell over from surprise.

"Walk him downstairs," Sarah suggested. Dad threw her a dirty look but got me to the door. We went out to the hall and down the narrow, dark-carpeted stairs without talking. Outside on Nelson Avenue he gestured at passersby and said loud enough for them to hear: "Puerto Ricans. Negroes. I don't mind, but Sarah's scared of the colored. We're moving to a new housing development in Long Island." I mumbled something. "If there's nothing there, if it's like the English new towns, don't worry, I'll organize something."

He was, he said, active in the Bronx section of the Social-Democratic Federation, a collection of old-time socialists, tough little Jews with long memories. Then, "You still a big time red?" My name he forgets, but not that. I wondered if he even remembered his letter disowning me? I wanted to say something that didn't sound contrite or weak. He'd hate that. "Dad," I said mimicking Popeye the Sailor Man, "I yam what I yam and that's what I yam."

That got him. He shrugged, "You're a funny kid, you know." For the first and only time I felt that, father and son, we both got it at the same time.

He walked me to the IRT subway stop a block away, boldly staring down the lounging teenagers we passed on front stoops who gave us the city scowl. The set of Dad's body, his vigilant eyes, dared them to take New York, his city, away from him. My old man. What balls.

We stopped for a traffic light on the corner. Nothing more to say.

At the IRT station he stopped and cocked his head at me. "Physically," he announced, "I'm a champ in my weight class. Emotionally, I'm yellow. Maybe that's where you get it from, Percy."

What a parting shot. He pointed me down the subway stairs. As I went down, he shouted his goodbye.

"I made my mark! I took part!"

He walked away.

❊ ❊ ❊

Dad died the following year in his Bronx apartment while watching John Wayne on TV in *She Wore A Yellow Ribbon.* From London, I rang his wife, Sarah, who was terribly kind. Did he say anything about me? After a long pause, she lied. "Of course. All the time. After all, you were his son."

❊ ❊ ❊

I *was* his son, too. Maybe not exactly *beau idéal* of what a real boy should be, but his son nonetheless. Not until I began researching Jennie's story did I realize how much of my life belonged to her, but also how much of it had been, possibly still is, devoted to gaining Leo Sigal's approval. All the time I thought I was acting autonomously I was fulfilling his pattern of kicking in doors that were wide open and bashing my head against doors made of stone. I wanted to be like him and to be liked by him for all the "incorrect" reasons—his macho swagger and Homburg-hat-cocked-over-one-eye style, his pugnacity, and his fighter's stance in the world. I admired him and probably still do. So today, like Jennie, he watches over me, Old Cyclops Eye forever pushing me to mix it up and face the music. "You're a tough kid," he used to tell me in my most cowardly moments, "so act tough." Camus and Sartre couldn't have said it better.

❊ ❊ ❊

The emotion comes too late, as it usually does. Waiting to give love is possibly the greatest sin of all. I am blessed by a mother who everyone but Joe and I believe is dead and gone. But at any moment I expect her to swoop up Joe in her arms as only grandmothers can.

Leo Sigal is something else. A part of me wants to protect Joe from the Leo-in-me, the troubled eagle wildly thrashing its wings, and part of me wants to have a long earnest talk with Dad about sons and fathers. Problems aside, it would be good, if only because my Joe, over five feet tall and big and strong, and I already have "issues" the more he becomes like a younger version of me. Joe listens to the "wrong" music and has the "wrong" friends and his changeup slider isn't what it could be and any moment now I expect him to reinvent the Kedzie alley rubber gun.

I want to break the cycle of misplaced hate and violence that probably began somewhere in the depths of a Russian forest as my father's father's father escaped through the birch trees from wildly plunging Cossack horsemen slashing their way with sabres to catch the Jew who drinks the blood of new-born babes on Passover eve. If responsibility begins in dreams, I want my son to live unshackled from anxieties he did not create, terrors and fears he doesn't own, the hidden, fist-in-the-mouth reflex signifying a human reaction to overwhelming chaos. It stops with me, maybe here.

Epilogue

Los Angeles, Today

Speed bonnie boat like a bird on the wing
Onward the sailors cry
Carry the lad that's born to be king
Over the sea to Skye
—Old English lullaby

Joe sometimes comes out with me jogging on the red-cindered track at Beverly Hills high school, where I go evenings before the setting sun backlights Century City against the *Hello, Dolly* set of Fox Studios. When I run alone, Jennie's voice speaks to me from behind the athletic scoreboard by the carcinogenic oil well just down the hill from the Century City high-rise where Bruce Willis stood off all those terrorists in *Die Hard*. These are my private moments with "Granma Jennie," as Joe calls her. My speaking out loud to her passes unnoticed by the trim, tanned Spandexed entertainment lawyers and aerobically top-of-the-line, sweater-tied-at-midriff, Oliver Peeples-shades-on-scalp Beverly Hills wives, all serious Botox and triple diamond and platinum renewal-vow rings, because almost all the joggers are chattering into neck-clamp cell phones, looking at least as loony as me talking into the dry California air.

From behind the scoreboard, Jennie passes the word. "Get Joe to drop the "Granma," will you? I may be gone, but I'm not *passé*." "Ma," I say, "I'll try, but you know what a stubborn kid he is." "I wonder where he gets it from," she says.

Then Joe shows up in his Carolina Mudcats baseball uniform and falls in step beside me. "How's Granma Jennie?" he asks casually.

"She says to stop calling her Granma," I say.

"Why?"

"Vanity," I say.

"What's vanity?" he asks.

"It goes with being a Sigal."

We do one slow lap. The sun is gone now but not the strong hot Santa Ana breeze.

"Can we go home now?" Joe asks.

"Say good-night to Jennie first."

Joe stops on the track so that the lawyers and second wives have to detour around him. He opens his arms in a wide panoramic embrace and turns in all four directions like a Native American to the elements.

"See you tomorrow, Jennie! I'm hungry."

Acknowledgments

This account of Jennie's life has involved a number of people who helped me peel away the layers of dust and evasion.

In the actual writing, thanks to Amy Scholder, who gave me the professional push I needed to see the whole in perspective.

A special thanks to Dr. Barry Cohen whose office and patience I used to lay out this book's pages.

To Sam Stoloff and Frances Goldin my gratitude for demonstrating perseverance above and beyond the call of duty.

This book could not have been written without the memories and assistance of the "Chicago gang": Ron Grossman and Diane Wagner, Jack Weinberg, and of course Studs Terkel, who fought hard to see this come to birth. I am also grateful for those graduates of Howland Elementary, Marshall High, and Jones Commercial High who wish to remain anonymous.

Over the years I have plundered the formidable Persily clan for stories, tales, fragments, and remembrances of Jennie

Persily and Leo Sigal. Thanks to Coleman (Charlie) Persily—viva the Lincoln Battalion!—his wife Pearl, and sons Fred and Harold, and Harold's wife Christy; cousin Ida, bless her; my cousins Claire and Bernard Persily; Joan Levinson, and Persilys no longer with us, Fannie and Clem.

Harriet Glickman, who knew Jennie so well has been an invaluable source of testimony.

Robert Berkovitz has been most generous in sharing memories of our life together and in GVS, the old neighborhood. His support and assistance have been invaluable.

In Los Angeles I have been encouraged by the shrewd advice of Frances Ring, as always.

Suzanne Potts helped to de-clutter my mind and my files. My thanks for their staunch support, and love of Joe, to Eliane Parisi and Alda Aguinaga.

For technical and moral support my hat is off to James Spottiswoode and Constance Meyer and their daughters Natasha and Tatiana, and to Roger Spottiswoode.

Corky Gordon kept my chapters safe and welcome as I wrote them.

My early reading of Grover Lewis's unfinished memoir "Goodbye If You Call That Gone" showed me how it could be done. Many thanks to Rae Lewis and to Grover now resting in Texas heaven.

And to all of the Tidwells, especially Joe and Sue, my anchor in life.

Index

About the Author

Clancy Sigal has published four novels, including *Going Away,* a National Book Award nominee. He was principal screenwriter for the 2002 film *Frida.* He is a reporter and ex-BBC correspondent and was based for many years in London. He worked closely with the charismatic "anti-psychiatrist" Dr. R. D. Laing; and knew Jimmy Hoffa. He is professor emeritus at University of Southern California's Annenberg School of Communication, and he lives in Los Angeles with his wife and son.